Shaen Corbet, Andrew Urquhart, Larisa Yarovaya (Eds.)
Cryptocurrency and Blockchain Technology

Batten–Corbet–Lucey Handbooks in Alternative Investments

Series editor
Jonathan A. Batten, Shaen Corbet and Brian M. Lucey

Volume 1

Cryptocurrency and Blockchain Technology

Edited by
Shaen Corbet, Andrew Urquhart, Larisa Yarovaya

DE GRUYTER

ISBN 978-3-11-065943-6
e-ISBN (PDF) 978-3-11-066080-7
e-ISBN (EPUB) 978-3-11-065952-8
ISSN 2629-3714

Library of Congress Control Number: 2020938034

Bibliographic information published by the Deutsche Nationalbibliothek
The Deutsche Nationalbibliothek lists this publication in the Deutsche Nationalbibliografie; detailed bibliographic data are available on the Internet at http://dnb.dnb.de.

Typesetting: VTeX UAB, Lithuania
Printing and binding: CPI books GmbH, Leck

www.degruyter.com

MIX
Papier aus verantwortungsvollen Quellen
FSC www.fsc.org
FSC® C083411

Contents

Andrew Urquhart and Larisa Yarovaya

Introduction to cryptocurrencies

Today, cryptocurrencies are getting more and more attention from investors, regulators, governments and media outlets alike, and therefore there is a requirement for a sound understanding of the economic and financial dynamics of these new assets. This book offers a broad range of chapters on varying topics of cryptocurrencies and acts as a foundation for anyone interested in these new assets and seeks to understand the issues and challenges of investing in these new, interesting and volatile markets. More importantly, this book will give you a solid understanding of important elements of cryptocurrencies, as well as clear overview of the current academic understanding of these assets.

Cryptocurrencies are a new form of digital money that is shifting the paradigm and challenging the traditional financial system. First introduced by Satoshi Nakamoto in his 2008 white paper, Bitcoin has grown into the most popular cryptocurrency as well as a global phenomenon. The technology behind Bitcoin (and most cryptocurrencies) is blockchain and a recent survey by Deloitte found that 53% of respondents say that blockchain technology has become a critical priority for their organizations in 2019 while 83% see compelling use cases for blockchain.[1] The Financial Times reports that business schools around the world are racing to offer lessons in blockchain and bitcoin and Professor Campbell Harvey stresses the need for students to engage with popular cryptocurrencies.[2]

According to EY FinTech adoption Index (2019)[3] adoption of FinTech services has grown from 16% in 2015 to 33% in 2017, and in 2019 it went as high as 64%. Furthermore, the awareness of FinTech grown significantly, and in 2019 around 96% of consumers are aware of at least one form of FinTech service available. Particularly, awareness of cryptocurrency has also increased in the recent years. The Financial Conduct Authority (FCA) examined the reasons of the popularity of cryptocurrency assets amongst consumers and the potential risks that this technology can cause. In October 2018, the FCA published a joint report with the Bank of England and HM Treasury, providing the main definitions and description of different categories of digital assets, and current regulatory perimeter.[4] Together with Revealing Reality research firm, the FCA published a report based on 31 qualitative interviews with cryptocurrency consumers shading the light on main motivations, beliefs and attitudes of cryptocurrency users.

---

1 https://www2.deloitte.com/content/dam/Deloitte/se/Documents/risk/DI_{2}019-global-blockchain-survey.pdf

2 https://www.ft.com/content/011cf9b6-69a7-11e8-aee1-39f3459514fd

3 see electronic version here: https://fintechauscensus.ey.com/2019/Documents/ey-global-fintech-adoption-index-2019.pdf

4 see full report, and additional FCA research here: https://www.fca.org.uk/publications/research/consumer-attitudes-and-awareness-cryptoassets-research-summary

https://doi.org/10.1515/9783110660807-001

Findings show that majority of respondents decided to buy cryptocurrencies following advice received from a friend or family member. It is interesting insight that consumers relied on family advice, or in some particular cases advice from taxi drivers, and not the advice of professional advisors or analysts, which indicates the power of word-of-mouth as a main channel of popularity of this investment assets. Would consumers be encouraged to invest in ETFs, derivatives, or other new investments assets, following family advice? Hard to tell, but probably not. This highlights the very unique features of the cryptocurrency phenomenon, that regardless the complexity of technology behind it, that undoubtedly is quite hard to understand by any regular consumer, the idea behind it seems to be mass appealing and exciting for uniformed investors and users. Furthermore, the role of media and social media in disseminating information about digital currencies was crucial.

Consumers relied on media in gathering information about cryptocurrencies and some of the majority of consumers indicate that social media play a key role in their decision to purchase a digital asset. However, according to the FCA survey conducted in December 2018 among 2,132 participants (70%) have not heard of cryptocurrencies or did not know what are they, and only 3% have bought cryptocurrency before. Among those who purchased cryptocurrency 8% completed 'deep research' before purchasing, while 16% conducted no research at all before purchasing.[5] The results of the survey conducted in December 2018 by Coinbase,[6] and published in June 2019, provides evidence of increased awareness of cryptocurrencies in the US. Particularly, 58% of Americans responded that they heard of Bitcoin, where the word *"Bitcoin"* was more popular search on Google than "*royal wedding*" or "*election results*".[7] Considering the fact that both surveys were conducted in the same time, we can conclude that awareness of cryptocurrencies was higher in the US than in the UK. So cryptocurrencies, what are they? There are many definitions of cryptocurrencies are available online, in this volume, we use the following generic definition of cryptocurrencies:

- ***Cryptocurrencies*** *are decentralised digital assets, that use cryptography to transfer of funds from one party to another without monetary authority influence.*

This generic definition is particularly applicable for the most widely known cryptocurrency and cryptocurrency market leader – Bitcoin. There are several unique characteristics of cryptocurrencies that make them attractive for users and investors. Particularly, cryptocurrencies offer many upgrades over traditional money or fiat currencies, such as the following:

5 see details here https://www.fca.org.uk/publication/research/cryptoassets-ownership-attitudes-uk-consumer-survey-research-report.pdf

6 https://blog.coinbase.com/the-united-states-of-crypto-55282c97855c

7 A YouGov study was conducted in December 2018 and included 2,000 U.S. Internet users over the age of 18 in the general population.

- **Decentralisation** which means that the data is not saved on a single computer or server but saved on millions of computers simultaneously. This means there is no central authority and that the blockchain cannot be tampered with without the agreement of all the nodes (participants).
- **Consensus** which means that the community of participants have for anything to happen. One way to reach this consensus is called "*mining*". It is part of the proof-of-work-system.
- **Transparency** which means that all transactions can tracked and users can see at all times who has added blocks.
- **Replacement of intermediaries** which means that there is no need for financial intermediaries (such as banks) to act as a "middleman" between two individuals wanting to exchange money. Also cryptocurrencies can transfer large sums of money across international borders in a matter of minutes while most banks take at least one business day.
- **Limited supply** which means that unlike fiat currencies, only a limited number will ever be produced which means it is not affected by inflation and is a scare asset that's unlikely to depreciate

These innovative features, combined with it's ability to be easily converted into traditional currencies, makes cryptocurrencies very attractive for investors around the globe. There are several types of cryptocurrencies that can be distinguished. According to above mentioned *Cryptoassets Taskforce* report by FCA, Bank of England, and HM Treasury, cryptoassets include: (i) exchange tokens; (ii) security tokens; and (iii) utility tokens, where cryptocurrencies like Bitcoin belong to the first group of the exchange tokens, and are primarily being used as a means of exchange or as an investment. Different categorisations is provided by Corbet et al. (2020) who allocated all digital assets into three categories: (i) currencies; (ii) blockchains/protocols; (iii) decentralised apps, where cryptocurrencies like Bitcoin also belong to the first group since their primarily role is money transfer. Overall, we can note that both classifications determine cryptocurrencies in the category of digital assets that have main function, such as transfer of funds, storage of value, and investment opportunities. One of the first debates in the academic literature was around the role cryptocurrencies play in the financial system, whether cryptocurrencies are a new form of money and can store value, or they are a new class of highly speculative investment assets. These debates we widely discussed in the media, and many suggested that true value of Bitcoin is zero (e. g. Cheah and Fry (2015)). However, late in 2017 when Bitcoin price skyrocketed from $1000 to nearly $20,000, further discussion of the true value of Bitcoin and other cryptocurrencies was emerging (Corbet et al., 2018a). With time, academics started looking at cryptoassets differently, by noticing the fact that investors who hold substantial sums of Bitcoins are not cashing out their positrons, indicating their strong belief that regardless of regulatory uncertainty, ethical considerations and a variety of environmental issues, cryptocurrencies still can store the value over time and Bitcoin especially is a valuable asset to hold in longer term.

The next chapter of this book focused on the current state of cryptocurrency research. While quite a detailed literature survey has been provided by Corbet et al. (2018b) already, this chapter offers more up-to-date review of the literature in this field, particularly, it highlights the main networks of cryptocurrency scholars and research groups that are leading the research in this field. Authors took into consideration several indicators like geographic location of the research teams and their institutions, number of published articles on cryptocurrencies and related topics, and last but not the least, amount of citations that each of the published manuscripts were able to generate over relatively short period of time after publications. This displays how rapidly cryptocurrency research evolved in the last few years, and provides some idea how to cryptocurrency scholars can collaborate to further advance this innovative field of finance.

The third chapter might be most useful for those who really want to dip into technological details of Blockchain and distributed ledger technology that cryptocurrencies are based on. If you just started your cryptocurrencies journey, after reading of the next chapter you will be able to find answer on several important questions, such as what is a double spending problem, mining, and proof-of-work algorithm? This chapter discussed the existing problems of Blockchain technology, such as scalability, oracle problem, and fork. It is a new and exciting technology, innovation that potential will destruct the financial services and other businesses, therefore a good understanding of Blockchain is important to successfully adopt to technological changes and use the applications of Blockchain that might be most relevant for your business or research. In comparison to various previous literature that covers technological aspect of cryptocurrencies, this chapter explains it in more accessible manner, that makes it easier to understand the technology and main terminology around it.

The following chapter focuses on the key issues of the Initial Coin Offerings (ICOs), and provides insightful examples of ICOs misusage, such as questionable motives of ICOs, criminality and ICO disappearance. The cases considered in this chapter received were discussed widely in the media, however, they are also important from theoretical perspectives, and provide interesting avenue for corporate finance researchers, and broader range of finance and business scholars. For example, when Kodak announced the release of their KODAKCoin, there was an immediate and significant price rise of Kodak shares, while after the announcement there was increased correlation between the price of Kodak shares and Bitcoin (Corbet et al., 2019). Further examples includes Facebook and Libra cryptocurrency, as well as Venezuelan Petro. This discussion will be particularly interesting for cryptocurrency-enthusiasts who are dedicated to promote the potential of the new technology, since this chapter highlights that entire sector has been susceptible to various frauds and scams that cannot be ignored. It concludes with comments on ICOs regulation.

Next, we provide practitioners with insights on the regulatory and legal aspects of cryptocurrency markets. This commentary and non-academic point of view on cryptocurrencies adds a great value to this volume, stimulating a dialog between practitioners and academics in the areas that are of great importance, such as business ethics. Also, there are regulatory issues as cryptocurrencies have been found to be used for illegal activities and the huge price fall of Bitcoin once the website Silk Road was taken down by the FBI 2013 Foley et al. (2019). Further, the Mt.Gox collapse in 2014 with over 650,000 Bitcoins stolen with an estimated value of $450 million at the time has led to many trust issues. A good understanding of legal and policy implications of cryptocurrency markets is essential for anyone who wants to participate in it as an investor or service provider.

Another important contribution is presented in the following chapter of this volume that focused on the market structure of cryptocurrencies, and explains how the cryptocurrencies are being trade. It provides details on existing types of exchanges, highlighting the differences between centralized and decentralized exchanges, and what can happen if the exchange will get hacked. This chapter is important read for everyone who is planning to invest in cryptocurrencies, or plan to conduct research in this area, but not yet understand the cryptocurrency exchanges mechanism. Cryptocurrency derivatives are also discussed, as a new investment assets and growing area of research. Furthermore, this section present an overview of the key issues of cryptocurrency trading, such as undercutting, short selling constraints, front running and griefing. Indeed, this is a useful read if you want to understand cryptocurrency trading better.

The main emphasis of the following chapter is placed on the financial characteristics of cryptocurrencies, its statistical properties, explosivity, volatility, and interconnectedness with other more traditional financial markets. In this chapter cryptocurrencies considered as an investment assets, and it is a useful read for investors interested to include cryptocurrencies in their investment portfolio. For instance, a recent paper by Platanakis and Urquhart (2020) shows that including Bitcoin in a well diversified portfolio consisting of bonds, stocks and commodities significantly improves the risk-adjusted returns of the portfolio. However cryptocurrencies are not without their controversies such as the unstable volatility. This is a major issue with all cryptocurrencies being accepted as a form of payment since the price can change dramatically on any given day. This is also an excellent direction for academic research, and opportunity to contribute to contagion, portfolio theory and diversification literature.

We then present a useful example of the research on the predictability between Bitcoin and the US technology stock returns. This paper used daily data covering the period 18 August 2011 to 15 April 2019 and Granger causality in moments methodology providing an evidence of a relationship between Bitcoin and US tech stock indices. This chapter is useful particularly for students and early career researchers who want to conduct the research in this area, since it clearly displays methodological details and results, as well demonstrate how the academic study should be structured and presented. This is also useful for a broad range of practitioners, and academics working in this area, since they are in continuous search of the methods to predict the Bitcoin prices. As a cryptocurrency market leader Bitcoin influence prices of other cryptocurrencies, therefore by predicting Bitcoin price and understanding which factors determine it investors can predict the behaviour of the cryptocurrency markets.

The growth of cryptocurrency markets, and increased mining difficulty of Bitcoin, caused increased of energy consumption of this sector which might results in wider environmental implications. The penultimate chapter discuss the environmental aspects of cryptocurrency markets, addressing the issue whether cryptocurrencies are a contributor to the climate problem. It is not very popular topic among cryptocurrency-enthusiasts, however, this issue concern public and the media, since it become increasingly important for consumers to understand the climate implications of the new technology before actually using it. By including this chapter to the volume we are making a statement that climate change issues should no longer be ignored by finance community, and climate finance area in general has a great importance. The impact of cryptocurrency energy consumption and growing FinTech adoption on environment, should be thoroughly investigated by researchers to provide evidence for policy makers and regulators alike to introduce necessary legislation to this area.

The final chapter summarises the findings, providing the recommendations for future research. Cryptocurrencies are likely here to stay and more cryptocurrencies will be developed every year with new, exciting and innovative features in the hope of attracting some of the attention the traditional cryptocurrencies have since their introduction. As cryptocurrencies fight for a level-standing in the financial system, a strong understanding of this asset class is required. While pioneer papers considered technological aspect of digital assets, this volume considered cryptocurrency from a wide range of finance and business perspectives. After reading this book, you will be able to:

- Understand the main technological aspects of cryptocurrencies, and define the basic Blockchain and cryptocurrency related terms and concepts.
- Distinguish between different types of cryptocurrencies.
- Understand where and how cryptocurrencies are traded, and what are the specific features of decentralised exchanges.
- Acknowledge the existing challenges of Blockchain technology and cryptocurrency trading.
- Discuss the main problems of ICOs misusage, fraud, and wide range of regulatory, ethical and legal concerns.
- Analyse cryptocurrency as financial assets, and predict behaviour of cryptocurrencies.
- Acknowledge environmental impacts of cryptocurrency energy consumption.
- Identify interesting direction for research to make contribution to existing knowledge.

Bibliography

Cheah, E.-T., and J. Fry (2015). Speculative bubbles in bitcoin markets? An empirical investigation into the fundamental value of bitcoin. *Economics Letters 130*, 32–36.

Corbet, S., C. Larkin, B. Lucey, and L. Yarovaya (2019). KODAKCoin: A blockchain revolution or exploiting a potential cryptocurrency bubble? *Applied Economics Letters* (forthcoming).

Corbet, S., C. J. Larkin, B. M. Lucey, A. Meegan, and L. Yarovaya (2020). Cryptocurrency reaction to FOMC announcements: Evidence of heterogeneity based on blockchain stack position. *Journal of Financial Stability 46*.

Corbet, S., B. Lucey, and L. Yarovaya (2018a). Datestamping the bitcoin and ethereum bubbles. *Finance Research Letters 26*, 81–88.

Corbet, S., A. Meegan, C. Larkin, B. Lucey, and L. Yarovaya (2018b). Exploring the dynamic relationships between cryptocurrencies and other financial assets. *Economics Letters 165*, 28–34.

Foley, S., J. R. Karlsen, and T. J. Putnins (2019). Sex, drugs, and bitcoin: How much illegal activity is financed through cryptocurrencies? *Review of Financial Studies 32*, 1789–1853.

Platanakis, E., and A. Urquhart (2020). Should investors include bitcoin in their portfolios? A portfolio theory approach. *British Accounting Review*, 100837.

Daisuke Adachi and Jun Aoyagi

Blockchain and economic transactions

1 Introduction

Cryptocurrency market values have skyrocketed, as exemplified in the Bitcoin. In the meanwhile, the transactions based on the cryptocurrency has also increased significantly over the last decade. At the same time, the concept of blockchain has become popularized since the rise of cryptocurrencies as the background technology of the cryptocurrency. In this chapter, we will outline the technical and economic aspects of cryptocurrencies and blockchain. The first set of questions we attempt to answer include, but not limited to: What is blockchain? What is the Bitcoin mining process? What is crypto-transactions?

Moreover, the blockchain is not only about Bitcoin. We have been observing the widened role of these new technologies in real economic transactions, as well as financial markets. Transactions of goods, commodity, and asset markets used to have nothing to do with blockchain-based operations, while nowadays, several essential products are traded with the help of the blockchain. For instance, a consulting firm EY advisory has oriented an empirical experiment of blockchain in a commodity market, e. g., wine transactions. What would be the impact of the blockchain adoption on the wine market? Why do we need blockchain in wine transactions? How does it change the wine market properties, such as the quality of wine, transaction prices?

After we give a brief discussion about the technical aspects of blockchain, we will provide thorough explanations on the role of cryptocurrencies and blockchains on the real economic transactions. In particular, we will focus on (i) how the blockchain affects information frictions in transactions and (ii) how it changes the landscape of markets, taking into account the spillover effects to all the players.

To streamline our discussions, we will not cover the details of cryptographic technology in blockchains.

Interested readers may refer to, for example, Harvey (2016) for general cryptography-based finance and to Antonopoulos (2014) for more detailed explanation on the cryptography used in the Bitcoin.

2 Technical aspect of blockchain

We begin our main discussions with the outline of the blockchain and related technologies, such as cryptocurrencies and the Bitcoin, following recent financial and economics studies.

https://doi.org/10.1515/9783110660807-002

2.1 Double spending

A good starting point is to discuss the role of blockchain in the Bitcoin trade: how and why Bitcoin differs from existing money and digital currencies. One of the characterizing issues in this regard is the double-spending problem. Suppose that Bob purchases a book online by using a mobile payment system. After the delivery of the book, he can hack into the online ledger and rewrite his account information to pretend that the transaction has not made and to retrieve his money. Physical money has addressed this issue by developing sophisticated printing technology, thereby making it difficult to forge bills. Furthermore, cash with a physical entity (coin and paper bill) cannot be used twice because it cannot be in Bob's pocket if Alice holds it in her hand.

Although it becomes increasingly hard to counterfeit physical bills, most of our daily transactions have become digital, e. g., debit card transactions, payment by PayPal, Venmo, Google Pay, just to name a few. The conventional digital currencies are subject to the double spending problem because it is vulnerable to information manipulations. If a ledger system has a flaw, Bob may manipulate ledger information and retrieve the money he paid. The problem is traditionally handled by setting some centralized agency with anti-manipulation security. Although it can be secure, it comes with a considerable cost, and users are concerned about the credibility issue.

What blockchain and the Bitcoin provide is a new solution to this issue. Decentralized management with a hard-to-rollback mechanism mitigates the problem. It distributes transaction information to a large number of nodes of participating computers. The data is timestamped and irreversible. A set of transaction records are impounded into a block, encrypted, and attached to the pre-existing chain of information. The process repeats over and over again to generate a sequence of chained blocks, i. e., the blockchain. As all the nodes have information about a state of the world, there must be a consensus mechanism that determines what is the correct state and what should be recorded in a block.

In what follows, we detail the critical concepts, decentralization, the consensus mechanism, and smart contracts in order.

2.2 Decentralization

The first building block is the decentralized management of information. Information is distributed to a large (potentially infinite) number of computers, and each of them keeps track of information. Firstly, this prevents a single point of failure, meaning that even when one node of the network fails, the system as a whole can keep track of the correct information.

Another benefit includes reducing market power and increasing competition. If a centralized player exerts her monopolistic power, she may have an incentive to manipulate and distort information in favour of her. As we discuss in the following subsection, information on the blockchain must be the consensus of the network. Thus, even if a single record keeper tries to manipulate information, it is almost impossible to achieve.[1]

In a nutshell, a centralized record keeper in the traditional record-keeping system is replaced by a large number of competitive record keepers (called "miners" in Bitcoin network) in the blockchain system. They competitively determine what information they impound into the blockchain system by a certain consensus mechanism, rather than a single centralized entity makes a decision on it.

2.3 Consensus

The second building block is how to reach the consensus. The mechanism must make the consensus hard to manupurate, and a critical technological advance, the cryptography, kicks in here.[2] A key element in reaching consensus is the selection of nodes that chooses the legitimate information. As there is no centralized player in the blockchain network, some terminal node has to make a decision. The process of selecting the node is unique to each application but, in the Bitcoin and other large blockchains (e. g., Ethereum), the consensus mechanism called Proof-of-Work (PoW) is employed. We focus on PoW in the following, although there are many other possibilities of consensus algorithm, such as Proof-of-Stake (Saleh, 2019).

PoW is a process that (i) asks each node in the network to solve computation-heavy cryptographic problems and (ii) rewards the first node that successfully solves the problem by giving the right to authorize the information and record it on the blockchain.

The cryptographic problem relies on a hash function. The hash function should satisfy several properties (e. g., uniformity, universality, deterministic function, defined range) that are desirable for the mining protocol explained below to work. Specifically, nodes are asked to find a solution to a mathematical problem of finding a correct value. The expected time until finding the solution is determined by the difficulty target. At the same time, it decreases as computing power, called hash power, that each node devotes to the problem becomes strong. Solving a problem requires high computation power, and this triggers a competition among nodes, i. e., if other nodes adopt higher hash power, you are less likely to win the race. This process of finding the value is called mining, as it is reminiscent of finding metal ore from a mine. When a node wins the race, the mining reward is paid in the Bitcoin, and she is entitled to record information on the blockchain.

---

1 These benefits in detail and the benefits of decentralization are further discussed in Chen et al. (2019).

2 For our purpose, we only discuss selective key elements of cryptography, leaving the details in technical writings, such as Antonopoulos (2014).

This helps explain why information on the blockchain is (almost) tamper-free. First, a malicious entity trying to rewrite information on a chain must accumulate enormous computing power that outrace the other participants in the network. Second, a potential attacker must find significant benefits of attack, i. e., returns from mining the Bitcoin must outweigh the cost of computing power.

Through the competition between decentralized record keepers, the total hash rate affects the quality of consensus. As we will discuss later, having a high hash rate may improve the quality of the consensus, as winning the race becomes more costly for each miner, and her incentive to manipulate information by devoting a large power diminishes. This incentive problem will be translated to the degree of information frictions in economic transactions, as we will discuss in the later section.

The Bitcoin's hash rate increased year by year from 2016 to autumn 2018, but the hash rate continued to decrease in line with the timing of the crash of the virtual currency market. During these times, companies may be forced to withdraw from the mining business. This observation will be a crucial ingredient to our economic analysis in Section 3.

2.4 Smart contract

Smart contracts itself have been an abstract concept that existed independent of blockchain. Szabo (1997) characterizes it as a contract that is executed automatically based on specified conditions without any centralized authorizations. Although the cryptographic security mechanism was simply one of the possible choices to implement the smart contract, the blockchain grows to be the primary mechanism that guarantees secure transactions in implementing smart contracts.

Blockchain, as the underlying technology, suits the objective of smart contracts quite well. Firstly, the decentralized information-keeping system with the consensus mechanism makes the deals verifiable and thus enforceable without relying on a centralized authority (i. e., the first condition of the smart contract). Moreover, Ethereum has invented a blockchain system that records information contingent on some prespecified conditions (i. e., the second condition of the smart contract). That is, a transaction is verified—i. e., information on payment and delivery is recorded as "correct" and becomes immutable—if and only if a specified condition is satisfied.

Not only does the smart contract makes the double spending extremely difficult, it also works as a new form of "warranty" on goods' quality. It is novel because information on which the contract is contingent is managed by the decentralized record keepers rather than a centralized authority. In Section 3, we study the concept of smart contract, what it entails, and the role of blockchain behind them in detail.

2.5 Existing problem

We have overviewed some of the favorable properties of blockchains so far. Although significantly mitigated by blockchain, there are still possible problems in an actual implementation of blockchain and smart contracts. Among them, we overview some technical issues. In general, thorough consideration gives an "impossible trinity" of blockchain in Abadi and Brunnermeier (2018). They compare the characteristic features of PoW, Proof-of-Stake, and centralized ledger. Their analysis establishes the fundamental problem between self-sufficiency, rent-free, and resource-efficiency.

2.5.1 Scalability

Among the technical problems of blockchain, we overview scalability and oracle problem. The problem of scalability, in general, emerges when the number of participants of the blockchain increase. Here, the participants include miners of the cryptocurrency and users. On the one hand, when the size of a miner pool increases, record-keeping becomes slow. In particular, the speed of transmitting the latest state of the blockchain hinges on the slowest node in the network. Since anybody can participate in the blockchain network, a low-performance node typically slows down the whole system.

On the other hand, if many users flood to the cryptocurrency, loadings in the blockchain network explode, which in many cases results in significant waiting time for transfers and increasing transaction fees. One manifestation of such a problem includes the congestion effect; a long queue for transaction approval may incentivize users to pay high transaction fees because miners work on transactions that yield a high commission. The congestion effect rises the overall cost of using the blockchain (Easley et al., 2019; Huberman et al., 2019).

2.5.2 Oracle problem

Oracle in the blockchain refers to sending data outside the blockchain to the blockchain. The blockchain can generate consensus on information that is accumulated in the blockchain system and make it immutable. However, original information must be introduced to the blockchain from an external source. This outside information must also be trusted to make the whole blockchain system secure. How to guarantee the trustworthiness is called the oracle problem.

For instance, in the wine blockchain, we want to establish that a grape variety stored in the blockchain has not been manipulated but nothing within the blockchain implies that the original information injected into the system is not a lie. This casts a doubt on the smart contract too. Suppose that you made a transaction of wine contingent on some conditions, such as “make payment if and only if the wine is 100% Cabernet Sauvignon from Napa, CA.” You are (almost) sure that no information manipulations are made after the information is impounded into the blockchain record-keeping system, i. e., once the blockchain guarantees that the bottle is 100% CabSau, it is hard to mix it with Pinot Noir and still claim it as 100% CabSau. However, you are not sure if the first-place information is correct. The blockchain node cannot distinguish the grape in the first place. We will come back to this issue when we analyze the implications for real economic transactions.

2.5.3 Fork

Recall that the blockchain adds blocks to the previous chains. Occasionally, nodes do not agree which blocks should be added to which existing chains. In this case, the blockchain splits at a point in the chain. The split is called fork. Forks are potentially detrimental to the whole blockchain system because it may undermine the consensus of the information stored in the chain. Several existing studies tackle the problem why the fork occurs. For example, Biais et al. (2019) study in the format of repeated games under which conditions miners follow the simple rule of Longest Chain Rule (LCR).

2.6 Some applications

Even though there is a couple of problems to be addressed as above, we have many examples of blockchain applications, which we will overview at this point. By so doing, we touch upon several cases where the blockchain successfully has solved the problems and opened new fields.

The first achievement that deserves mentioning is that the cryptocurrencies freed part of the settlement risks that were inherent in security markets. In this context, settlement risks entail the failure of delivery of the security by the seller while receiving the payment, or vice versa. A smart contract may achieve the delivery versus payment (DvP) mechanism through the automated blockchain infrastructure without any central authority. In particular, Chiu and Koeppl (2019) argues that the main advantage of blockchain in this case is “it can speed settlement, both by getting rid of a fragmented post-trade infrastructure and by implementing a more flexible settlement cycle.”

Blockchain has also made a significant change to financial contract designs in a dynamic environment.

Traditionally, financial contracts are contingent on the event only, that make the contracts static. However, the blockchain stores information in chronological order with time stamps. Therefore, new financial contracts emerged that depend on the event that happened, but also the timing of the event. By so doing Tinn (2017) showed that the optimal contract between the parties is the one that dynamically adjust the profit sharing rules.

Furthermore, blockchain opened a new tension between decentralized consensus and information distribution that are inseparable from each other. Namely, to achieve the decentralized consensus, the blockchain needs to have the information verified by the participating nodes. For this purpose, it needs to distribute (sometimes sensitive) data. Cong and He (2018) take insights from this possibility and applied to the problems of tacit collusions. They find that although the blockchain may achieve higher competition by mitigating the problem of incomplete contracts, it potentially induces collusion among sellers.

We have overviewed the forefront understanding of blockchain technologies, the problems, and applications. Throughout the section, we constrained ourselves in the realm of financial transactions. From now, we open ourselves to a broader perspective, including real economic transactions. To have a new view of the technology that we study in the next section, consider the hash rate in a new way. In particular, one may view the hash rate as a supply product of the Bitcoin market since it transmits to the output, the Bitcoin tokens. For example, Pagnotta and Buraschi (2018) apply the idea to analyze the behavior of the Bitcoin's prices and hash rates. By pushing this idea further to the real economic transactions, we will consider the broader potential implications of blockchain in the next section.

3 Implications to the real economic transactions

Another issue arises when we carefully consider how markets and participants react to the blockchain adoption in the environment that economists often call as general equilibrium. By reviewing the study by Aoyagi and Adachi (2018), we will go over the potential impacts of blockchains and cryptocurrencies on the real economy beyond finance.

3.1 Background

Examples of real economic transactions under consideration may be massive and expanding. A number of blockchain-based platforms for trading have been launched, including those for wine (EY Advisory and Consulting) fresh foods (Walmart), jewelry (HyperLedger), arts and photography (Kodak), security (tZero), and cryptocurrency (Waves, IDEX, Steller, Oasis, OKEx, Cashaa, and more). In the following analysis, we call these goods, commodities, and assets as "goods" or "products" collectively.

To give an idea of the real economic transactions, consider the case of wine blockchain by EY Advisory and Consulting. The blockchain was built as a solution to track wine origins and quality in all ecosystems involved in wine distribution: producers, distributors, logistics, and insurance companies. The blockchain offers tokens for transactions. The use of the tokens enables the tracking of a wine shipment, warehouses storage and deliveries, and insurance compensation for the shipping process and the buying and selling of the bottle. In other words, distributors and consumers can order wine directly from the platform and track shipping status, including custom clearance and storage in real-time.

As can be seen from this example, blockchain adoption in transactions of goods can be generalized as follows. First, the blockchain includes cryptocurrencies that is a digital token that works as a means of trade. Second, miners keep monitoring the transaction that involves cryptocurrencies and blockchain. Finally, users, including sellers and buyers, may use the tokens to trade goods.

In the below consideration, we will give an entire economic transaction system involving the blockchain as follows. A cryptocurrency token is exchanged in the mining markets. The miners join the market, and the token is given to reward their efforts of record-keeping. The users of the token are twofold—the buyers (Bob) of the goods (coffee) and the sellers (Alice). The users may transact with or without the cryptocurrency. If they do not use it, they need to resort to the traditional method of payment. It is worthwhile to emphasize again that we separate two types of agents, miners, and users. Given the dichotomy, the questions are raised in the following.

3.2 Questions

Since our interest is the broad implications on the real economic transactions, we need to be careful about posing a correct question to ask. We begin by asking a somewhat abstract motivation and bring ourselves down to a more particular and precise question. This process starts by asking: what is the general equilibrium (GE) implications to economic transactions of blockchain adoption? In our context, GE means that we are interested in the joint determination of economic variables, including prices of goods, trading volume, market quality, as well as blockchain-related variables, such as the value of cryptocurrencies and miner pool sizes. Discussions so far have explored the mechanism and incentive of each participant (e. g., miners). In the real economy, they interacts to form the overall economic system. What do the economic outcomes of our interest look like, such as the price and volume of the cryptocurrency traded, the sorting of users that use cryptocurrency, the quality of the goods traded? What will happen when the cost of cryptocurrency mining increases? Would the decentralized transaction space be better than the one that is operated by a single centralized record-keeper?

These motivations lead us to a natural question–why do users use blockchain to trade goods, beyond double-spending? The short answer to this question is asymmetric information. To understand this better, let us further ask ourselves: what is the economic meaning of the blockchain? As we have seen, the blockchain is technically a collection of technologies and concepts that enable the decentralized information keeping system. This defining feature is inseparably connected to the recent flood of the applications to the goods markets. In particular, in the real economy, there is an increasing demand for knowledge about the source of the goods. Partly due to the changes in the international regulations and decreases in the shipping and communication costs, the supply chains get complicated. For instance, the global supply chains of iPad and Boeing 787 are prohibitively enormous. Understanding the whole structure of the chain of these products is almost impossible (Antras, 2015).

Even before jumping to such extreme examples, wine production is already sophisticated enough that the blockchain found it useful to help the problem we discuss below. The wine production contains at least the following steps: cultivation and harvesting of grape and other ingredients, brewing, shipping, vintage, and delivery. All these steps are indispensable for letting the final consumers enjoy the quality bottle. If these steps were done within one player in home-production and sales, there would be a minimal problem of quality counterfeiting. However, such an all-in-one approach of production is not scalable, and a typical market structure involves multiple parties along the supply chain. Furthermore, at any given stage of the production, it is typically difficult to verify the quality of the products up to the stage.

In this case, what economists often call as the lemon problem arises. Namely, no buyers may verify the quality of the inputs they purchase. Furthermore, the cost of producing low-quality ones is typically lower (imagine counterfeiting the grape variety by rewriting the low-quality one to the high-quality one). Therefore, the transactions are contaminated by low-quality goods. The lemon translates directly into the low-quality bottles of wine and possibly leads to the collapse of high-quality wine markets (Akerlof, 1970). Therefore, there is a great demand for correctly knowing the quality of the upstream goods other parties produce.

3.3 Role of blockchain in economic transactions

The key concept in the lemon problem is information asymmetry that only the seller knows the quality, while the buyer does not. A potential (and historical) solution to this problem is introducing a centralized record keeper. However, typically, the solution is costly, as we discussed above. The blockchain has the potential to address the problem. As we have discussed, the blockchain's technical aspects allow smart contracts. The involved parties may use the pre-specified conditions under which the transaction is completed in the contract protocol. If the requirement stating that only the high-quality goods may be transacted is not satisfied, either of the parties may terminate the transaction without actual changes in the ownership of goods and money. By doing this, we may potentially achieve that the goods transacted under smart contracts backed by the blockchain may be reliable to be high-quality.

The above configurations are likely. However, there is still a margin of how reliable the information stored in the blockchain. As we discussed in the sections above, given the oracle problem, there is no way to guarantee the information conveyed in any protocols is true for sure. What blockchains can do is to mitigate the uncertainty in the information. We call the level of uncertainty as "security" of the blockchain. When the security is high, the uncertainty of the information stored is low, and vice versa.

How is the security level determined? Naturally, the security level is high when the underlying technology, such as the program codes written to operate the blockchain, is robust and sophisticated. However, it is not the end of the story. It is critical to recognize and emphasize the role of miners and the size of miner pools. The size matters because of the decentralized property of the blockchain—the more miners participate, the less the benefit of cheating is. We will detail the specific mechanisms below. At this point, we only claim two. First, there is a concept of the security level of the blockchain. Second, it has to be determined at the end of the analysis.

3.4 Miner-side analysis

We then move on to the analysis of players in the market in detail—miners, users of the token separated by the buyers and sellers of the goods. We then come back to combining all the considerations to determine the prediction of the economy.

The crucial first question regarding the miner side is: how do the blockchain miners enter the mining pool? As we discussed in the technical section, the miners join the pool and engage in the mining process (most likely equipped with ASIC in case of PoW protocol) if and only if it is profitable to do so. When is the entry profitable? For simplification, we focus on the role of the price of the cryptocurrency attached to the blockchain. In other words, miners enter when the price of cryptocurrency is high. We acknowledge, in reality, there are many aspects to be concerned when determining profitability. Furthermore, Aoyagi and Adachi (2018) show that our analysis may be extendable to the case of blockchain without cryptocurrencies.

The second key question is: given entry, how are the security levels of the chain achieved and maintained? To answer this question, we look into the partially verifiable false-reporting and reputation costs. In particular, let us consider the simplified reporting system the miners or record keepers may tell the truth or lie. Whenever profitable for the keeper, (s)he can tell a lie, risking verification by a third party. In this case, (s)he would suffer from the reputation loss due to the misreporting. This consideration disciplines the keeper. In this situation, the security level is determined according to the size of the mining pool. Namely, as the mining pool gets massive, chances of winning to add the block are lower. Hence it does not worth risking the reputation cost for many miners. Thus, a large mining pool increases the overall security level of the information stored in the blockchain. Note that this resembles the positive network effect studied in Pagnotta and Buraschi (2018).

3.5 User-side analysis

Although the above considerations for the miner side are relatively common in the study of blockchains and cryptocurrency, it is relatively understudied how the user side of the blockchain interact with miners. In fact, users are also expected to actively respond to the features of the blockchain, the security level, and the price of cryptocurrencies—obviously, the secure the blockchain is, the value for the user increases. The cheaper the cryptocurrency price is, the more valuable it is for buyers of the goods transacted, the less for sellers. Given the discussions above, we consider these points in detail under the dual markets where the products may be sold and purchased in the traditional market where the means of payment is cash or traditional digital currencies, and the blockchain-based market where the transaction is done in the cryptocurrency based on the blockchain. In particular, to participate in the blockchain-based market and make a purchase, the buyer must hold the cryptocurrency token beforehand. Therefore, there is a link between the users and miners of the blockchain in the following sense. On the one hand, the users demand cryptocurrency since they want to purchase the goods whose quality information is stored in the blockchain system. On the other hand, the miners supply cryptocurrency through record keeping.

Under this situation, the non-monotonicity of the demand for cryptocurrencies in the security level emerges as a surprising result. Put differently, it is not always the case that as the blockchain becomes secure the demand for the cryptocurrency increases. Given that the higher security enhances the value of blockchain-based market for product transactions, this may be a surprising result. We overview why and how this result may emerge due to the congestion effect below.

Intuitively, as the security level goes up, the demand for the blockchain-based good increases as the chance of getting high-quality goods is higher. This security effect increases the demand for cryptocurrency that is needed for the transaction therein. However, at the same time, as more buyers flood into the blockchain-based market, the price for the cryptocurrency goes up. The price surge drives out some of the buyers who would have stayed otherwise. This congestion effect may reduce the quantity of cryptocurrency demanded since the size of the blockchain market shrinks. Therefore, there are two conflicting forces, the positive security effect and the negative congestion effect, that makes the prediction non-monotonic. In particular, Aoyagi and Adachi (2018) discuss the further detail of the conditions behind this finding and more specific prediction about the non-monotonicity.

Readers should also notice that the value of cryptocurrency here is real values rather than a bubble. The cryptocurrency and underlying blockchain help mitigating the information friction problem, which yields the real economic gain. The actual economic value because of reducing the lemon problem is also a characterizing feature of this analysis.

3.6 Analysis of changes

Combining the thorough thought experiments about both miners and users, we can consider a rich analysis of the effect of the change of external economic conditions on any features we are interested in the investigation, such as cryptocurrency prices and the security level of blockchain. This analysis is typically useful in testing our considerations above. Although the full details are relegated to Aoyagi and Adachi (2018), we give two examples of their studies.

When is blockchain more efficient than the centralized system? We may regard the above analysis as nesting the case with a centralized authority. One can see this by considering the case with only one conceptual "miner" that is allowed to enter the token-generating system. The miner, we call as the centralized authority, does not mine since it does not have to keep the record in a decentralized manner anymore. Instead, it just gives the credentials to all the transactions that come across the system. What would the centralized authority do? Since now it may choose the security level without the distributed consensus mechanism, it would do so to optimize its interest, in this case, the price of the token they would receive upon authorization. Here, again, the non-monotonic cryptocurrency price structure matters—the centralized authority would take advantage of it and select the optimal security level for itself, without considering the appropriate security levels for other parties. Aoyagi and Adachi (2018) detail under which circumstances the security level under the distributed ledger system with blockchain is higher than that with the centralized ledger. In this sense, our consideration is complete with highlighting the benefit of decentralization.

The second analysis is regarding the following prediction about the change in the cost to operate ASIC (e. g., ASIC machine price, electricity price). When the cost increases, fewer miners enter the mining pool. Effectively this enhances the cryptocurrency prices because the entry must be more profitable for miners that may cover the increased cost of mining. We overviewed that the demand for cryptocurrency may decrease or increase in the security level of blockchain. If it is falling, then we expect that the cryptocurrency price increases. This prediction confirms the intuition discussed by the previous studies. If it is increasing, then somewhat surprisingly, the increase in the cost of mining may potentially decrease the price of the cryptocurrency. This prediction is first introduced by Aoyagi and Adachi (2018) but is yet to be formally tested in the real-world data.

Although not comprehensive, we have been witnessing some supporting evidence for our story. An example comes from the wine blockchain project outlined above. For example, a few wine seller companies introduced the wine blockchain under the empirical experiments conducted by EY Advisory and Consulting. The result includes the increased unit price of the bottle. This result is consistent with our story since the wine blockchain is meant to improve the information stocked throughout the supply chain tamper-free, making the average quality of the bottles to the final consumers improved. The higher quality translates into higher prices. More thorough empirical studies are expected to challenge the story outlined in this section.

4 Conclusion

In this chapter, we overviewed the technical aspects and the potential implications for real economic transactions. Throughout the analysis, we emphasized the role of decentralization and smart contract for our purpose, leaving a large set of interesting aspects blockchains unexplained. We only begin to witness the profound real economic consequences in a subset of economic transactions. However, as our technical section suggested, we have sophisticated technical backgrounds that such impacts are to come. We hope the current monograph helps the reader to frame the blockchain and the economic implications.

Bibliography

Abadi, Joseph, and Markus Brunnermeier (2018). *Blockchain economics*, Technical Report, mimeo, Princeton University.

Akerlof, George (1970). The market for lemons. *Quarterly Journal of Economics 84*(3), 488–500.

Antonopoulos, Andreas M. 2014. *Mastering bitcoin: Unlocking digital cryptocurrencies.* O'Reilly Media, Inc.

Antras, Pol (2015). *Global production: Firms, contracts, and trade structure.* Princeton University Press.

Aoyagi, Jun, and Daisuke Adachi (2018). Economic implications of blockchain platforms. Available at SSRN, 3132235.

Biais, Bruno, Christophe Bisiere, Matthieu Bouvard, and Catherine Casamatta (2019). The blockchain folk theorem. *The Review of Financial Studies 32*(5), 1662–1715.

Chen, Long, Lin William Cong, and Yizhou Xiao (2019). A brief introduction to blockchain economics. Available at SSRN.

Chiu, Jonathan, and Thorsten V. Koeppl (2019). Blockchain-based settlement for asset trading. *The Review of Financial Studies 32*(5), 1716–1753.

Cong, Lin William, and Zhiguo He (2018). *Blockchain disruption and smart contracts.*

Easley, David, Maureen O'Hara, and Soumya Basu (2019). From mining to markets: The evolution of bitcoin transaction fees. *Journal of Financial Economics.*

Harvey, Campbell (2016). *Cryptofinance.*

Huberman, Gur, Jacob Leshno, and Ciamac C. Moallemi (2019). An economic analysis of the bitcoin payment system. *Columbia Business School Research Paper*, 17–92.

Pagnotta, Emiliano, and Andrea Buraschi (2018). An equilibrium valuation of bitcoin and decentralized network assets. Available at SSRN 3142022.

Saleh, Fahad (2019). Blockchain without waste: Proof-of-stake. Available at SSRN 3183935.

Szabo, Nick (1997). Formalizing and securing relationships on public networks. *First Monday 2*(9).

Tinn, Katrin (2017). *Blockchain and the future of optimal financing contracts.*

Shaen Corbet and Brian Lucey

An analysis of the development of cryptocurrency research

1 Introduction

The aim of this chapter is to provide a short overview of cryptocurrency research as of the end of 2019. We do this by means of a scientometric analysis, which has been used across a wide-ranging number of disciplines. We do not provide here a critical literature review per se. Rather, our ambition is to present the pathway through which research has flowed in the past decade. To do so we draw on similar pieces of work across other disciplines, such as that of sustainability and sustainability development (Olawumi and Chan (2018)), the development of building information systems (Zhao (2017), He et al. (2017)), food authentication (Danezis et al. (2016)), biotic identification (Ruaro and Gubiani (2013)) and even at the level of products, such as algae, biohydrogen and biodiesel (Konur (2011, 2012a,b)). With regards to examples as to how such research can provide benefit to broad disciplines, Rotolo et al. (2015) developed a definition of 'emerging technologies' and linked the conceptual effort with the development of a framework for the operationalisation of technological emergence, which could then be used to trace the development of research over time. Serenko et al. (2010) conducted a meta-analysis of prior scientometric research of the knowledge management using 108 scientometric studies of the discipline and subjecting each meta-analysis techniques. Further, Corbet et al. (2019) provides such a review as of early 2019, what we aim for here is to analyse the development of this area of research in terms of its intellectual structure. Lowry et al. (2013) investigated journal quality and the association for information systems, specifically analysing as to whether expert journal assessments add value? The authors conclude that bibliometric measures provide very similar results to expert-based methods in determining a tiered structure of IS journals, thereby suggesting that bibliometrics can be a complete, less expensive, and more efficient substitute for expert assessment.

The rapid development of cryptocurrencies as a financial product appears to have taken many regulatory systems by surprise. While research to uncover the many systemic repercussions of this digital finance evolution continues to expand at pace, much evidence points toward substantially differing characteristics associated with these new financial products relative to traditional financial products on which much regulation has been honed over time. The development of cryptocurrencies and the surrounding research associated at both the narrow-product level (namely, Bitcoin or Ethereum individually) or at the broad-level (all cryptocurrencies) has been further advertised by the unprecedented price appreciations that have taken place across a number of assets, particularly that of Bitcoin. These products have therefore offered substantial opportunities to a number of speculative investors, not to mention a

https://doi.org/10.1515/9783110660807-003

transmission vehicle through which those with illicit needs can take advantage of regulatory circumvention. Research, beginning with such humble beginnings through the work of Nakamoto (2009) has expanded to analyse technical, sociological, legal, financial and economical aspects of the product. However, such research has recently begun to question if this price evolution could be a symptom of other deeper issues such as the presence of financial bubbles (Corbet et al. (2018a); Fry (2018)), or as to whether the product is now unfortunately overcome with illegality. In recent works to identify such illicit tactics, Griffins and Shams (2018) investigated Tether's influence in Bitcoin and other cryptocurrency prices to find that purchases with Tether were timed following market downturns and resulted in significant increases in the price of Bitcoin. Further, less than 1% of the hours in which Tether experienced significant transactions is associated with 50% of the increase in Bitcoin prices and 64% of other top cryptocurrencies, drawing the damning conclusion that Tether was used to provide price support and manipulate cryptocurrency prices. Along with this source of instability, cryptocurrency exchanges as well as individual currencies have experienced several sophisticated hacking events, further damaging the confidence in this asset class. Further, Gandal et al. (2018) identified the impact of suspicious trading activity on the Mt.Gox Bitcoin exchange theft, when approximately 600,000 Bitcoins were attained. The authors demonstrated that the suspicious trading likely caused the spike in price in late 2013 from $150 to $1,000, most likely driven by one single actor. These two significant pieces of research have fine-tuned the focus of regulators, policy-makers, and academics alike, as the future growth of cryptocurrencies cannot be sustained at pace with such significant questions of abnormality remaining unanswered.

This chapter focuses distinctly on the pathway that such cryptocurrency research has taken. Further, we attempt to provide oversight of the key areas that appear to have been under-resourced with academic coverage and as to where we observe current trends to be focused. The rest of the chapter is as follows: in Section 2 we provide a very short review of the key developments in cryptocurrency research to date. In Section 3 we explain the data and methodologies used to analyse the research and carry out the bibliometric analysis. In Section 4 we provide the results of this analysis, while in Section 5 we conclude.

2 The development of cryptocurrency research: A very short review

Since the product's evolution through the work of Nakamoto (2009), Bitcoin has developed as an investment asset that have no association with any higher authority, specific country, tangible asset or firm, and the value of it is based on the security of an algorithm which is able to trace all transaction (Corbet et al. (2020)). Corbet et al.

(2019) provided a thorough overview of the empirical literature based on the major topics that have been associated with the market for cryptocurrencies since their development as a financial asset. Anonymity and decentralisation of cryptocurrency attracted attention from both users and investors, which caused enormous growth of market capitalisation and price of Bitcoin. Corbet et al. (2018a) while utilising the bubble identification methodology of Phillips et al. (2011), found clear evidence of periods in which Bitcoin and Ethereum were experiencing bubble phases. Urquhart (2016) investigated the efficiency of Bitcoin using a battery of robustness tests to find that returns are significantly inefficient over their selected full sample, but when dividing the same sample, Bitcoin presented evidence of becoming more efficient. Recent findings by Sensoy (2018) also report that Bitcoin prices both in terms US dollar and euros have become more efficient. Similar research has been conducted on the newly developed Bitcoin futures market (Corbet et al. (2018); Katsiampa et al. (2019a); Katsiampa et al. (2019b)). Further research areas have developed with focus on trading rules (Corbet et al. (2019c)); portfolio design (Akhtaruzzaman et al. (2019)); the creation of derivatives product exchanges (Akyildirim et al. (2019a)); implied volatility (Akyildirim et al. (2019b)); and market cross-correlations and interactive dynamics (Akyildirim et al. (2019b), Corbet et al. (2018b, 2019a)).

In Table 1 we observe the descriptive statistics for the data used in this bibliometric analysis using all available between the first observation, identified as the work of Nakamoto (2009) until that of November 2019. The research is separated between two distinct types, firstly, that relating to a digital currency directly, such as Bitcoin for example, and secondly, broad coverage of cryptocurrencies as a research topic. Figure 1 presents evidence of the dramatic growth in research based on this new product during the time analysed. We clearly observe that research surrounding individual products account for approximately twice that of broad cryptocurrency research. There are 521 separate sources of coverage for research by product, however, only 323 sources for that relating to the sector. With regards to citations, product-level research focused on 10,773 other pieces of work, while topic-level research accounted for 3,739 citations, however, product-level research has generated 9.22 cites per document while topic-wide research generated 6.99. There is evidence of increased multi-authorship on topic-level research, with an average of 2.65 authors per paper, substantially above the average of 1.99 for product-level research. To date, 3,742 authors have worked on research relating to cryptocurrencies whether narrow or broad.

In Table 2 we observe the top citations sources by author as ranked by the number of articles and associated fractional citations. In terms of both narrow and broad areas of research, we can identify a number of authors that are prevalent across both research-types. In Table 3 we observe the top citations across countries based by both narrow and broad research types. In terms of narrow-based research, we observe that the United States have produced, to this point, the largest number of research articles, however, in terms of quality, measured by the number of citations, the UK possesses a far more substantial level of cites per article (12.5) in comparison to the United States

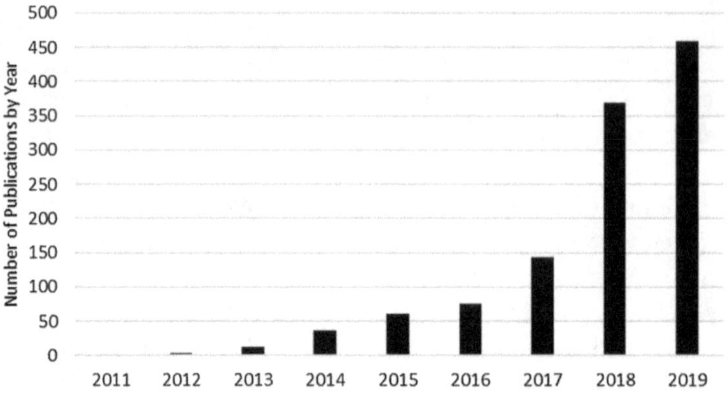

(a) Broad Area-Based Research

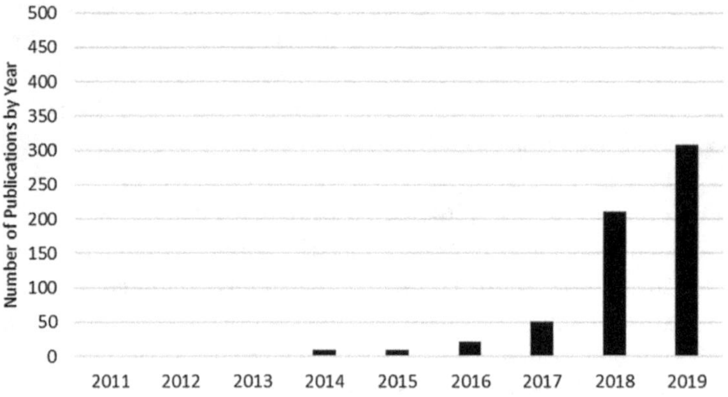

(b) Narrow Product-Based Research

Figure 1: Number of observations based on research designation.

Note: The above data was compiled as of November 2019.

(7.2). Both Lebanon and Switzerland possess the largest number of cites per article, but these estimates are provided with the caveat of quite a low number of articles published (13 and 14 respectively). Considering broad-based research, China has provided far more research articles. Again, the UK stands out through the possession of a considerable number of cites per article, considering the substantial number of research papers that have been published. However, both Ireland and Lebanon lead the way in terms of citations per article (27.8 and 17.7 respectively).

In Table 4, we observe the top journals in terms of research output and citations. In terms of both narrow and broad types of research, Finance Research Letters has published the largest number of papers and is closely followed by Economics Letters, who possess are larger number of citations in both categories. Both of these journals are closely followed by Applied Economics Letters and IEEE Access. It becomes quickly

Table 1: Descriptive Statistics based on the selected dataset.

Measure	By product	By topic	Total
Documents	1,169	535	1,704
Sources (Journals, Books, etc)	521	323	844
Citations	10,773	3,739	14,512
Average citations per document	9.22	6.99	8.52
Authors	2,326	1,416	3,742
Authors of single authored documents	274	137	411
Authors of multi authored documents	2,052	1,279	3,331
Documents per author	0.50	0.38	0.46
Authors per document	1.99	2.65	2.20

Note: The above data was compiled as of November 2019.

Table 2: Top citation sources by author.

Narrow Product-Based Research				Broad Area-Based Research			
Rank	Author	Articles	Fractional	Rank	Author	Articles	Fractional
1	Bouri E.	12	9.9	1	Bouri E.	26	15.3
2	Roubaud D.	12	9.9	2	Roubaud D.	23	17.2
3	Corbet S.	8	6.9	3	Li X.	12	8.7
4	Katsiampa P.	8	10.6	4	Liu J.	12	0.4
5	Lucey B.	8	6.9	5	Lucey B.	11	16.6
6	Li X.	7	7.7	6	Corbet S.	11	17.6
7	Urquhart A.	7	11.9	7	Gupta R.	9	21.6
8	Yarovaya L.	6	4.5	8	Li Y.	9	0.2
9	Tiwari A. K.	5	0.5	8	Katsiampa P.	8	16.8
10	Wang Y.	5	4.3	9	Mensi W.	8	13.5
11	Choo K.-K. R.	4	1.9	10	Urquhart A.	8	19.6
12	Delgado-Segura S.	4	1.3	11	Kristoufek L.	7	11.3
13	Herrera-Joancomartí J.	4	1.3	12	Liu X.	7	1.3
14	Li H.	4	6.3	13	Luther W. J.	7	4.3
15	Li Y.	4	0.5	14	Selmi R.	7	13.6
16	Ludermir T. B.	4	1.6	15	Tiwari A. K.	7	18.4
17	Luther W. J.	4	7.9	16	Yarovaya L.	6	8.2
18	Marchesi M.	4	3.0	17	Al-Yahyaee K. H.	6	9.8
19	Shen D.	4	3.5	18	Bouoiyour J.	6	15.5
20	Stosic D./Stosic T.	4	1.6	19	Herrera-Joancomartí J.	6	0.0

Note: The above data was compiled as of November 2019.

evident that the letters-format of research appears to be most popular amongst cryptocurrency researchers. This is most likely due to the fast-moving nature of the research area and the ability to quickly disseminate research in a reputable and visible

Table 3: Top citation sources by country.

Narrow Product-Based Research					Broad Area-Based Research				
Rank	**Country**	**Articles**	**Cites**	**Cites/Article**	**Rank**	**Country**	**Articles**	**Cites**	**Cites/Article**
1	United States	126	907	7.2	1	United States	230	2,247	9.8
2	United Kingdom	70	877	12.5	2	China	152	971	6.4
3	China	59	434	7.4	3	United Kingdom	127	2,067	16.3
4	Russian Federation	35	69	2.0	4	France	76	968	12.7
5	India	33	83	2.5	5	India	68	256	3.8
6	Australia	31	173	5.6	6	Australia	65	670	10.3
7	France	31	342	11.0	7	Germany	57	816	14.3
8	Italy	29	158	5.4	8	Italy	52	386	7.4
9	Spain	28	307	11.0	9	Spain	49	716	14.6
10	South Korea	26	309	11.9	10	South Korea	46	407	8.8
11	Germany	24	115	4.8	11	Russian Federation	42	109	2.6
12	Ukraine	22	56	2.5	12	Canada	31	203	6.5
13	Canada	19	105	5.5	13	Lebanon	30	531	17.7
14	Brazil	18	86	4.8	14	Ireland	26	722	27.8
15	Ireland	16	42	2.6	15	Netherlands	23	132	5.7
16	Malaysia	16	11	0.7	16	Brazil	22	77	3.5
17	Japan	15	10	0.7	17	Japan	22	140	6.4
18	Switzerland	14	176	12.6	18	Switzerland	22	342	15.5
19	Lebanon	13	241	18.5	19	South Africa	21	311	14.8
20	South Africa	12	34	2.8	20	Greece	19	155	8.2

Note: The above data was compiled as of November 2019.

Table 4: Top ten journals as defined by both broad and narrow product-based research.

Narrow Product-Based Research				Broad Area-Based Research			
Rank	**Source**	**Documents**	**Citations**	**Rank**	**Source**	**Documents**	**Citations**
1	Finance Research Letters	66	1,005	1	Finance Research Letters	42	287
2	Economics Letters	38	1,380	2	Economics Letters	20	583
3	IEEE Access	29	273	3	IEEE Access	13	161
4	Future Generation Computer Systems	19	227	4	Applied Economics	7	75
5	International Review of Financial Analysis	17	192	5	Applied Economics Letters	7	13
6	Applied Economics Letters	10	167	6	Computer Law and Security Review	6	20
7	Applied Economics	9	242	7	Future Generation Computer Systems	6	97
8	Computer Fraud and Security	7	62	8	Communications of the ACM	5	109
9	Financial Innovation	7	55	9	Electronic Commerce Research and Applications	4	19
10	Future Internet	7	185	10	Business Horizons	3	14

Note: The above data was compiled as of November 2019.

Table 5: Top ten articles as defined by both broad and narrow product-based research.

Narrow Product-Based Research	
1	Tschorsch, F. and Scheuermann, B., 2016. Bitcoin and beyond: A technical survey on decentralized digital currencies. IEEE Communications Surveys & Tutorials, 18(3), pp. 2084–2123.
2	Yli-Huumo, J., Ko, D., Choi, S., Park, S. and Smolander, K., 2016. Where is current research on blockchain technology? – a systematic review. PloS one, 11(10), p. e0163477.
3	Böhme, R., Christin, N., Edelman, B. and Moore, T., 2015. Bitcoin: Economics, technology, and governance. Journal of Economic Perspectives, 29(2), pp. 213–38.
4	Urquhart, A., 2016. The inefficiency of Bitcoin. Economics Letters, 148, pp. 80–82.
5	Cheah, E. T. and Fry, J., 2015. Speculative bubbles in Bitcoin markets? An empirical investigation into the fundamental value of Bitcoin. Economics Letters, 130, pp. 32–36.
6	Dyhrberg, A. H., 2016. Bitcoin, gold and the dollar – A GARCH volatility analysis. Finance Research Letters, 16, pp. 85–92.
7	Khan, M. A. and Salah, K., 2018. IoT security: Review, blockchain solutions, and open challenges. Future Generation Computer Systems, 82, pp. 395–411.
8	Kristoufek, L., 2015. What are the main drivers of the Bitcoin price? Evidence from wavelet coherence analysis. PloS one, 10(4), p. e0123923.
9	Dwyer, G. P., 2015. The economics of Bitcoin and similar private digital currencies. Journal of Financial Stability, 17, pp. 81–91.
10	Katsiampa, P., 2017. Volatility estimation for Bitcoin: A comparison of GARCH models. Economics Letters, 158, pp. 3–6.
Broad Area-Based Research	
1	Li, X., Jiang, P., Chen, T., Luo, X. and Wen, Q., 2017. A survey on the security of blockchain systems. Future Generation Computer Systems.
2	Zheng, Z., Xie, S., Dai, H. N., Chen, X. and Wang, H., 2018. Blockchain challenges and opportunities: A survey. International Journal of Web and Grid Services, 14(4), pp. 352–375.
3	Fernández-Caramés, T. M. and Fraga-Lamas, P., 2018. A Review on the Use of Blockchain for the Internet of Things. IEEE Access, 6, pp. 32979–33001.
4	Fry, J. and Cheah, E. T., 2016. Negative bubbles and shocks in cryptocurrency markets. International Review of Financial Analysis, 47, pp. 343–352.
5	Bouri, E., Molnár, P., Azzi, G., Roubaud, D. and Hagfors, L. I., 2017. On the hedge and safe haven properties of Bitcoin: Is it really more than a diversifier?. Finance Research Letters, 20, pp. 192–198.
6	Garcia, D., Tessone, C. J., Mavrodiev, P. and Perony, N., 2014. The digital traces of bubbles: feedback cycles between socio-economic signals in the Bitcoin economy. Journal of the Royal Society Interface, 11(99), p. 20140623.
7	Phillip, A., Chan, J. S. and Peiris, S., 2018. A new look at Cryptocurrencies. Economics Letters, 163, pp. 6–9.
8	Kim, Y. B., Kim, J. G., Kim, W., Im, J. H., Kim, T. H., Kang, S. J. and Kim, C. H., 2016. Predicting fluctuations in cryptocurrency transactions based on user comments and replies. PloS one, 11(8), p. e0161197.
9	Dai, J. and Vasarhelyi, M. A., 2017. Toward blockchain-based accounting and assurance. Journal of Information Systems, 31(3), pp. 5–21.
10	Kouicem, D. E., Bouabdallah, A. and Lakhlef, H., 2018. Internet of things security: A top-down survey. Computer Networks, 141, pp. 199–221.

Note: The above data was compiled as of November 2019.

manner. Applied Economics, Future Generation Computer Systems and International Review of Financial Analysis are journals that would be considered to produce more substantial pieces or work closely these short-form research outputs. There also appears to be quite a coherent grouping of computer-based research outputs along with both economics and finance-based research outputs.

The top articles as defined by citations, as per late-2019 are presented in Table 5. In terms of citations, Tschorsch and Scheuermann (2016) had produced the most cited paper in terms of narrow-focused cryptocurrency research, providing a technical survey of decentralised digital currencies in the IEEE Communications Surveys & Tutorials. With regards to broad-based cryptocurrency research, Li et al. (2017) produced a survey on the security of blockchain systems in the journal Future Generation Computer Systems. While much of this research focuses specifically on the technical elements of Bitcoin and cryptocurrency at large, some of the most well known pieces of research relating directly to economics and finance research include that of Cheah and Fry (2015) who provided an empirical investigation into the fundamental value of Bitcoin; Bouri et al. (2017) who investigated as to whether Bitcoin was a diversifier through its hedge and safe-haven properties; and Urquhart (2016) who analysed Bitcoin in terms of its efficiency as a product. Research from Economics Letters and Finance Research Letters appear to be most pronounced. This is further supported in Table 6 where we observe the combined number of cryptocurrency-based research citations (inclusive of both broad- and narrow-based research). In terms of broad citations, Economics Letters is the most visible research outlet with 1,269 citations, but this is closely followed by both Finance Research Letters and Physica A. Then follows International Review of Financial Analysis, PLOS One, Applied Economics, Applied Economic Letters and Econometrica. We can clearly observe broad cross-discipline coverage, with research spanning economics, finance, physics, communications, technological, sociological and econometric-based topics.

3 Data selection and methods

3.1 Methods

Bibliometrics, the analysis of citation and author networks, as well as its close relative scientometrics, have had significant traction in areas outside finance. In the life sciences, medicine and nursing especially, Cochrane Reviews, deep systemic reviews of an area incorporating meta analyses and bibliometrics, are seen as the gold standard for evidence. A search for "bibliometrics or scientometrics" in Scopus will show that close to a quarter of all papers in this area are in Medicine. The next largest lies in Library and Archival science. In the UK the 2021 Research Evaluation Framework reference documents suggest that bibliometrics will be a major and indeed en-

Table 6: Journals ranked by the number of overall cryptocurrency citations (both broad and narrow-based).

Rank	Source	Citations
1	Economics Letters	1,269
2	Finance Research Letters	977
3	Physica A	706
4	international Review of Financial Analysis	399
5	PLOS One	338
6	Applied Economics	253
7	Applied Economics Letters	227
8	Econometrica	225
9	IEEE Access	204
10	Communications of the ACM	183
11	Journal of Finance	168
12	Physical Review E	154
13	Research in International Business & Finance	152
14	Journal of Financial Economics	151
15	Energy Economics	122
16	Financial Cryptography & Data Security	120
17	Review of Financial Studies	119
18	Journal of Econometrics	97
19	Journal of Finance	95
20	Quantitative Finance	91
21	American Economic Review	84
22	Expert Systems with Applications	73
23	Journal of Financial Stability	73
24	MIS Quarterly	72
25	Biometrika	71
26	Nature	71
27	Journal of Economic Perspectives	62
28	Future Internet	55
29	Economic Modelling	53
30	Journal of International Financial Markets, Institutions & Money	51

Note: The above data was compiled as of November 2019.

hanced component in both suggested submission strategies and in how the review panels form judgements[1] More critically, Jappe et al. (2018) provides a (Sociologically focused) overview of the influence of bibliometrics and scientometrics on research evaluation and funding bodies. Levine-Clark and Gil (2008), Vieira and Gomes (2009), Franceschet (2010) and Mongeon and Paul-Hus (2016) – which concludes that each has advantages but all should, ideally, be used. Considerable data cleaning would be

1 See https://thebibliomagician.wordpress.com/2018/08/13/metrics-in-latest-ref-documents/ for a discussion and further linkages.

required however to create a blended database of all. In addition, not all meta data are present in all three data bases, in particular Google Scholar.[2]

Core bibliometric approaches involve surfacing the linkages between papers or articles. Here we use, unless otherwise indicated, the number of articles to weight collaboration and linkage. Thus linkages are stronger when say two authors collaborate with each other on 10 papers than would be the case where another two authors collaborate on 5. These linkages lend themselves nicely to graphical presentation, being in essence network models. Graphic models rely on nodes and edges (See Kosnik (2018)) where the nodes here are determined by the individual units of analysis (authors, countries etc) and the edges the linkages between them. In all cases we apply fractional counting, whereby authorship or nationality among other characteristics are scaled to the number of occurrences. Therefore an author appearing in a paper with five others has their linkages weighted $\frac{1}{6}$. Linkages are, unless otherwise noted, based on number of documents. The thicker the connecting lines in the networks the higher the weight. The package VOSviewer was used for this analysis, supplemented by Gephi[3] and the R package Bibliometrix[4] (Aria and Cuccurullo (2017)).

3.2 Data

We use the Scopus database as our source of record. For the analysis in this paper all data are sourced from Scopus, as this captures the widest range of papers with complete reference sets and author/institution metadata in a consistent form. From the authors knowledge of the area we are confident that no significant academic source of papers was omitted. We chose 1990 as a starting point for the research as the further back in any bibliometric database one goes the more scant becomes the coverage. This issue is discussed in Michels and Schmoch (2012) and in Harzing and Alakangas (2016). Finally, all citation measures, unless otherwise noted, are inclusive of self citation. Waltman (2016), S5.3, contains an extensive discussion of self citation and its effects on scientometric measures and analyses. The conclusion of this section is that in large scale analyses self citation does not overly bias or distort findings. Nor is there any clear finding that for authors, as opposed to say countries or institutions, self citation should pose a problem for scientometric analysis, overall. We break out our analyses into two categories, narrow product based research, examining individual cryptocurrencies, and broader area based research looking at the entirety of the research

2 One issue with all databases, discussed in Mongeon and Paul-Hus (2016) is that they tend to have an over representation of English language journals at the expense of others.

3 for analysis of centrality measures and checking of the consistency of the graphs generated from VOSviewer.

4 for preliminary data analysis and measures of author and country dominance.

As per Corbet et al. (2019b), we further estimate the applicability of Lotka's Law (Chung and Cox (1990)) to the dataset. Lotka's law suggests that the number of publication by authors is best described as an inverse square law. Lotka's Law is formulated as $A = K/X^n$, where K and n are constants. Usually $n = 2$ is the number of authors publishing n papers and X represents the number publishing one paper. This implies that the number of authors publishing X number of articles is a fixed ratio, 2, to the number of authors publishing a single article. We used the R package Bibliometrix (Aria and Cuccurullo (2017) for this analysis. The search strategy used for the broad-based analysis was:

(TITLE-ABS-KEY(cryptocurrency OR cryptocurrencies...)
(TITLE-ABS-KEY(...OR digital currency OR digital currencies)
AND PUBYEAR >2010
AND(LIMIT-TO(DOCTYPE,"ar"))
AND(LIMIT-TO (SUBJAREA,"ECON" OR "FIN"))
AND(EXCLUDE(PREFNAMEAUID,"UndefinedUndefined")) (1)

While the search strategy used for the narrow-based analysis was:

(TITLE-ABS-KEY(Bitcoin OR Ethereum OR Litecoin)
AND PUBYEAR >2010
AND(LIMIT-TO(DOCTYPE,"ar"))
AND(LIMIT-TO (SUBJAREA,"ECON" OR "FIN"))
AND(EXCLUDE(PREFNAMEAUID,"UndefinedUndefined")) (2)

The last two exclusions were required due to large numbers of papers being returned which were opinion or reportage from The Economist Newspaper, classified as articles by Scopus. All data were downloaded as both CSV and as plaintext, where all information was selected. This allows for the analysis of inward and outward citations, of abstracts and of a wide variety of other bibliometric areas. The usage of the terms "cryptocurrency", "cryptocurrencies", "digital currency" and "digital currencies" enabled the analysis of broad-based cryptocurrency research. While the search of terms relating to "Bitcoin", "Ethereum" and "Litecoin" enabled a search of more narrow-focused product level research.

4 Results

So what do we find when we examine research in economics and finance as it pertains to cryptocurrencies?

We first note a great rise in the numbers of articles, whether broad-based or more narrowly-based, with the great bulk arriving in the 2018-19 period. This is a very new

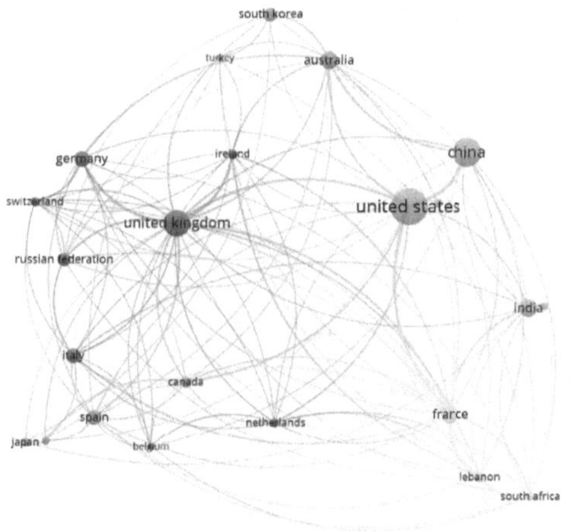

(a) Narrow Product-Based Research

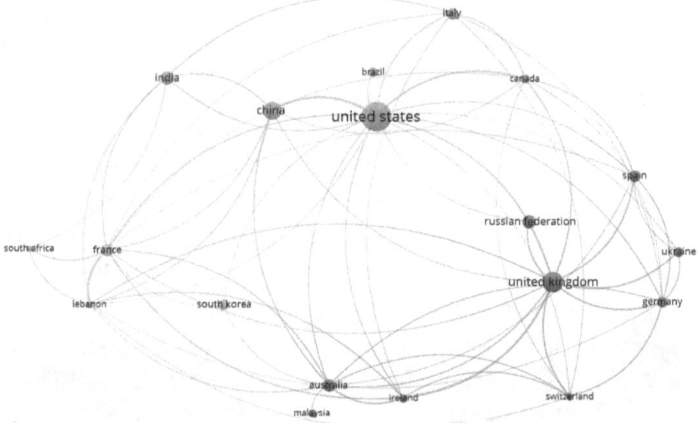

(b) Broad Area-Based Research

Figure 2: Co-authorship patterns across countries.

Note: The above figure we see the coauthorship as analysed using clusters of the countries represented in the field. The top panel represents all research based on narrow product-based research (that is Bitcoin for example). The middle panel represents broad area-based research. The lower panel represents all analysed research. The above figure is prepared using VOSviewer which is a software tool for constructing and visualising bibliometric networks. The above data was compiled as of November 2019.

area. A Google trends search of cryptocurrency or cryptocurrencies will illustrate this, with essentially no searches until early 2017. This is of course not surprising given that the Bitcoin ledger did not open until 2009. However, what is notable is the very significant uptick in research from 2017 to 2018, matching the rise in the Bitcoin price when

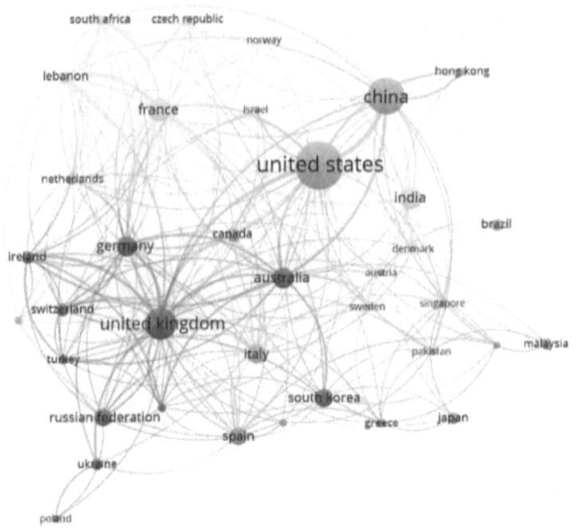

(c) Combination of Research Types

Figure 2: (continued)

the notion of such currencies really began to penetrate into the public and apparently the academic conscience.

We also evaluated the bibliometrics, per se, of the papers. Core bibliometric approaches involve surfacing the linkages between papers or articles. These linkages lend themselves nicely to graphical presentation, being in essence network models. In all cases we apply fractional counting, whereby authorship or nationality etc is scaled to the number of occurrences. Therefore an author appearing in a paper with five others has their linkages weighted $\frac{1}{6}$. Linkages are, unless otherwise noted, based on number of documents. The thicker the connecting lines in the networks the higher the weight, documents generally. The package VOSviewer was used for this analysis.

First we examine, in Figure 2 the nature of coauthorship. This allows us to look into who is working with whom. Figure 2 positions this in terms of national collaboration. We split this into three lobes: narrow products in (a), broad areas in (b) and overall in (c) The size of the nodes indicates the number of units, documents here, while the thickness of the lines indicates the strength of the linkages. Colours and shades represent clusters based on linkages and collaboration. Starting at (c) we see four main lobes of collaborative research, one each centred on the UK, the US, France and Spain. US-based authors collaborate strongly with China, surprising perhaps given the restrictions on cryptocurrencies in place in China. The UK grouping is essentially Europe, with Germany, Ireland and Russia well represented. Australia is also present in this grouping, as is Poland and Ukraine linked via Russia. The French grouping includes India and South Africa, while the Spanish group is more diffuse, with weaker links and a much more geographically spread nature. The broad product-based network is much sparser, with three clusters, including that of the US, UK and France.

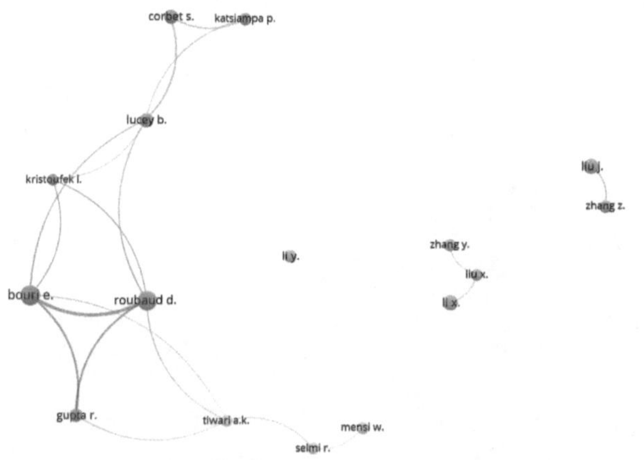

(a) Narrow Product-Based Research

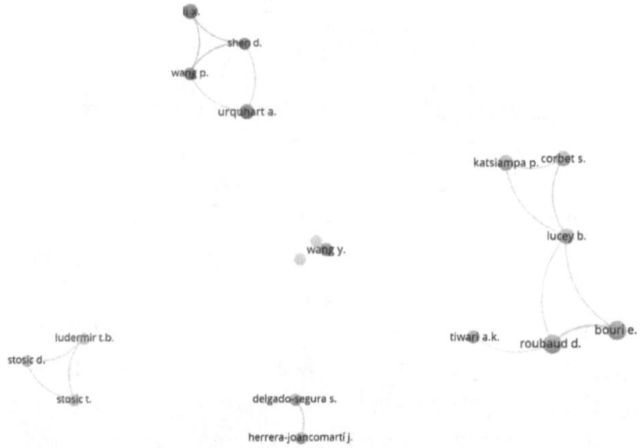

(b) Broad Area-Based Research

Figure 3: Co-authorship patterns across authors.

Note: The above figure we see the coauthorship as analysed using clusters of the authors represented in the field. The top panel represents all research based on narrow product-based research (that is Bitcoin for example). The middle panel represents broad area-based research. The lower panel represents all analysed research. The above figure is prepared using VOSviewer which is a software tool for constructing and visualising bibliometric networks. The above data was compiled as of November 2019.

The narrow product based research shows the four clusters, suggesting that first, collaboration in this area is "bottom up", focusing on products and specific instances of cryptocurrency, and second that this suggests a gap in exploiting broad conceptual areas.Examining individuals collaboration we see a very sparse network, regardless of how we cut the focus – there are islands of collaboration but these are archipelago in format. Enormous synergies exist in collaboration potential. The present authors

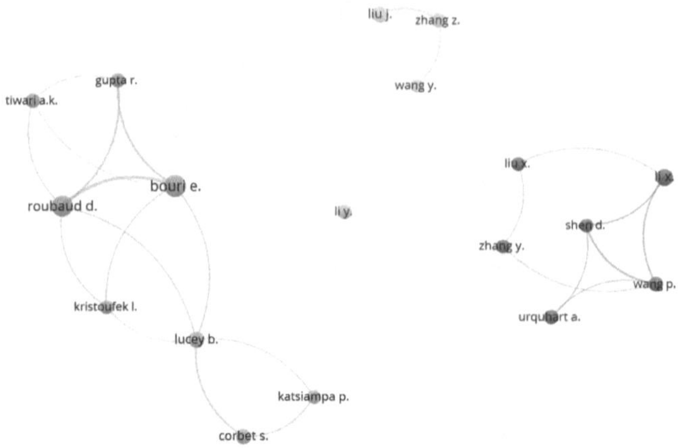

(c) Combination of Research Types

Figure 3: (continued)

appear as crucial nodes in a number of networks, but these are isolated, suggesting that we should ourselves practice what we preach!

In Figure 3 we observe a number of distinct research clusters based on both narrow and broad research. There is evidence of a number of clusters of authors that are prevalent across both types. This is also evident when considering the combination of both types of research, with further connections and segregation evident between these clusters and the topics on which each focus. Figure 4 shows a citation network of publishing sources. This is a network composed where we examine how often each element (here, journal or periodical) cites another. Again, the larger the node the more publications, the stronger the citation strength, the more often a source cites another, the thicker the linkage line. Also we again subdivide into networks, broad subject areas (b) and narrow product-based research (a).

Overall a strong pattern of main players emerges. Clearly also there are two main clusters – one is focused on the financial economics of the area, revolving around publications in Economics Letters, Finance Research Letters and International Review of Financial Analysis, while the other is a more technical cluster, with Physica A and computing journals. These are however intermingled. This is clearer in the broad area, with a third cluster emergent on law, security and commerce. Again there is a divergence between products and broad concerns. What seems evident is that collaborative opportunities for research do exist but also there is a degree of intellectual silo-ing here. There are very few citation linkages between the law/commerce/technical journals and the financial research journals.

We can deeper dive into the networks looking at cross national citation patterns. Shown in Figure 5 are two networks. The narrow based products show a very clear bilobal pattern. There is clear national segregation with the network of researchers from France and its satellites not really citing strongly the larger group of nations re-

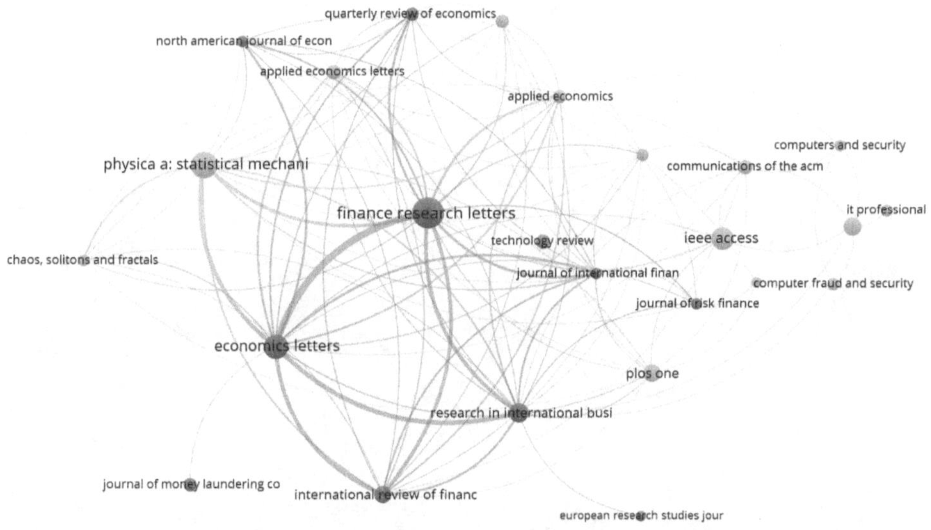

(a) Narrow Product-Based Research

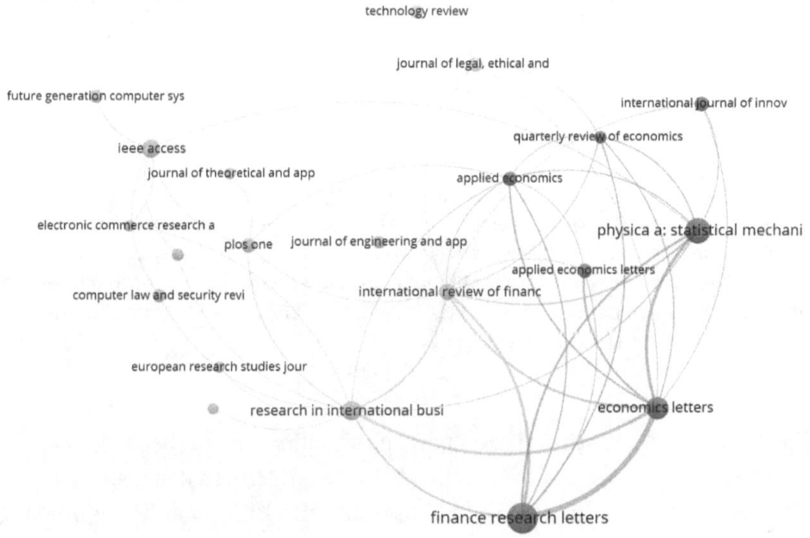

(b) Broad Area-Based Research

Figure 4: Citation pattern across sources.

Note: A citation network is a graphical representation of how often elements of the graph cite each other. We show this in the above figure for sources, and the table showing cluster memberships are shown above. The top panel represents all research based on narrow product-based research (that is Bitcoin for example). The lower panel represents broad area-based research. The above figures are prepared using VOSviewer which is a software tool for constructing and visualising bibliometric networks. The above data was compiled as of November 2019.

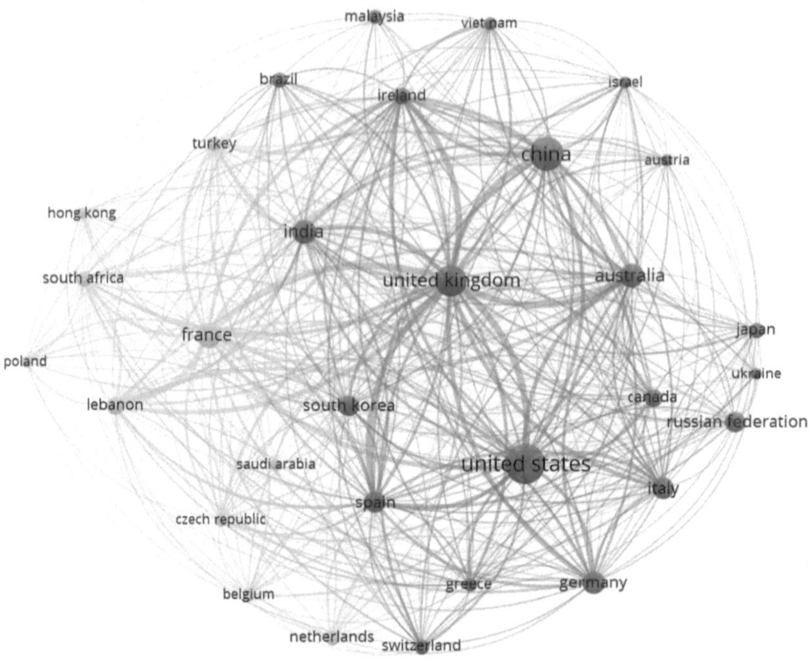

(a) Narrow Product-Based Research

Figure 5: Citation pattern across countries.

Note: A citation network is a graphical representation of how often elements of the graph cite each other. We show this in the above figure for sources, and the table showing cluster memberships are shown above. The top panel represents all research based on narrow product-based research (that is Bitcoin for example). The lower panel represents broad area-based research. The above figures are prepared using VOSviewer which is a software tool for constructing and visualising bibliometric networks. The above data was compiled as of November 2019.

volving around UK and USA. Why this is unclear. The situation regarding broader areas of research is less polarised; we see three lobes of more or less equal size and importance, one around China, one around the UK and one the USA, all with significant linkages each to the other. The inference is that when it comes to the broad architecture of cryptocurrencies we see significant international intellectual cross pollination but not when it comes to applications.

Shown in Figure 6 is a citation heatmap of articles published by country. The deeper the shade the more highly cited are these papers, normalised by the mean number of citations of all papers. We see that papers from France, Lebanon, USA, China and UK are highly cited despite, for example, Lebanon not being a major "source" of papers. So on what are authors working? In Figures 7 and 8 we see an analysis which surfaces this. In figure 7 we see an analysis of abstract words, while in 8 we see keywords. Each article requires authors to provide keywords when they submit a paper,

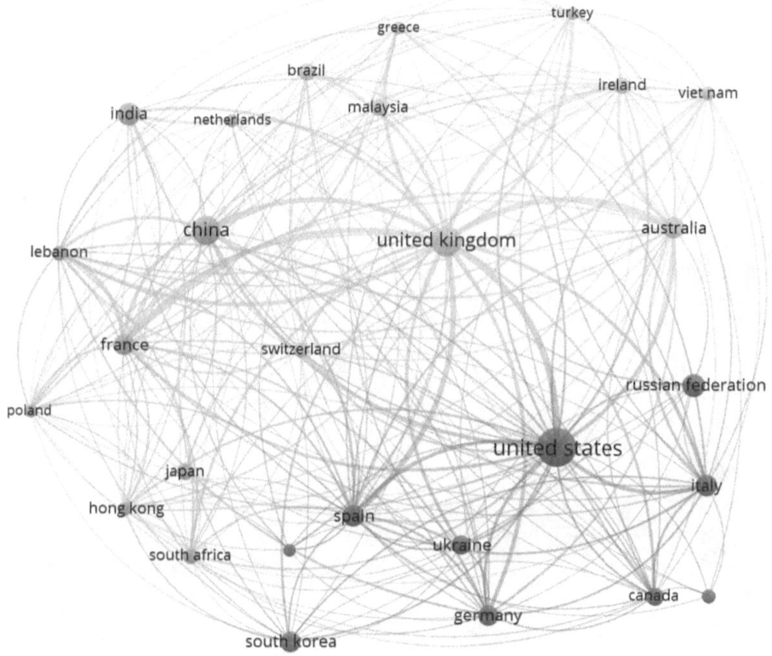

(b) Broad Area-Based Research

Figure 5: (continued)

usually up to 6. Shown in Figure 8 is a keyword cooccurance network. Again, as usual, the nodes of the network are the units of analysis, here either regular words in Figure 7, or keywords in Figure 8. The size is the relative frequency, the linkage thicknesses the number of times each are represented together. Examining first the abstract network, we notice four clear clusters. Three- computers (far right), economics (top left) and systems (bottom left) are each quite cohesive and also distinct from each other. There is a cluster linking these, but it is quite diffuse, which we can label Money. Not surprisingly this is at the centre of the entire network,these being cryptocurrencies after all. What is interesting is what is missing – there is no evidence here of a sustained research aim at cybercriminality, despite the concerns people have adduced since the start of the cryptocurrency era. No do we see a coherent cluster on environmental issues, nor on legal aspects. Overall the research community appears to be concerned with the technical, the financial aspects as well as with the technical aspects of designing the structures. This suggests that there exists, as much as we have seen earlier in author and country collaboration, great potential for "filling in the gaps" in research, through interdisciplinary research.

Specifically, when we turn our attention to the author provided keywords, in Figure 8, we see a different picture. Recall that the keywords are what the authors themselves

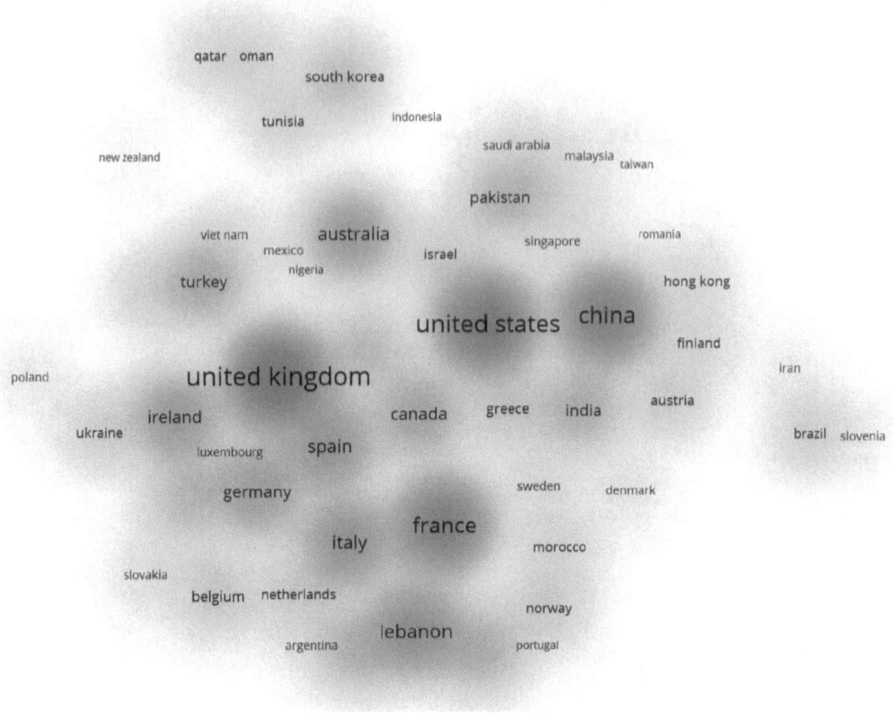

Figure 6: Heatmap presenting citation pattern across countries (Full Sample).

Note: A citation network is a graphical representation of how often elements of the graph cite each other. We show this in the above figure for sources, and the table showing cluster memberships are shown above. The above figure is prepared using VOSviewer which is a software tool for constructing and visualising bibliometric networks. The above data was compiled as of November 2019.

believe best represent the material. As we have done before we split the analysis three ways: (a) shows products, (b) areas and (c) overall. For overall we see five clusters. From the right we see a cluster on the information structure of cryptocurrencies, one on security, then on the top one on design tolerances, a large cluster on the financial economics of cryptocurrencies and finally one that examines the micro-structure and investment potential thereof. It is striking that we do not see this reflected in the abstracts – it suggests that what authors think, or wish for readers to think, they are examining is at variance with what is actually examined.

Figure 9 provides a similar analysis when we combine author keywords with the indexing keywords provided by the publishers, which are often the basis for bibliometric software such as Scopus or Web of Science to use. A further concept in scientometric analysis is that of bibliometric coupling. This refers to the degree of similarity which reference sets share. Think of two articles, each with say 20 references; in article A 5 each come from 4 other journals, in article B they come from 4 also but only 2

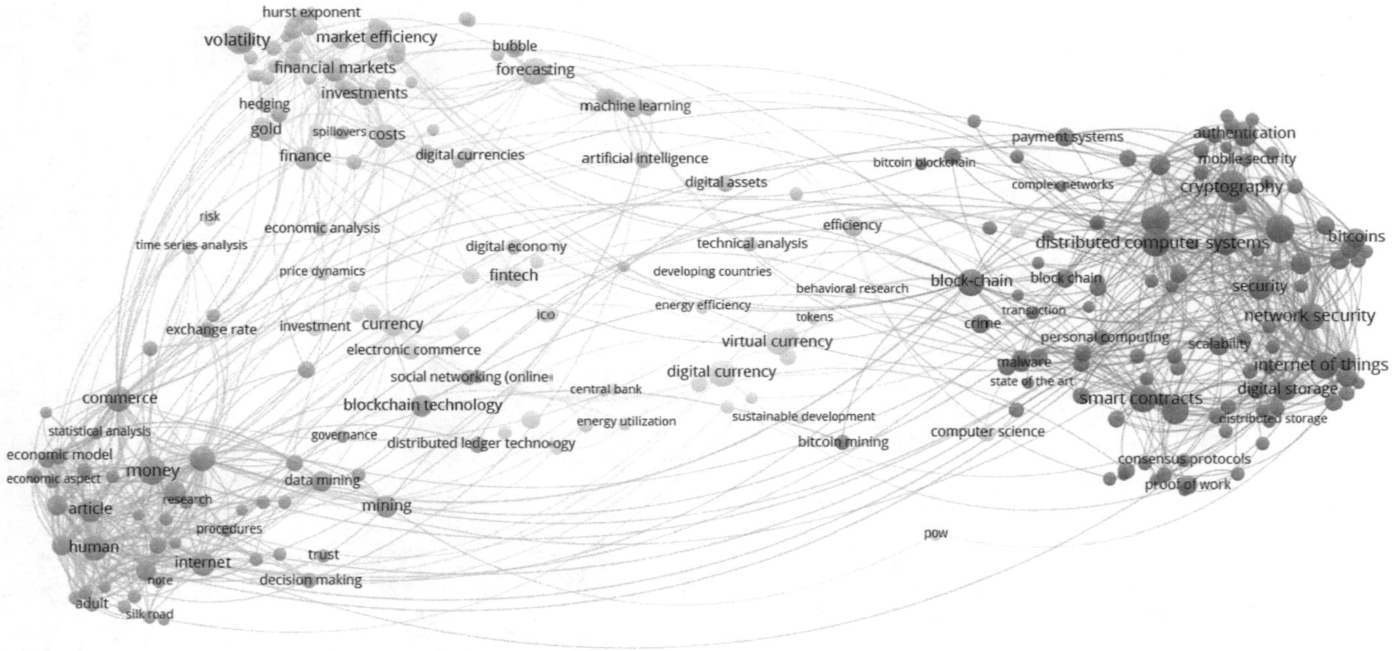

Figure 7: Abstract Keyword Cooccurance.

Note: The above figure is prepared using VOSviewer which is a software tool for constructing and visualising bibliometric networks. The above data was compiled as of November 2019.

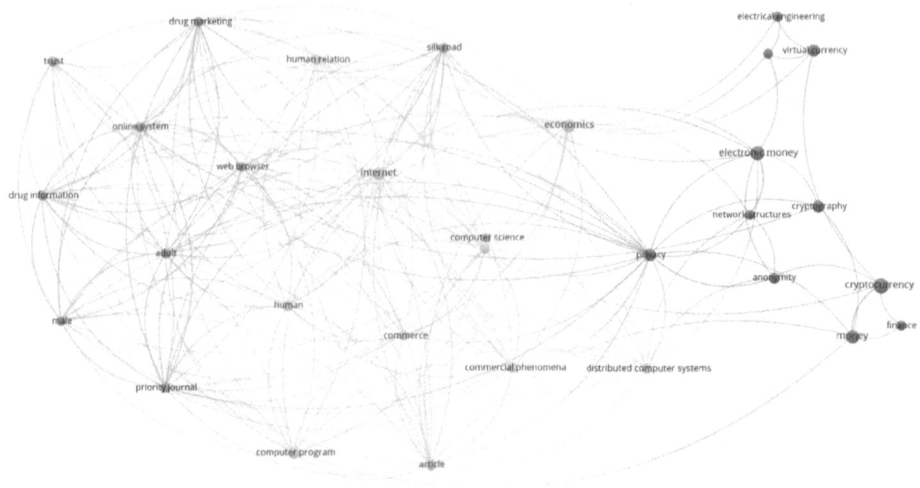

(a) Narrow Product-Based Research

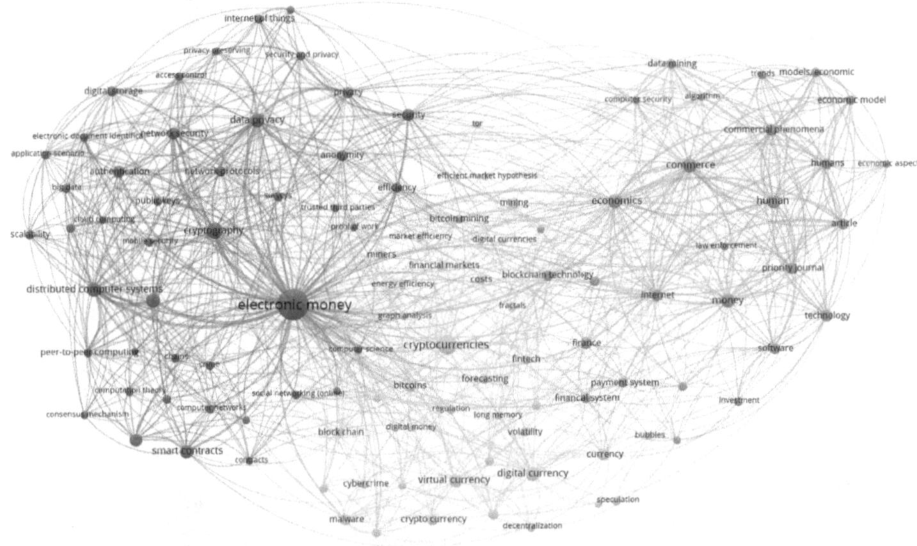

(b) Broad Area-Based Research

Figure 8: Abstract Keyword Cooccurance.

Note: In the above figure we create networks of terms. In the case of material exported from Scopus it is possible to use some or all of the Author Keywords, the publisher created Index Keywords, and the Abstract. We show this in the above figure for sources, and the table showing cluster memberships are shown above. The top panel represents all research based on narrow product-based research (that is Bitcoin for example). The middle panel represents broad area-based research. The lower panel represents all analysed research. The above figure is prepared using VOSviewer which is a software tool for constructing and visualising bibliometric networks. The above data was compiled as of November 2019.

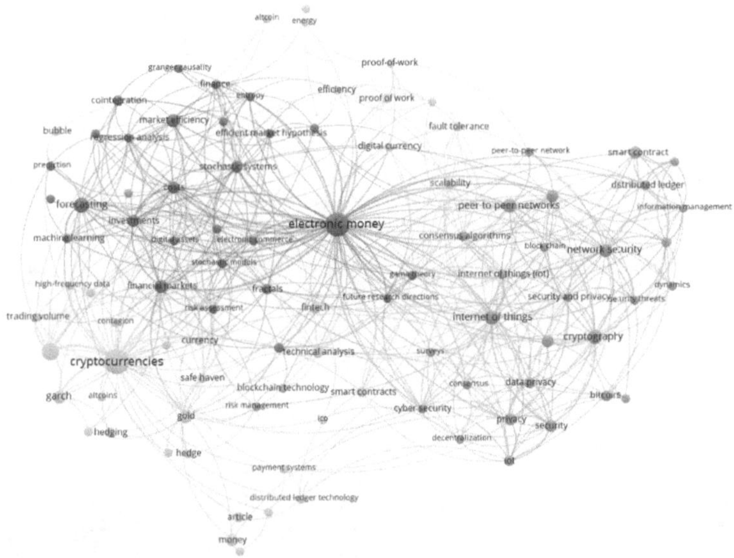

(c) Combination of Research Types

Figure 8: (continued)

of the 4 are common. This set of two articles are coupled together by having common sources. However, if all references in each of the articles came from the same set of journals they would be more closely coupled. Thus we can construct a network where the linkages are the number of times that two journals are cited in common, the nodes are the journals themselves. This allows us to look at the extent to which research shares common roots or otherwise. Shown in Figure 10 through 11 is a representation of bibliometric coupling based on sources, that is to say seeing how often pools of research draw their references from the same journals. Figure 10 is for narrow product based research and Figure 11 for areas.

For narrow products we see two clusters; again a common theme in this research is that there tends to be islands of research with limited spillover. Researchers in products – Bitcoin, Ethereum etc – draw references and one can reasonably infer inspiration form either CS or financial economics literature but rarely from both. In CS the IEEE Access open access journal is dominant, followed bu PLOS One. It is interesting to see two open access journals as primary sources. In the larger and more diffuse economics and finance research cluster we see Finance Research Letters and Physica A as the dominant sources followed closely by Economics Letters. A marked preference is clear for shorter more focused papers in this area.

Focusing on broader areas as per Figure 11 we see four clusters of reference sources. The economics cluster has split into two – one centred around Physica A is a more quantitative orientated set, including Quantitative Finance and Econometrica, the other still centres on the letters journals. A third cluster now emerges, blending

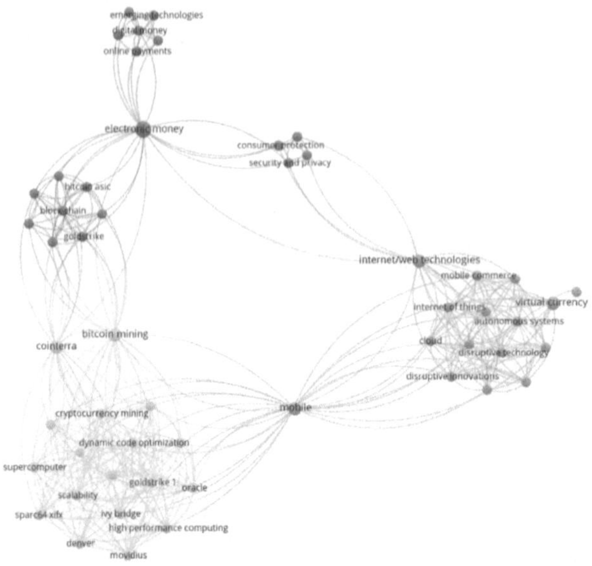

(a) Pre-2015 Keyword Cooccurance

Figure 9: Overall Keyword Cooccurance.

Note: In the above figure we create networks of terms. In the case of material exported from Scopus it is possible to use some or all of the Author Keywords, the publisher created Index Keywords, and the Abstract. We show this in the above figure for sources, and the table showing cluster memberships are shown above. The top panel represents the keyword cooccurance for the period before 1 January 2015. The middle panel represents the keyword cooccurance for the period between 1 January 2015 and 31 December 2018. The lower panel represents the keyword cooccurance for the period after 1 January 2019. The above figure is prepared using VOSviewer which is a software tool for constructing and visualising bibliometric networks. The above data was compiled as of November 2019.

economy and technical issues, with no clear dominant source. The clusters are closer to each other in addition. A takeaway here might be that when it comes to conceptual areas researchers draw, as might be expected, from a wider and deeper well of primary sources than is the case for products. This is potentially problematic as products are embedded within the overall information and economic paradigms of their creation.

Finally in Figure 12 we see the evolution of the bibliometric coupling over time for products. In the top panel, we observe the clusters of research when analysing the period prior to 2015. We observe scientific interest from PLOS One and Science, some interest from journals in economics and finance, such as Econometrica, and other areas such as computer science and the environment. Interestingly, there is also a significant cluster of work relating to money laundering, presenting evidence that forthcoming issues with regards to these new digital products were identifiable far in advance of their eventual occurrence. In the period 2015 through 2018, we can observe the clear expansion of coverage across multiple research disciplines. The largest clusters sur-

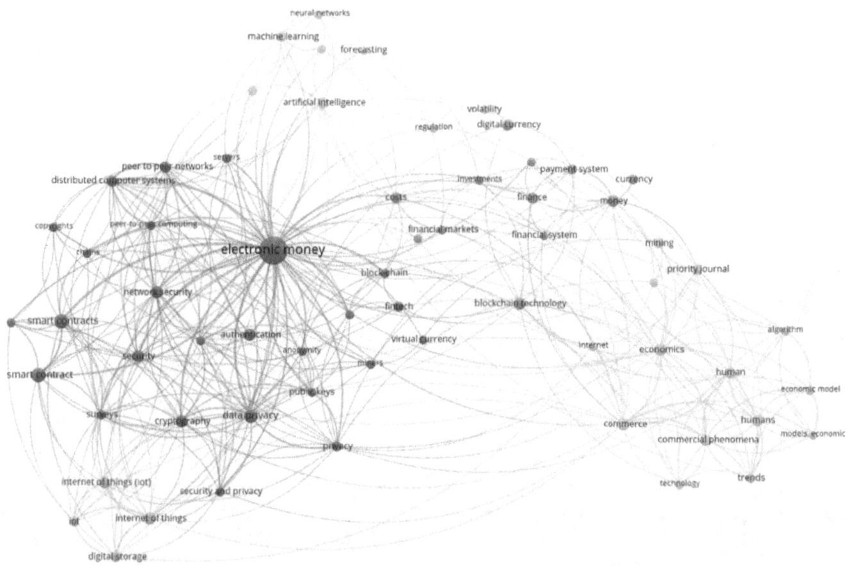

(b) Keyword Cooccurance between 2016 and 2018

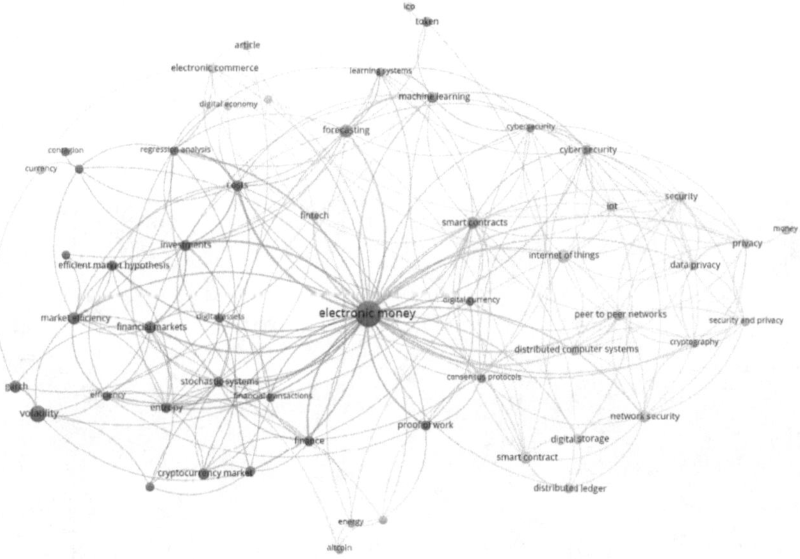

(c) Post-2018 Keyword Cooccurance

Figure 9: (continued)

round that of Physica A and PLOS One, focusing on the technical aspects surrounding the underlying characteristics of cryptocurrency, while Finance Research Letters and Economics Letters focus on the financial and pricing implications. In the lower panel,

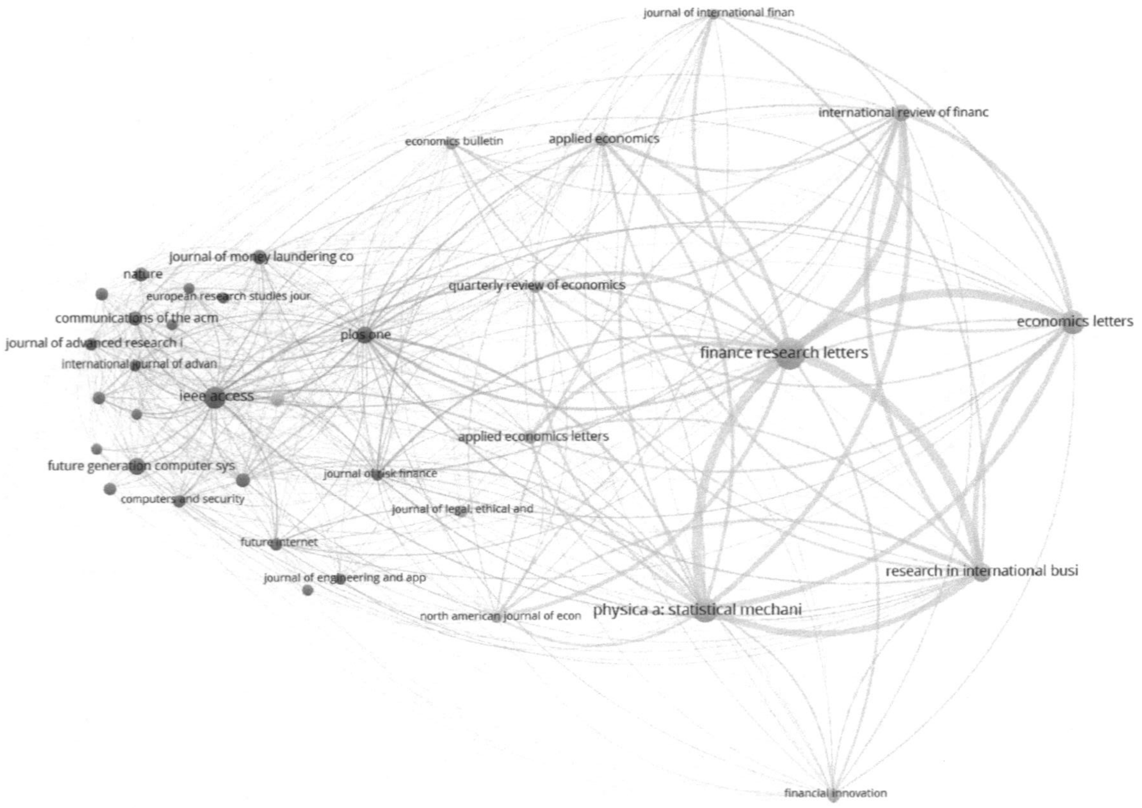

Figure 10: Bibliometric Coupling.

Note: The above figure presents a bibliometric coupling for sources. The above figure is prepared using VOSviewer which is a software tool for constructing and visualising bibliometric networks. The above data was compiled as of November 2019.

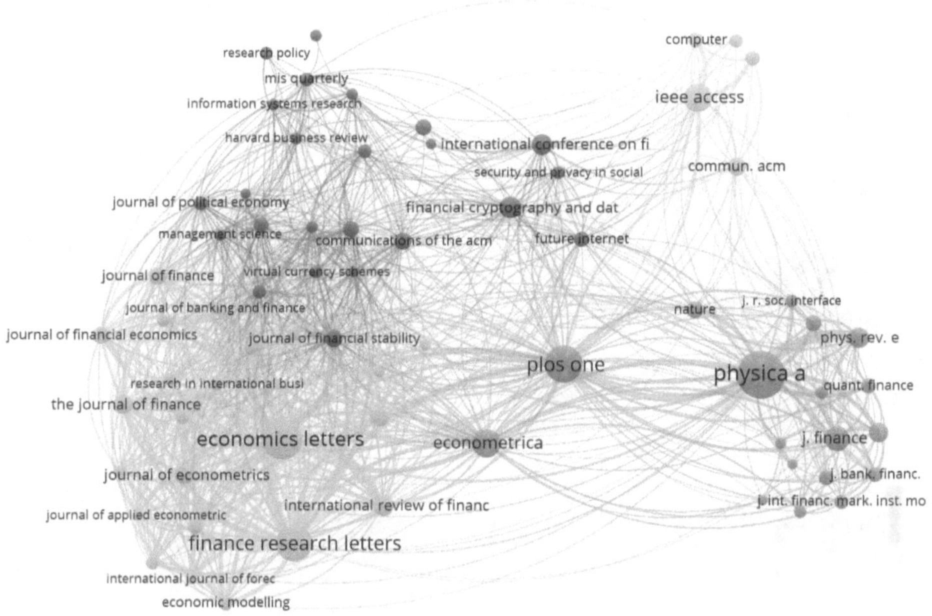

Figure 11: Bibliometric Coupling by Cited Sources.

Note: The above figure presents a bibliometric coupling for sources. The above figure is prepared using VOSviewer which is a software tool for constructing and visualising bibliometric networks. The above data was compiled as of November 2019.

we observe the research clusters for the period post-2018, identifying further expansion of research coverage along with several distinct areas of research.

5 Conclusions

Cryptocurrencies are a novel, and sometimes controversial financial instrument. Regardless of whether one believes them to be a passing fad, the future of money or somewhere in between, they have emerged as one of the most interesting and discussed financial assets of the last decade. We find here that these assets have had greatly increased research activity focused on them over the last two years. This research however is characterised by being rather fragmented. It is fragmented in a significant sense across products and broad areas. While islands of research do connect they do so in very limited ways. There are parallel, mostly non-overlapping research initiatives drawing inspiration form the technical and the economic literature but limited "interdisciplinary" research. It is our hope that this handbook goes some way to providing an overview of the areas of research and will spark greater cooperation.

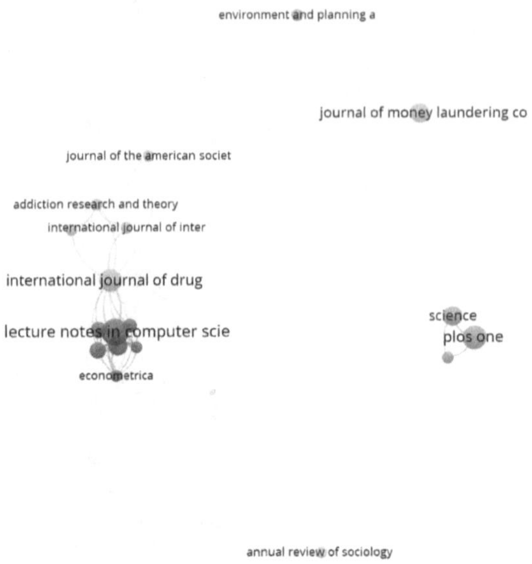

(a) Pre-2015 Research Citations

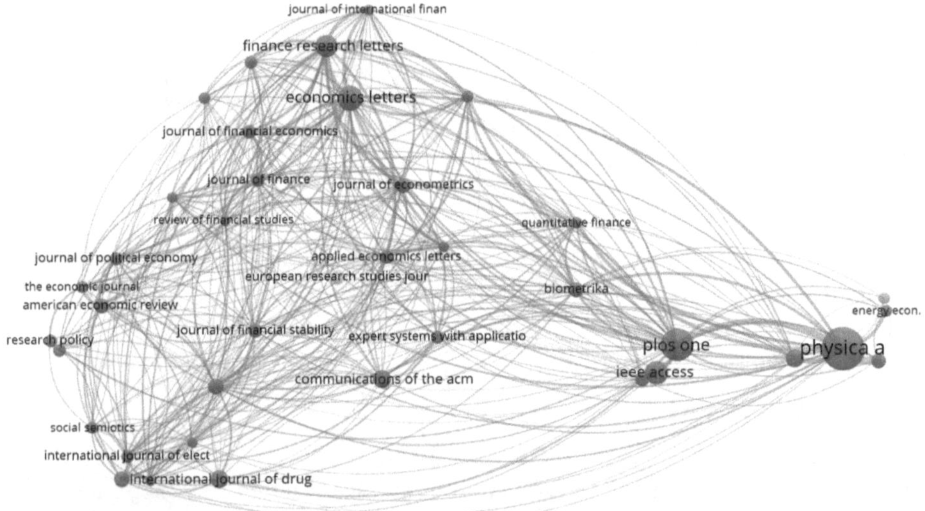

(b) Research Citations 2015 through 2018

Figure 12: Bibliometric cited sources over time.

Note: The above figure presents a bibliometric coupling for sources over time. The top panel represents the bibliometric cited sources for the period before 1 January 2015. The middle panel represents the bibliometric cited sources for the period between 1 January 2015 and 31 December 2018. The lower panel represents the bibliometric cited sources for the period after 1 January 2019. The above figure is prepared using VOSviewer which is a software tool for constructing and visualising bibliometric networks. The above data was compiled as of November 2019.

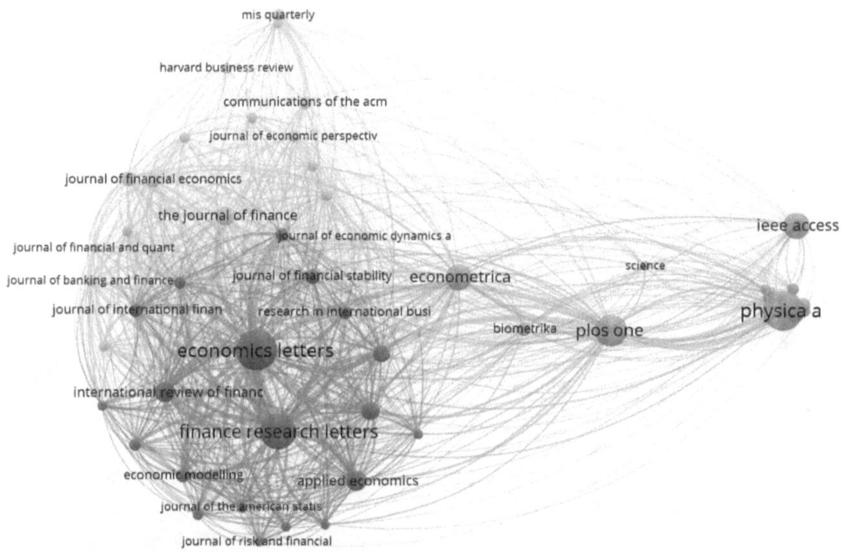

(c) Post-2018 Research Citations

Figure 12: (continued)

Bibliography

Akhtaruzzaman, M., A. Sensoy, and S. Corbet (2019). The influence of bitcoin on portfolio diversification and design. *Finance Research Letters*. Available online at: https://doi.org/10.1016/j.frl.2019.101344.

Akyildirim, E., S. Corbet, P. Katsiampa, N. Kellard, and A. Sensoy (2019a). The development of bitcoin futures: Exploring the interactions between cryptocurrency derivatives. *Finance Research Letters*. Available online at: https://doi.org/10.1016/j.frl.2019.07.007.

Akyildirim, E., S. Corbet, B. Lucey, A. Sensoy, and L. Yarovaya (2019b). The relationship between implied volatility and cryptocurrency returns. *Finance Research Letters*.

Aria, M., and C. Cuccurullo (2017). Bibliometrix: an R-tool for comprehensive science mapping analysis. *Journal of Informetrics 11*(4), 959–975.

Bouri, E., P. Molnár, G. Azzi, D. Roubaud, and L. I. Hagfors (2017). On the hedge and safe haven properties of bitcoin: Is it really more than a diversifier? *Finance Research Letters 20*, 192–198.

Cheah, E.-T., and J. Fry (2015). Speculative bubbles in bitcoin markets? An empirical investigation into the fundamental value of bitcoin. *Economics Letters 130*, 32–36.

Chung, K. H., and R. A. Cox (1990). Patterns of productivity in the finance literature: A study of the bibliometric distributions. *the Journal of Finance 45*(1), 301–309.

Corbet, S., D. Cumming, B. Lucey, M. Peat, and S. Vigne (2019a). The destabilising effects of cryptocurrency cybercriminality. *Economics Letters*.

Corbet, S., M. Dowling, X. Gao, S. Huang, B. Lucey, and S. A. Vigne (2019b). An analysis of the intellectual structure of research on the financial economics of precious metals. *Resources Policy 63*: 101416.

Corbet, S., V. Eraslan, B. Lucey, and A. Sensoy. 2019c. The effectiveness of technical trading rules in cryptocurrency markets. *Finance Research Letters 31*, 32–37.

Corbet, S., C. Larkin, B. Lucey, A. Meegan, and L. Yarovaya (2020). Cryptocurrency reaction to FOMC announcements: Evidence of heterogeneity based on blockchain stack position. *Journal of Financial Stability 46*: 100706.

Corbet, S., B. Lucey, M. Peat, and S. Vigne (2018). Bitcoin futures-what use are they? *Economics Letters 172*, 23–27.

Corbet, S., B. Lucey, A. Urquhart, and L. Yarovaya (2019). Cryptocurrencies as a financial asset: A systematic analysis. *International Review of Financial Analysis 62*, 182–199.

Corbet, S., B. Lucey, and L. Yarovya (2018a). Datestamping the bitcoin and ethereum bubbles. *Finance Research Letters 26*(1), 81–88.

Corbet, S., A. Meegan, C. Larkin, B. Lucey, and L. Yarovaya (2018b). Exploring the dynamic relationships between cryptocurrencies and other financial assets. *Economics Letters 165*, 28–34.

Danezis, G., A. Tsagkaris, F. Camin, V. Brusic, and C. Georgiou (2016). Food authentication: Techniques, trends & emerging approaches. *TrAC – Trends in Analytical Chemistry 85*, 123–132.

Franceschet, M. (2010). A comparison of bibliometric indicators for computer science scholars and journals on web of science and Google scholar. *Scientometrics 83*(1), 243–258. Cited by 85.

Fry, J. (2018). Booms, busts and heavy-tails: The story of bitcoin and cryptocurrency markets? *Economics Letters 171*, 225–229.

Gandal, N., J. Hamrick, T. Moore, and T. Oberman (2018). Price manipulation in the bitcoin ecosystem. *Journal of Monetary Economics 95*, 86–96.

Griffins, J., and A. Shams. 2018. Is bitcoin really un-tethered? Available at SSRN: https://ssrn.com/abstract=3195066, 13 June 2018.

Harzing, A.-W., and S. Alakangas (2016). Google scholar, scopus and the web of science: A longitudinal and cross-disciplinary comparison. *Scientometrics 106*(2), 787–804.

He, Q., G. Wang, L. Luo, Q. Shi, J. Xie, and X. Meng (2017). Mapping the managerial areas of building information modeling (BIM) using scientometric analysis. *International Journal of Project Management 35*(4), 670–685.

Jappe, A., D. Pithan, and T. Heinze (2018). Does bibliometric research confer legitimacy to research assessment practice? A sociological study of reputational control, 1972–2016. *PloS one 13*(6):e0199031.

Katsiampa, P., S. Corbet, and B. Lucey (2019a). High frequency volatility co-movements in cryptocurrency markets. *Journal of International Financial Markets, Institutions and Money 62*, 35–52.

Katsiampa, P., S. Corbet, and B. Lucey (2019b). Volatility spillover effects in leading cryptocurrencies: A Bekk-Mgarch analysis. *Finance Research Letters 29*, 68–74.

Konur, O. (2011). The scientometric evaluation of the research on the algae and bio-energy. *Applied Energy 88*(10), 3532–3540.

Konur, O. 2012a. The evaluation of the research on the biodiesel: A scientometric approach. *Energy Education Science and Technology Part A: Energy Science and Research 28*(2), 1003–1014.

Konur, O. 2012b. The evaluation of the research on the biohydrogen: A scientometric approach. *Energy Education Science and Technology Part A: Energy Science and Research 29*(1), 323–338.

Kosnik, L.-R. (2018). A survey of JEL codes: What do they mean and are they used consistently? *Journal of Economic Surveys 32*(1), 249–272.

Levine-Clark, M., and E. L. Gil (2008). A comparative citation analysis of web of science, scopus, and Google scholar. *Journal of Business & Finance Librarianship 14*(1), 32–46.

Li, X., P. Jiang, T. Chen, X. Luo, and Q. Wen (2017). A survey on the security of blockchain systems. *Future Generation Computer Systems*.

Lowry, P., G. Moody, J. Gaskin, D. Galletta, S. Humpherys, J. Barlow, and D. Wilson (2013). Evaluating journal quality and the association for information systems senior scholars' journal basket via bibliometric measures: do expert journal assessments add value? *MIS Quarterly: Management*

Information Systems 37(4), 993–1012.
Michels, C., and U. Schmoch (2012). The growth of science and database coverage. *Scientometrics 93*(3), 831–846.
Mongeon, P., and A. Paul-Hus (2016). The journal coverage of web of science and scopus: A comparative analysis. *Scientometrics 106*(1), 213–228. Cited by 88.
Nakamoto, S. (2009). *Bitcoin: A peer-to-peer electronic cash system*, Technical report, Manubot.
Olawumi, T., and D. Chan (2018). A scientometric review of global research on sustainability and sustainable development. *Journal of Cleaner Production 183*, 231–250.
Phillips, P. C., Y. Wu, and J. Yu (2011). Explosive behavior in the 1990's Nasdaq: When did exuberance escalate asset values? *International Economic Review 52*(1), 201–226.
Rotolo, D., D. Hicks, and B. Martin (2015). What is an emerging technology? *Research Policy 44*(10), 1827–1843.
Ruaro, R., and Ã. Gubiani (2013). A scientometric assessment of 30 years of the index of biotic integrity in aquatic ecosystems: Applications and main flaws. *Ecological Indicators 29*, 105–110.
Sensoy, A. (2018). The inefficiency of bitcoin revisited: A high-frequency analysis with alternative currencies. *Finance Research Letters*.
Serenko, A., T. Hardie, N. Bontis, L. Booker, and K. Sadeddin (2010). A scientometric analysis of knowledge management and intellectual capital academic literature (1994–2008). *Journal of Knowledge Management 14*(1), 3–23.
Tschorsch, F., and B. Scheuermann (2016). Bitcoin and beyond: A technical survey on decentralized digital currencies. *IEEE Communications Surveys & Tutorials 18*(3), 2084–2123.
Urquhart, A. (2016). The inefficiency of bitcoin. *Economics Letters 148*, 80–82.
Vieira, E., and J. Gomes (2009). A comparison of scopus and web of science for a typical university. *Scientometrics 81*(2), 587–600. Cited by 88.
Waltman, L. (2016). A review of the literature on citation impact indicators. *Journal of Informetrics 10*(2), 365–391.
Zhao, X. (2017). A scientometric review of global bim research: Analysis and visualization. *Automation in Construction 80*, 37–47.

Paraskevi Katsiampa

Financial characteristics of cryptocurrencies

1 Introduction

Over the last decade, cryptocurrency markets have remarkably evolved. Cryptocurrencies as a medium of exchange could seem attractive to potential users as a result of their user anonymity, low transaction costs stemming from no intermediary involvement, and the fact that an increasing number of retailers has started accepting Bitcoin payments enabling cryptocurrency users to purchase goods, including illegal ones. Notwithstanding, cryptocurrencies are primarily traded for speculation purposes instead of as a traditional medium of exchange due to the fact that they can provide their users with the potential of reaching extremely high gains in very short periods of time, despite concerns about risks associated with their unprecedented price fluctuations raised by economists and financial institutions. Furthermore, cryptocurrencies resemble more financial assets rather than fiat currencies due to their volatility, persistence, heavy tail behaviour, and vulnerability to speculative bubbles, among other properties. This chapter will therefore discuss the financial characteristics of cryptocurrencies. We will start by looking at their statistical properties and then learn about their properties that make them resemble financial assets, but also about interdependencies of cryptocurrencies as well as their relationship with mainstream financial assets.

2 Statistical properties of cryptocurrencies

Since the introduction of Bitcoin, the cryptocurrency market has rapidly developed, with numerous altcoins having been introduced. Although Bitcoin has been the most popular cryptocurrency due to the fact that it constitutes the first implementation of the concept of a digital currency, as of August 2019 there are more than 2500 cryptocurrencies in existence with the total market capitalisation being estimated to exceed $246 billion (coinmarketcap.com, accessed on 29th August 2019). As illustrated in Figure 1, while Bitcoin represented about 94% of the total estimated market capitalisation in May 2013, its market share dropped to 33% in January 2018, as a result of the increase in popularity and, thus, in market capitalisation of more recently launched cryptocurrencies which have been attracting significant trading volumes. Such fluctuations in Bitcoin' market share have raised concerns about Bitcoin's long-term sustainability as well as about the increased competition between cryptocurrencies (Dowd, 2014).

In this section, we consider several major cryptocurrencies and analyse their statistical properties. We restrict to cryptocurrencies that have been in existence for three

https://doi.org/10.1515/9783110660807-004

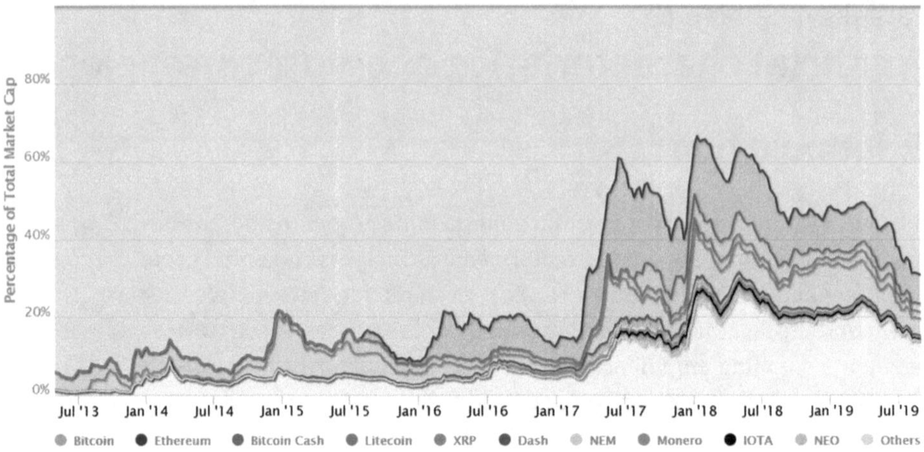

Figure 1: Cryptocurrencies' market share in terms of total market capitalisation.

Source: https://coinmarketcap.com/coins/

years with a market capitalisation in excess of 500 million US Dollars (as of 18th August 2019). The cryptocurrencies meeting these criteria are Bitcoin, Ether, Ripple, Litecoin, Monero, Stellar Lumen, Dash, NEO, and Ethereum Classic. Table 1 lists several characteristics, including the market capitalisation and 24-hour trading volume, of the considered cryptocurrencies as of 18th August 2018, with their total market capitalisation reaching approximately $228 billion, therefore representing circa 96% of the total market capitalisation of cryptocurrencies in circulation, with Bitcoin's market capitalisation in particular being 185 US Dollars, a figure that is about nine times higher than that of, e. g., Ether, the second largest cryptocurrency. The dataset therefore consists of daily closing prices for these nine cryptocurrencies from 9th September 2015 (as the earliest date available for NEO) to 15th August 2019. The data were sourced at https://coinmarketcap.com/coins/ and the prices are listed in US Dollars.

Figure 2 depicts the time plots of the daily closing prices of the nine cryptocurrencies considered over their common sample covering the period from 9th September 2016 to 15th August 2019. It can be noticed that the prices of the altcoins would be stable until the end of the first quarter of 2017, whereas the prices of Bitcoin would steadily increase. However, from the second quarter of 2017 until the end of 2017 there were severe price fluctuations leading to a significant and rapid growth in the prices of all the cryptocurrencies, while from the beginning of 2018 onwards all prices started declining. Nevertheless, not all prices shared an identical trend of decline in 2018. Moreover, while all cryptocurrencies experienced price appreciations again in 2019, the price increase was more significant for Bitcoin and Litecoin, with the price of the latter somewhat mirroring the price of Bitcoin. Figure 2 therefore illustrates that all prices seem to move in a similar pattern and to be correlated, especially during the growth pe-

Table 1: Characteristics of cryptocurrencies.

Cryptocurrency	Symbol	Market capitalisation	Price	24-hour trading volume	Circulating supply
Bitcoin	BTC	$185,022,920,955	$10,345.81	$12,999,813,869	17,883,850
Ether	ETH	$20,884,307,088	$194.49	$5,969,012,024	107,377,901
Ripple	XRP	$12,122,901,988	$0.282646	$1,216,547,019	42,890,708,341*
Litecoin	LTC	$4,809,876,077	$76.27	$2,743,241,606	63,063,843
Monero	XMR	$1,510,667,110	$88.02	$80,774,014	17,161,841
Stellar	XLM	$1,389,769,435	$0.070785	$66,660,569	19,633,542,514*
Dash	DASH	$854,767,039	$95.11	$130,360,202	8,987,307
NEO	NEO	$696,953,952	$9.88	$232,179,408	70,538,831*
Ethereum Classic	ETC	$629,472,339	$5.58	$365,608,038	112,806,644

Notes: Values as of 18th August 2018. Prices listed in US Dollars. * indicates not mineable.
Source: https://coinmarketcap.com/coins/

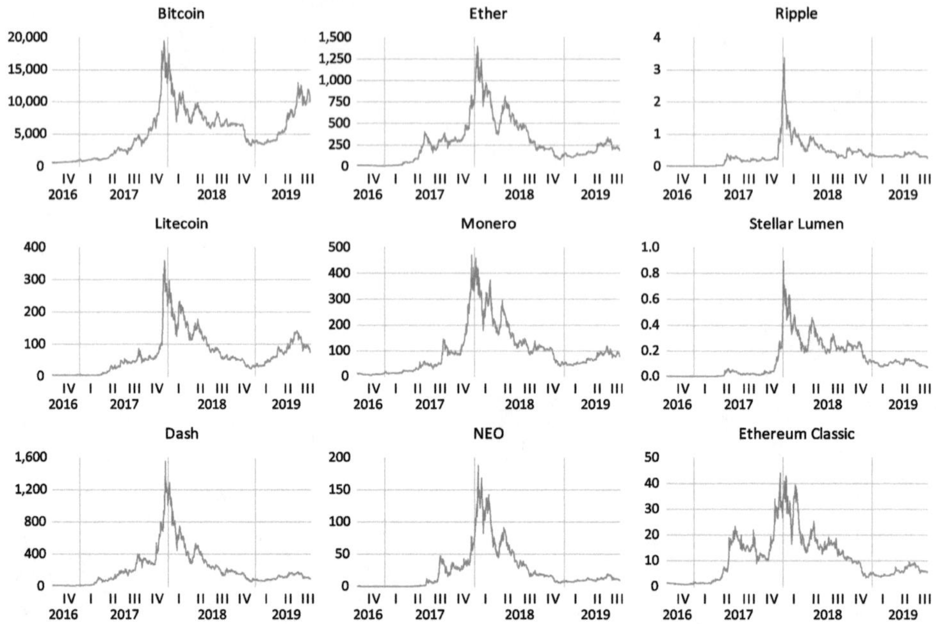

Figure 2: Daily closing prices of cryptocurrencies (in US Dollars).

riod. Indeed, the Pearson correlation coefficient, which measures the strength of the association between two variables, for the different pairs of cryptocurrencies' prices (reported in Table 2) confirms this fact, since all the correlation coefficients are positive – ranging from 0.6832 to 0.9480 – and significant. Interestingly, this result is true not only for any Bitcoin-altcoin pair as could have been expected, due to the fact that most altcoin buy and sell orders are executed in Bitcoin, but also for any other pair of altcoins.

Summary statistics for the cryptocurrencies' logarithmic price return series defined as the first difference of the logarithmic prices on two consecutive days over the common sample period are reported in Panel A of Table 3. Interestingly, while the average daily closing price returns are positive for all the cryptocurrencies considered, ranging from 0.13% (Ethereum Classic) to 0.36% (Ripple), suggesting that the highest return on average was obtained for Ripple over the common sample period from 9th September 2016 to 15th August 2019, the median is positive only for Bitcoin and Ether. The standard deviation ranges from 4.27% (Bitcoin) to 9.44% (NEO), indicating that cryptocurrencies with lower market capitalisation exhibit larger variability. Moreover, while the price returns of Bitcoin are negatively skewed suggesting that Bitcoin's return distribution has a longer left tail over the common sample period, the opposite result holds for the price returns of all the altcoins. Nevertheless all cryptocurrency price returns exhibit high kurtosis and thus have heavy tails, with Bitcoin exhibiting the lowest and Ripple the highest excess kurtosis. Furthermore, the Jarque-

Table 2: Correlation matrix of cryptocurrency prices.

	Bitcoin	**Ether**	**Ripple**	**Litecoin**	**Monero**	**Stellar**	**Dash**	**NEO**	**Ethereum Classic**
Bitcoin	1.0000								
Ether	0.7827***	1.0000							
Ripple	0.7350***	0.8437***	1.0000						
Litecoin	0.9067***	0.8861***	0.8222***	1.0000					
Monero	0.8607***	0.9381***	0.8631***	0.9367***	1.0000				
Stellar	0.7163***	0.8476***	0.8867***	0.7679***	0.8421***	1.0000			
Dash	0.7822***	0.8807***	0.8015***	0.8740***	0.9387***	0.6832***	1.0000		
NEO	0.6853***	0.9480***	0.7956***	0.8219***	0.9048***	0.8312***	0.8239***	1.0000	
Ethereum Classic	0.7302***	0.9136***	0.7435***	0.8228***	0.8859***	0.6952***	0.9055***	0.8256***	1.0000

Note: *** significant at the 1% level.

Bera test confirms the departure from normality for all the cryptocurrency price return series.

It is worth mentioning that in a study of the tail behaviour of the returns of Bitcoin, Ether, Ripple, Bitcoin Cash, and Litecoin, using an extreme value analysis and estimating Value-at-Risk and Expected Shortfall as tail risk measures, Bitcoin Cash, which was more recently launched compared to the other cryptocurrencies, was found to have the highest potential gain and loss and to thus be the riskiest cryptocurrency, while Bitcoin and Litecoin were found to be the least risky cryptocurrencies, and hence position in these two could be viewed safer than in their counterparts (Gkillas and Katsiampa, 2018). These results indicated that more recently launched cryptocurrencies are riskier than cryptocurrencies that have been in existence for several years and seem to be relatively more mature. It is also worth mentioning that cryptocurrencies have much higher volatility and exhibit heavier tail behaviour than traditional currencies, and are therefore riskier than fiat currencies.

Finally, cryptocurrency price returns are stationary but exhibit volatility clustering. They also exhibit asymmetric reverting behaviour (Corbet and Katsiampa, 2018) and long memory (Cheah et al., 2018; Jiang et al., 2018; Phillip et al., 2018) providing evidence against the efficient market hypothesis, as will be discussed in the next section.

3 Cryptocurrency market efficiency

The notion of market efficiency dates back to as early as in 1970s. A market in which prices always "fully reflect" all available information is called "informationally efficient" (Fama, 1970). There are three forms of informational efficiency, namely (i) weak form of efficiency, where prices reflect the information contained in the previous prices, (ii) semi-strong form of efficiency, where prices reflect all public information, and (iii) strong form of efficiency, if prices reflect all public and private information. Market efficiency is therefore related to the ability of a market to reflect the information in a quick and efficient manner. In an efficient market, asset prices are not predictable following a random walk, and the extent to which a market is efficient has been an important aspect of capital markets, since it affects investors' profitability. For this reason, there is vast literature examining the efficiency of different financial markets. Since cryptocurrencies are primarily used for speculation purposes, several studies have explored the market efficiency of cryptocurrencies as well, even though the efficient market hypothesis could seem inappropriate to explain cryptocurrency prices because it assumes that prices always reflect and are driven by relevant information as well as that investors behave rational in terms of immediately incorporating all available information in an unbiased manner (Brauneis and Mestel, 2018). Empirical tests of cryptocurrency market efficiency are therefore mostly related to testing

Table 3: Descriptive statistics for cryptocurrencies' price returns.

	Bitcoin	Ether	Ripple	Litecoin	Monero	Stellar	Dash	NEO	Ethereum Classic
Mean	0.0026	0.0026	0.0036	0.0028	0.0018	0.0033	0.0020	0.0027	0.0013
Median	0.0031	0.0000	−0.0033	−0.0002	−0.0003	−0.0037	−0.0006	−0.0025	−0.0002
Maximum	0.2251	0.2901	1.0274	0.5103	0.4303	0.7231	0.4377	0.8012	0.4577
Minimum	−0.2075	−0.3155	−0.6163	−0.3952	−0.2932	−0.3664	−0.2432	−0.5225	−0.4353
Std. Dev.	0.0427	0.0582	0.0804	0.0631	0.0650	0.0872	0.0617	0.0944	0.0675
Skewness	−0.1106	0.2881	2.8467	1.2041	0.3858	2.0334	0.8128	1.1078	0.2222
Kurtosis	6.6568	7.0185	37.766	12.723	6.8469	17.8599	9.1410	15.0770	9.8051
Jarque-Bera	598.356***	734.772***	55330.58***	4473.508***	686.311***	10582.13***	1799.152***	6721.493***	2073.428***

Note: *** significant at the 1% level.

for price predictability in terms of randomness, with the informational efficiency of cryptocurrency markets depending on several factors.

Few such important factors affecting whether cryptocurrency markets appear to be informational efficient or not are related to the sample time period under investigation as well as the data and method employed. The results of a battery of robust tests, namely the Ljung–Box test, Runs tests, Bartels test, AVR test, BDS test and R/S Hurst, for the daily logarithmic price returns of Bitcoin over the period of the first six years since Bitcoin started being traded revealed that Bitcoin returns were not weakly efficient (Urquhart, 2016). When the sample was split into two equal subsample periods, the results for the first sub-sample were consistent with those for the whole sample period. However, the results of the Ljung-Box test and AVR test for the second sub-sample covering the period from 1st August 2013 to 31st July 2016 indicated that Bitcoin is efficient in the latter period, and hence Bitcoin may becoming more efficient over time. Nevertheless, a power transformation of the Bitcoin price returns of the form r_t^m, where m is an odd integer, over the same period of time covering the first six years since Bitcoin started being traded results in the transformed Bitcoin returns to actually be efficient according to the results of several tests, including the Ljung–Box test, Runs tests, Bartels test, and BDS test, among others (Nadarajah and Chu, 2017). Moreover, the results of various long-range dependence estimators (including the Centred Moving Average-squared absolute fluctuation, Centred Moving Average-mean absolute fluctuation, Periodogram-Least Squares, Periodogram-Least Absolute Deviation) while allowing for time variation for the logarithmic price returns for a period spanning over the first seven years since Bitcoin was launched have also shown that the Bitcoin market is informational efficient (Tiwari et al., 2018). On the other hand, contradictory results to those listed above have been found for the logarithmic price returns over the time period from 1st December 2010 to 30th November 2017 due to the fact that the Bitcoin market exhibits long-term memory and a high degree of inefficiency ratio (defined as the percentage of inefficient windows among the total number of windows) as well as due to rejecting null hypotheses of randomness in most sub-periods (Jiang et al., 2018).

Nevertheless, the Bitcoin market informational efficiency also depends on the data frequency under consideration, with the higher the data frequency, the lower the pricing efficiency being. More specifically, although there has been found some evidence of efficiency in the Bitcoin market at the daily level of data when testing the martingale hypothesis using different variance ratio tests, there are indications of informational inefficiency at higher data frequencies (Zargar and Kumar, 2019). Moreover, even at intraday level (e. g., 15-, 20-, 30-, 40-, and 45-min), the higher the data frequency, the lower the pricing efficiency is (Sensoy, 2019).

The degree of informational efficiency of cryptocurrency markets also depends on the market itself. For instance, there exists non-homogeneous informational inefficiency across Bitcoin markets in Europe, USA, Australia, Canada, and UK, as a result of different long memory estimates, with the considered Bitcoin markets being moderate to highly inefficient enabling investors to capture speculative profits (Cheah et al., 2018). Moreover, although it has been shown that both the Bitcoin markets in terms of US Dollars and Euros have become more informationally efficient over time at the intraday level since the beginning of 2016, the Bitcoin market in terms of US Dollars is slightly more efficient than the Bitcoin market in terms of Euros, with Bitcoin markets in terms of Euros therefore providing a more profitable trading environment at the intraday level (Sensoy, 2019).

In addition, the informational efficiency of cryptocurrency markets further depends on the cryptocurrency under examination. While most previous studies have mainly examined the efficiency of Bitcoin markets due to its dominance in the cryptocurrency markets, market inefficiencies exist not only for Bitcoin but also for altcoins. Although there is a heterogeneous pattern of inefficiency across the different cryptocurrencies and despite the fact that the degree of persistence indicating inefficiency changes over time for the different cryptocurrencies, Bitcoin seems to be the cryptocurrency passing most of the statistical tests of price randomness, therefore representing the most efficient cryptocurrency (Brauneis and Mestel, 2018; Caporale et al., 2018).

The efficiency of cryptocurrency markets seems to also depend on the form of efficiency under examination. Most studies in the literature have examined the weak form of efficiency. On the other hand, Vidal-Tomás and Ibañez (2018) examined the semi-strong efficiency of daily Bitcoin price returns in the Bitstamp and Mt.Gox exchanges through an event study with monetary policy and Bitcoin news, and found that Bitcoin did not respond to monetary policy news and is therefore semi-strong form inefficient with regards to this kind of news, as a result of the absence of any kind of control from central banks on Bitcoin. However, when focusing on events that are related to features of Bitcoin, the cryptocurrency was found to respond to negative events in both the Bitstamp and Mt.Gox markets, while it responded to positive news only in the Bitstamp market, indicating that Bitcoin has become more efficient over time in relation to its own events after the bankruptcy of Mt.Gox. Nevertheless, while studying the evolving predictability in the logarithmic price returns of Bitcoin, Khuntia and Pattanayak (2018) found evidence supporting the Adaptive Market Hypothesis, according to which markets evolve due to events and structural changes and adapt, suggesting that the market efficiency of Bitcoin varies in degree at different times and therefore evolves with time. Consequently, the existence of behavioural bias and occurrence of some events can change efficiency, enabling speculators to take advantage of such events at times, thus making it unrealistic to assume perfectly efficient or inefficient markets as per the Efficient Market Hypothesis.

Furthermore, besides the market, cryptocurrency, sample period, data frequency, method employed, and form of efficiency under investigation, the informational efficiency of cryptocurrency markets seems to depend on several other factors, such as the liquidity, degree of maturity, size, and volatility of the market. More specifically, liquidity has a positive and significant impact on the informational efficiency of cryptocurrency markets suggesting that cryptocurrencies become more efficient as liquidity increases (Brauneis and Mestel, 2018; Sensoy, 2019; Wei, 2018). The market size as measured by market capitalisation has also been found to be positively related to efficiency (Brauneis and Mestel, 2018), while Bitcoin as the oldest, most mature, and most commonly used cryptocurrency is the most efficient one (Brauneis and Mestel, 2018; Caporale et al., 2018). On the other hand, volatility has a negative effect in the informational efficiency of Bitcoin prices (Sensoy, 2019).

Based on the above, although cryptocurrency markets exhibit inefficiencies, the degree of inefficiency depends on several factors including the sample time period under investigation, the data, data frequency, and method employed, the cryptocurrency under investigation as well as the maturity, liquidity, and volatility of the market, among others. However, the most efficient cryptocurrency is Bitcoin, which is the most mature and dominant one.

It is worth noting, though, that, despite the fact that Bitcoin started being traded over a decade ago, cryptocurrencies still constitute a relatively new asset class and are still rather in their infancy. As it is common for informational inefficiencies to exist in new and smaller equity markets (Bekaert and Harvey, 2002), the existence of long-term memory and inefficiency findings in cryptocurrency markets are not surprising. Moreover, due to these characteristics, cryptocurrency markets are frequently compared with emerging markets, which exhibit greater inefficiency compared to developed markets (Bekaert and Harvey, 2002). Furthermore, such results are also related to the irrational behaviour of investors and the lack of a reasonable pricing mechanism (Jiang et al., 2018).

4 Bubbles

Few decades ago, the efficient market hypothesis considered in the previous section was widely accepted by academic financial economists. However, since then it has been frequently criticised, primarily due to the fact that asset prices are at least partially predictable. According to the survey by Beechey et al. (2000), although the efficient market hypothesis "is the right place to start when thinking about asset price formation", it "cannot explain some important and worrying features of asset market behaviour". One such feature is related to the bubble behaviour followed by crashes that different assets may exhibit. The efficient market hypothesis assumes that the current prices of securities are close to their fundamental values and that investors are rational, implying that bubbles and crashes cannot occur (Abreu and Brunnermeier, 2003). However, throughout history there have existed several popular examples of bubbles followed by crashes, including the famous Dutch tulip mania in the 1630s as well as the Internet stock boom of the 1990s.

According to Kindleberger (1991), a bubble can be defined "as a sharp rise in price of an asset or a range of assets in a continuous process, with the initial rise generating expectations of further rises and attracting new buyers – generally speculators interested in profits from trading in the asset rather than its use of earning capacity", with the rise being frequently "followed by a reversal of expectations and a sharp decline in price often resulting in a financial crisis". Financial asset bubbles in particular are viewed as inflations of prices beyond expectations based on fundamental economic features only.

Nonetheless, what occurs in markets depends on the traders' reaction to specific news and events. Indeed, changes in asset prices originate from the collective behaviour of several market participants instead of fundamental values (Kaizoji, 2000). Interestingly, even though investors might realise that prices are in excess of fundamental values, they could conjecture that the bubble will continue to expand and yield large positive returns (McQueen and Thorley, 1994), and thereby rationally remain in the market, since expectations leading to self-fulfilling speculative bubbles are consistent with fully rational, informed behaviour (Hamilton and Whiteman, 1985).

Although bubbles – and manias – do not follow an identical path, different bubbles exhibit some similar features, such as extensive public and media interest and over-valuation compared to historical averages – features which have clearly been present in cryptocurrency markets. Moreover, despite the fact that there can be speculation without a bubble, a bubble cannot occur without speculation. Consequently, due to the extent of public and media attention, the fact that cryptocurrencies have experienced periods of rapid price appreciations followed by sharp declines as well as the extent of speculation in cryptocurrency markets, several studies have investigated whether cryptocurrency markets exhibit speculative bubbles. In an early study – long before the unprecedented cryptocurrency price appreciations that occurred in 2017, Cheung et al. (2015), applying the Phillips et al. (2013) methodology to Bitcoin prices from the Mt. Gox exchange over the period 2010–2014, detected several short-lived bubbles as well as three large bubbles during the period 2011–2013 lasting between 66 and 106 days. The authors further found that the bursting of these large bubbles seems to coincide with certain major events that occurred in the exchange, namely an online attack leading to \$8.75 million in Bitcoin being stolen from the Mt. Gox exchange in June 2011, the incident in which trading at Mt. Gox was suspended for two days in April 2013, as well as Mt. Gox's decision to suspend all Bitcoin withdrawals on 7th February 2014 and to shut down its trading activities on 25th February. On the other hand, Corbet et al. (2018b) investigated whether underlying fundamentals related to Bitcoin and Ether, such as the blockchain position, the hashrate, and liquidity as measured by the volume of daily transactions, can be designated as drivers of price growth that could generate the conditions and environment in which a pricing bubble could thrive over the period between 2009 and 2017. In their study, it was found for Bitcoin that, although some periods where each of the fundamental drivers showed a bubble were identified, most bubbles were indicated as from the price alone, whereas for Ether, even scantier signals of bubbles, which were concentrated in the early 2016 and mid-2017 periods, were observed. The authors concluded that, although Bitcoin has been in a bubble phase since its price exceeded the landmark of $1000, there is a lack of clear evidence of a persistent bubble in the Bitcoin and Ether markets, without this suggesting that their prices are correct, though. Bubbles were also identified in the more recent study of Su et al. (2018), which analysed Bitcoin prices in terms of both CNY and USD and found that exogenous shocks enable the outset of bubbles, with important financial crises causing long-term and large-scale bubbles while short-term bubbles being triggered by domestic economic events, and that bubbles burst as a result of authorities' intervention, suggesting that governments can limit speculation in Bitcoin markets and stabilise its price.

Moreover, Cheah and Fry (2015) showed using methods originating in Econophysics that similar to other asset classes Bitcoin prices are prone to speculative bubbles, that the bubble component contained within Bitcoin prices is substantial, and that interestingly the fundamental value of Bitcoin is zero. Later, Fry and Cheah (2016) found evidence of a negative bubble in the prices of both Bitcoin and Ripple, concluding that over the period in question Ripple was over-priced compared to Bitcoin. More recently, using a theoretical refinement of the model in Cheah and Fry (2015), Fry (2018) found evidence of bubbles in the prices of both Bitcoin and Ether but no evidence of a bubble in Ripple once accounting for heavy-tails and liquidity risk, indicating technical advantages and reduced levels of speculation in Ripple compared to Bitcoin. On the other hand, no conclusive evidence of a bubble was found in the price of Bitcoin Cash, which could, however, be due to its reduced sample size compared to other cryptocurrencies which were launched much earlier.[1]

To sum up, the investigation of booms and crashes in financial markets has been a subject of interest among academics for decades. Recently the literature on bubbles and crashes in cryptocurrency markets has started emerging as well. While the bubble behaviour in altcoin markets seems to depend on both the cryptocurrency and period under investigation, Bitcoin has exhibited several bubbles since its launch. The explanation to cryptocurrencies' bubble behaviour lies merely in their very own nature: cryptocurrencies develop bubbles because they are simply objects of speculation without intrinsic value (Cheung et al., 2015). This fact has led to numerous bubbles of different magnitude with various incidents, such as online hacking attacks stealing Bitcoins and the decision of Chinese regulators to ban cryptocurrency trading, making them burst. Nevertheless, the risk-management implications are ambiguous since bubbles do not constitute a prerequisite for the occurrence of boom–bust episodes (Fry, 2018).

1 Bitcoin Cash was only launched in July 2017.

5 Volatility

Financial time series, such as stock prices and exchange rates, often exhibit the phenomenon of volatility clustering, where large changes tend to be followed by large changes, of either sign, and small changes tend to be followed by small changes. Since various types of news and other exogenous shocks could have an impact on an asset's price, the returns of financial assets tend to exhibit time-varying volatility, such that markets could be more tranquil during certain periods and more turbulent during others. Consequently, understanding and modelling time-varying volatility is of high importance in different areas, such as asset pricing, portfolio selection, and financial risk management. For instance, investors in stock markets are particularly interested in the volatility of stock prices, since higher levels of volatility could lead not only to huge gains but also to huge losses, therefore imposing larger risks. Volatility also has important implications for interval and density forecasting, since correct confidence intervals and density forecasts in the presence of time-varying volatility require time-varying confidence interval widths and time-varying density forecast spreads (Diebold, 2019).

Of course, it is well known that cryptocurrencies' prices exhibit a lot of fluctuations, including many violent ones, with several studies having found evidence of volatility clustering in the price returns of cryptocurrencies.[2] Interestingly, the volatility in cryptocurrency markets increased around the announcement of trading in Bitcoin futures (Corbet et al., 2018a). In fact, the price volatility of cryptocurrencies is significantly higher than the volatility of widely used currencies and financial assets, making forecasting of cryptocurrencies' prices a more challenging task compared to forecasting the prices of, e. g., exchange rates and stock indices. Many studies on the volatility of cryptocurrencies have employed Generalised Autoregressive Conditional Heteroskedasticity (GARCH) models, which are broadly applied in financial econometrics, mainly in modelling the volatility of stock prices and foreign exchange rates, as they are able to explain and forecast the volatility of financial time series, showing that cryptocurrency price volatility is significantly affected by both its own past shocks and past volatility.

One interesting finding in the literature on the volatility of Bitcoin is that, in contrast to what is frequently observed in financial returns, when studying the price volatility of Bitcoin at univariate level, there is no significant asymmetric effect between positive and negative past errors in the current levels of Bitcoin's volatility, known as leverage effect, irrespective of the data frequency. Consequently, negative return shocks do not have a greater impact on the conditional volatility of Bitcoin than positive shocks of equal magnitude, as commonly witnessed in different financial markets. On the other hand, another interesting finding, which is similar to what

2 For instance, Urquhart (2017) found evidence of significant price clustering in Bitcoin.

is observed in several financial returns, though, is that Bitcoin's volatility is best described by both a short-run and a long-run component (Katsiampa, 2017; Conrad et al., 2018; Troster et al., 2018; Vidal-Tomás and Ibañez, 2018). More specifically, in a comparison of several GARCH-type models, such as the simple GARCH, Exponential GARCH, GJR-GARCH, Asymmetric Power GARCH, Component GARCH, and Asymmetric Component GARCH, the Component CARCH model of Engle and Lee (1999), which decomposes the aggregate volatility into a long-run (permanent) component and a short-term (transitory) component and which has been found to outperform the simple GARCH model in financial applications (Christoffersen et al., 2008), was found to explain the Bitcoin price volatility better than other GARCH-type models, including models that allow for different responses of the volatility to positive and negative past shocks – i. e., the Exponential GARCH, GJR-GARCH, and Asymmetric CGARCH models (Katsiampa, 2017). The AR-CGARCH model under the Generalised Error Distribution (GED) has also been found to achieve the best out-of-sample forecasting performance for Bitcoin returns according to the root mean squared error (RMSE) when compared to several GARCH-type models under different error distributions (Troster et al., 2018).

Nevertheless, not only does Bitcoin exhibit heteroskedasticity but also altcoins are characterised by volatility clustering both at daily and intraday frequency. In a comparison of different GARCH-type models for several cryptocurrencies, it was found that among all the GARCH-type models fitted, the Integrated GARCH (IGARCH) model gave the best fit for Dash, Litecoin, Maidsafecoin, and Monero, and the simple GARCH model gave the best fit for Ripple, whereas the GJR-GARCH model, which takes asymmetric effects of positive and negative shocks in the conditional variance into consideration, gave the best fit for Dogecoin. Consequently, similar to Bitcoin and unlike many financial assets, the conditional volatility of most altcoins is not characterised by significant asymmetric effects between positive and negative past errors. Brauneis and Mestel (2018) further confirmed heteroscedasticity at the daily level for sixty-eight out of the seventy-three cryptocurrencies considered in their dataset.

Cryptocurrencies' price volatility also exhibit long memory, structural breaks, and jumps. More specifically, it has been found that the volatility in different Bitcoin markets exhibits long-range dependence, although after accounting for structural breaks, long memory in the mean and variance of cryptocurrencies decreases. Breaks in some cryptocurrencies' conditional variance were also found in Katsiampa (2019) who found that – contrary to Ether, Ripple, and Stellar – Bitcoin and Litecoin exhibit one structural breakpoint each in the conditional variance. Furthermore, cryptocurrencies' price returns and volatility exhibit jumps. Nevertheless, while jumps to mean returns have been found to only have contemporaneous effects, jumps to volatility are permanent.

All in all, although the optimal model describing or forecasting the volatility of the cryptocurrencies could depend not only on the cryptocurrency under investigation but also on the sample period, there are some findings that can be generalised.

First of all, cryptocurrencies exhibit volatility clustering, irrespective of the data frequency (daily, intraday, or monthly). Secondly, most cryptocurrencies do not exhibit significant asymmetric effect between positive and negative past errors in the current levels of their price volatility. Thirdly, some cryptocurrencies exhibit structural breaks in the conditional variance. Moreover, cryptocurrencies display long-memory in the conditional variance, despite the fact that, after accounting for structural breaks, long memory in the mean and variance of cryptocurrencies decreases. Another interesting finding is that while Bitcoin's volatility seems to be described by both a short-run and a long-run component, this does not seem to be true for altcoins, since the altcoins' volatility seems to be better described by more simple GARCH-type models. However, it is worth noting that volatility is lower in more liquid cryptocurrency markets (Wei, 2018), and cryptocurrency investors and traders should consider cryptocurrencies' volatility dynamics for improving their risk management.

Finally, it is worth noting that, in contrast to traditional assets, cryptocurrencies are subject to additional sources of risk including forks, price manipulation, and hacking, among others, all of which further contribute to their price volatility. In addition, despite the fact that cryptocurrencies constitute decentralised digital currencies, significant Bitcoin volatility has been found to be generated by decisions related to both adjusting interest rates and introducing quantitative easing made by the central banks of the US, EU, UK, and Japan, with decisions related to quantitative easing having been found to have generated the most significant influence (Corbet et al., 2017), therefore suggesting that cryptocurrencies are not completely independent of government actions but rather remain vulnerable to policy announcements.

6 Interdependencies of cryptocurrency markets

As mentioned in the introduction of this chapter, as of August 2019 the total number of cryptocurrencies has surpassed 2500, following the success of Bitcoin which led to the emergence of various alternative digital currencies (altcoins). Although most of them – including Bitcoin, Ether, Ripple, and Litecoin, among others – are based on Blockchain technologies, each cryptocurrency has some features that distinguish one from another. For instance, Litecoin is characterised by faster transaction confirmation times and improved storage efficiency than Bitcoin, with the block generation time being 2.5 minutes per block for Litecoin compared to 10 minutes per block for Bitcoin, and the maximum limit of coins being four times higher than that of Bitcoin; Ether constitutes the digital token of Ethereum, an open-source Blockchain-based platform featuring smart contracts, which is supported by several industry giants through the Enterprise Ethereum Alliance foundation; whereas Ripple has been adopted by banks as settlement infrastructure technology, as it connects banks, payment providers, digital asset exchanges and corporates via the RippleNet, which aims to improve the speed of financial transactions, with payments settling in only four seconds. On the other hand, Lumen represents the digital coin of the Stellar network, which is an open source, distributed and community owned technology that processes financial transactions, with the platform aiming to connect banks, payment systems and people, while contributing to financial inclusion focusing on developing markets. Lumen can be used for fast mobile payments and micropayments with very small fees. Monero provides its users with untraceability of their operations, a feature that could attract people interested in evading law enforcement.

Nevertheless, despite the fact that different features of cryptocurrencies can influence their prices and stability (Yi et al., 2018), cryptocurrencies' also have several similarities and it could be expected that the prices of Bitcoin and altcoins are interdependent, not only due to Bitcoin's dominance within the market but also due to the fact that most altcoin orders are executed in Bitcoin. Indeed Bitcoin and altcoin markets are interdependent, with Bitcoin being the dominant contributor of return and volatility spillovers among cryptocurrencies (Koutmos, 2018), and cryptocurrency users therefore face undifferentiated risks (Gkillas and Katsiampa, 2018). Moreover, the interdependencies between Bitcoin and altcoins are significantly stronger in the short-run than in the long-run, with macro-financial indicators influencing the price formation of altcoins in the long-run to a slightly greater extent than Bitcoin does (Ciaian and Rajcaniova, 2018).

However, besides understanding interlinkages of the prices and returns, it is also important to understand volatility co-movements and spillover effects among cryptocurrencies. Volatility spillovers are commonly observed in the behaviour of financial assets, and comprehending covariances and correlations is of paramount importance to investors who are interested in understanding the risk of their portfolios (Coudert et al., 2015), since high levels of volatility interlinkages can limit the benefits of diversification. Understanding volatility co-movements and spillovers in cryptocurrency markets can assist market participants with improving their knowledge of the information transmission mechanisms and interdependencies within cryptocurrency markets, therefore enabling them make more informed decisions as well as adjust their portfolios accordingly.

The total volatility connectedness in cryptocurrencies increased constantly after December 2016 (Yi et al., 2018). It has been shown that irrespective of the data frequency (daily or intraday), the conditional covariances of cryptocurrencies are significantly affected by cross products of past error terms and previous covariance terms while also capturing asymmetric effects of both good and bad news, and hence significant volatility co-movements between cryptocurrencies and time-varying conditional correlations which are mostly positive exist (Aslanidis et al., 2019; Katsiampa, 2018, 2019; Katsiampa et al., 2019a). Consequently, conditional correlations between cryptocurrencies do not remain constant but rather behave differently over different time periods. Nevertheless, when comparing conditional correlations between Bitcoin, Dash, Monero, and Ripple, correlations between cryptocurrencies and Monero are found to be more stable across time compared to the correlations of the other pairs of cryptocurrencies, whereas the most variable correlation is found between Ripple and Dash (Aslanidis et al., 2019). Moreover, the cryptocurrencies' conditional variance, covariance, and correlation plots exhibit several spikes indicating that they seem to have been susceptible to various news related to cryptocurrencies, such as Chinese authorities shutting down China-based cryptocurrency exchanges.

In addition, cryptocurrencies not only exhibit volatility co-movements but also volatility spillover effects. Interestingly, though, not only Bitcoin spillovers over altcoins. Instead, there are bidirectional spillovers between cryptocurrency markets, even though cryptocurrencies with higher capitalisation are more likely to spread volatility shocks to others (Yi et al., 2018). Katsiampa et al. (2019b) examined the conditional volatility interlinkages and correlations between three pairs of cryptocurrencies, namely Bitcoin-Ether, Bitcoin-Litecoin, and Ether-Litecoin, and found evidence of bi-directional shock transmission effects between Bitcoin and both Ether and Litecoin, and uni-directional shock spillovers from Ether to Litecoin, as well as bi-directional volatility spillover effects between all the three pairs.

It is also worth noting that when considering portfolios consisting of cryptocurrencies only, diversification is more efficient in the short to medium runs (Omane-Adjepong and Alagidede, 2019). Moreover, in terms of selecting between naïve (using equal weights) and optimal (Markowitz) diversification in portfolios consisting of cryptocurrencies only, there is very little difference in performance between the two types of diversification, supporting the findings of (DeMiguel et al., 2007) that naïve diversification is as good, if not better, than optimal diversification (Platanakis et al., 2018).

Consequently, cryptocurrencies show strong interdependencies both in the conditional mean and variance equation. Despite the fact that Bitcoin still remains the dominant cryptocurrency, there are bidirectional spillovers between cryptocurrency markets. Understanding the degree of connectedness and market spillover effects is of great importance in order for cryptocurrency users and traders to make more informed decisions with regards to appropriate trading strategy selection and risk management, especially since cryptocurrency users face undifferentiated risks.

7 Cryptocurrencies and financial assets

Despite the fact that Bitcoin and altcoins are digital currencies designed to work as a medium of exchange, they are primarily used for speculation and investment purposes rather than as alternative currencies or medium of exchange, where some investors employ them as a hedge against stocks or other assets. It is therefore of high importance for cryptocurrency investors to understand the relationship between cryptocurrencies and mainstream financial assets as well as cryptocurrencies' hedging and diversification ability for appropriate risk and portfolio management.

According to Baur and Lucey (2010),

- *"A hedge is defined as an asset that is uncorrelated or negatively correlated with another asset or portfolio on average."*
- *"A diversifier is defined as an asset that is positively (but not perfectly correlated) with another asset or portfolio on average."*
- *"A safe haven is defined as an asset that is uncorrelated or negatively correlated with another asset or portfolio in times of market stress or turmoil."*

Consequently, unlike a safe haven, neither a hedge nor a diversifier reduces losses in extreme market conditions.

Several studies[3] have investigated the relationship between Bitcoin and different mainstream assets, all of which have found consistent results showing Bitcoin and other cryptocurrencies not being correlated with financial assets and commodities, such as stocks, bonds, gold, and oil, with Bitcoin therefore being isolated from other markets, with no specific asset playing a dominant role in influencing cryptocurrency market. Interestingly, cryptocurrencies are uncorrelated with traditional asset classes both in normal times and in periods of financial turmoil (Baur et al., 2018). Similar results have been found to hold for the relationship between Bitcoin and different currencies which have shown that Bitcoin is not correlated with currencies either.[4]

Nevertheless, the relationship between Bitcoin and other financial assets is a continuous process that varies over time (Ji et al., 2018), and Bitcoin's hedging and safe haven properties seem to vary between different horizons (Bouri et al., 2017). For instance, although an early study assessing whether Bitcoin can act as a hedge and safe haven for major world stock indices, bonds, oil, gold, the general commodity index and the US dollar index, found that overall Bitcoin is a poor hedge, is appropriate merely for diversification purposes, and can only serve as a strong safe haven against weekly extreme down movements in Asian stocks (Bouri et al., 2017), some more recent studies have found that, by adding Bitcoin, the portfolio performance improves, even though this is primarily due to the increase in returns than in the reduction of volatility (Kajtazi and Moro, 2019), that a short position in Bitcoin allows hedging the risk of investment against various financial assets and that hedging strategies involving gold, oil, emerging stock markets and Bitcoin reduce considerably a portfolio's risk, in comparison to a portfolio composed of gold, oil and stocks from emerging

3 Examples of such studies include, e. g., those of Baur et al. (2018), Bouri et al. (2017), Corbet et al. (2018c), Ji et al. (2018), and Yermack (2015).

4 The reader can be referred to, e. g., Baur et al. (2018), Corbet et al. (2018c), Giudici and Abu-Hashish (2019), Guesmi et al. (2019), Ji et al. (2018), Urquhart and Zhang (2019), and Yermack (2015).

stock only (Guesmi et al., 2019). Bitcoin can be also used as a hedge against stocks in the Financial Times Stock Exchange Index, but also as a hedge against the American dollar in the short-term (Dyhrberg, 2016). Moreover, Conrad et al. (2018) found that Bitcoin volatility is negatively related to US stock market volatility, indicating that Bitcoin can act as a safe-haven. On the other hand, Urquhart and Zhang (2019), who assessed the relationship between Bitcoin and different currencies at the hourly frequency concluded that Bitcoin can act as an intraday hedge for the Swiss Franc, Euro and GBP, but acts as a diversifier for the Australian dollar, Canadian dollar and Japanese yen. The latter study also found that Bitcoin is a safe haven during periods of extreme market turmoil for the Canadian dollar, Swiss Franc and GBP. It is also worth noting that Bitcoin futures cannot mitigate the risk inherent in the underlying spot market and therefore are not an effective hedging tool (Corbet et al., 2018a).

Investors always search for alternative investment opportunities and instruments for their portfolios. Cryptocurrencies are different from mainstream assets and provide investors with such an alternative mainly due to the high returns they can offer. Consequently, understanding cryptocurrencies' relationship with other financial assets is of high importance to investors in order to make more informed decisions. Cryptocurrency markets have very low correlations with mainstream assets and are therefore isolated from financial and commodity markets, such as equity, gold, oil, and currency markets, and no specific asset plays a dominant role in influencing cryptocurrency markets. However, the relationship between cryptocurrencies and mainstream assets varies over time, and therefore cryptocurrencies' hedging and safe haven properties vary between horizons.

8 Summary

In this chapter, we considered several financial characteristics of cryptocurrency markets. As discussed, cryptocurrencies are characterised by heavy tail behaviour, very high volatility, persistence, large abrupt price swings, and vulnerability to speculative bubbles, among other properties, all of which lead cryptocurrencies to resemble more financial assets rather than fiat currencies. Moreover, cryptocurrency markets exhibit some informational inefficiencies, which, however, depend on several factors. Finally, cryptocurrencies are highly connected to each other but isolated from mainstream assets, with their hedging and safe haven properties varying over time.

Despite the fact that the first cryptocurrency was introduced over a decade ago, cryptocurrencies seem to constitute a different type of asset class which seems to still be in its infancy. Cryptocurrencies are primarily used for speculation purposes instead of as a traditional medium of exchange, despite the fact that they hold high investment risk and despite concerns about risks associated with their price fluctuations raised by economists and financial institutions, with their price discovery being driven by uninformed investors.

Bibliography

Abreu, D., and M. K. Brunnermeier (2003). Bubbles and crashes. *Econometrica 71*(1), 173–204.

Aslanidis, N., A. F. Bariviera, and O. Martínez-Ibañez (2019). An analysis of cryptocurrencies conditional cross correlations. *Finance Research Letters 31*, 130–137.

Baur, D. G., and B. M. Lucey (2010). Is gold a hedge or a safe haven? An analysis of stocks, bonds and gold. *Financial Review 45*(2), 217–229.

Baur, D. G., K. Hong, and A. D. Lee (2018). Bitcoin: Medium of exchange or speculative assets? *Journal of International Financial Markets, Institutions and Money 54*, 177–189.

Beechey, M., D. Gruen, and J. Vickery (2000). *The efficient market hypothesis: A survey*. Sydney: Reserve Bank of Australia.

Bekaert, G., and C. R. Harvey (2002). Research in emerging markets finance: Looking to the future. *Emerging markets review 3*(4), 429–448.

Bouri, E., P. Molnár, G. Azzi, D. Roubaud, and L. I. Hagfors (2017). On the hedge and safe haven properties of bitcoin: Is it really more than a diversifier? *Finance Research Letters 20*, 192–198.

Brauneis, A., and R. Mestel (2018). Price discovery of cryptocurrencies: Bitcoin and beyond. *Economics Letters 165*, 58–61.

Caporale, G. M., L. Gil-Alana, and A. Plastun (2018). Persistence in the cryptocurrency market. *Research in International Business and Finance 46*, 141–148.

Cheah, E. T., and J. Fry (2015). Speculative bubbles in bitcoin markets? An empirical investigation into the fundamental value of bitcoin. *Economics Letters 130*, 32–36.

Cheah, E. T., T. Mishra, M. Parhi, and Z. Zhang (2018). Long memory interdependency and inefficiency in bitcoin markets. *Economics Letters 167*, 18–25.

Cheung, A., E. Roca, and J. J. Su (2015). Crypto-currency bubbles: An application of the Phillips–Shi–Yu (2013) methodology on Mt. Gox bitcoin prices. *Applied Economics 47*(23), 2348–2358.

Christoffersen, P., K. Jacobs, C. Ornthanalai, and Y. Wang (2008). Option valuation with long-run and short-run volatility components. *Journal of Financial Economics 90*(3), 272–297.

Ciaian, P., and M. Rajcaniova (2018). Virtual relationships: short-and long-run evidence from BitCoin and altcoin markets. *Journal of International Financial Markets, Institutions and Money 52*, 173–195.

Conrad, C., A. Custovic, and E. Ghysels (2018). Long-and short-term cryptocurrency volatility components: A GARCH-MIDAS analysis. *Journal of Risk and Financial Management 11*(2), 23.

Corbet, S., and P. Katsiampa (2018). Asymmetric mean reversion of bitcoin price returns. *International Review of Financial Analysis*.

Corbet, S., G. McHugh, and A. Meegan (2017). The influence of Central Bank monetary policy announcements on cryptocurrency return volatility. *Investment Management & Financial Innovations 14*(4), 60.

Corbet, S., B. Lucey, M. Peat, and S. Vigne (2018a). Bitcoin futures—What use are they? *Economics Letters 172*, 23–27.

Corbet, S., B. Lucey, and L. Yarovaya (2018b). Datestamping the bitcoin and ethereum bubbles. *Finance Research Letters 26*, 81–88.

Corbet, S., A. Meegan, C. Larkin, B. Lucey, and L. Yarovaya. (2018c). Exploring the dynamic relationships between cryptocurrencies and other financial assets. *Economics Letters 165*, 28–34.

Coudert, V., K. Hervé, and P. Mabille (2015). Internationalization versus regionalization in the emerging stock markets. *International Journal of Finance and Economics 20*(1), 16–27.

DeMiguel, V., L. Garlappi, and R. Uppal (2007). Optimal versus naive diversification: How inefficient is the 1/*N* portfolio strategy? *The review of Financial studies 22*(5), 1915–1953.

Diebold, F. X. (2019). *Econometric data science: A predictive modeling approach*. Retrieved from: https://www.sas.upenn.edu/~fdiebold/Teaching104/Econometrics.pdf.

Dowd, K. (2014). New private monies: A bit-part player? *Institute of Economic Affairs Monographs, Hobart Paper* 174.

Dyhrberg, A. H. (2016). Hedging capabilities of bitcoin. Is it the virtual gold? *Finance Research Letters 16*, 139–144.

Engle, R. F., and G. Lee (1999). A long-run and short-run component model of stock return volatility. In *Cointegration, causality, and forecasting: A festschrift in honour of clive WJ Granger*, edited by R. F. Engle and H. White. Oxford University Press.

Fama, E. (1970). Efficient capital markets: A review of theory and empirical work. *Journal of finance 25*(2), 383–417.

Fry, J. (2018). Booms, busts and heavy-tails: The story of bitcoin and cryptocurrency markets? *Economics Letters 171*, 225–229.

Fry, J., and E. T. Cheah (2016). Negative bubbles and shocks in cryptocurrency markets. *International Review of Financial Analysis 47*, 343–352.

Giudici, P., and I. Abu-Hashish (2019). What determines bitcoin exchange prices? A network VAR approach. *Finance Research Letters 28*, 309–318.

Gkillas, K., and P. Katsiampa (2018). An application of extreme value theory to cryptocurrencies. *Economics Letters 164*, 109–111.

Guesmi, K., S. Saadi, I. Abid, and Z. Ftiti (2019). Portfolio diversification with virtual currency: Evidence from bitcoin. *International Review of Financial Analysis 63*, 431–437.

Hamilton, J. D., and C. H. Whiteman (1985). The observable implications of self-fulfilling expectations. *Journal of Monetary Economics 16*(3), 353–373.

Ji, Q., E. Bouri, R. Gupta, and D. Roubaud (2018). Network causality structures among bitcoin and other financial assets: A directed acyclic graph approach. *The Quarterly Review of Economics and Finance 70*, 203–213.

Jiang, Y., H. Nie, and W. Ruan (2018). Time-varying long-term memory in bitcoin market. *Finance Research Letters 25*, 280–284.

Kaizoji, T. (2000). Speculative bubbles and crashes in stock markets: An interacting-agent model of speculative activity. *Physica A: Statistical Mechanics and its Applications 287*(3–4), 493–506.

Kajtazi, A., and A. Moro (2019). The role of bitcoin in well diversified portfolios: A comparative global study. *International Review of Financial Analysis 61*, 143–157.

Katsiampa, P. (2017). Volatility estimation for bitcoin: A comparison of GARCH models. *Economics Letters 158*, 3–6.

Katsiampa, P. (2018). Volatility co-movement between bitcoin and ether. *Finance Research Letters*.

Katsiampa, P. (2019). An empirical investigation of volatility dynamics in the cryptocurrency market. *Research in International Business and Finance*.

Katsiampa, P., S. Corbet, and B. Lucey (2019a). High frequency volatility co-movements in cryptocurrency markets. *Journal of International Financial Markets, Institutions and Money*.

Katsiampa, P., S. Corbet, and B. Lucey (2019b). Volatility spillover effects in leading cryptocurrencies: A BEKK-MGARCH analysis. *Finance Research Letters 29*, 68–74.

Khuntia, S., and J. K. Pattanayak (2018). Adaptive market hypothesis and evolving predictability of bitcoin. *Economics Letters 167*, 26–28.
Kindleberger, C. P. (1991). *Bubbles. In the world of economics*, 20–22. London: Palgrave Macmillan.
Koutmos, D. (2018). Return and volatility spillovers among cryptocurrencies. *Economics Letters 173*, 122–127.
McQueen, G., and S. Thorley (1994). Bubbles, stock returns, and duration dependence. *Journal of Financial and Quantitative Analysis 29*(3), 379–401.
Nadarajah, S., and J. Chu (2017). On the inefficiency of bitcoin. *Economics Letters 150*, 6–9.
Omane-Adjepong, M., and I. P. Alagidede (2019). Multiresolution analysis and spillovers of major cryptocurrency markets. *Research in International Business and Finance 49*, 191–206.
Phillip, A., J. Chan, and S. Peiris (2018). A new look at cryptocurrencies. *Economics Letters 163*, 6–9.
Phillips, P. C., S. P. Shi, and J. Yu (2013). Testing for multiple bubbles 1: Historical episodes of exuberance and collapse in the S&P 500. Research Collection School Of Economics.
Platanakis, E., C. Sutcliffe, and A. Urquhart (2018). Optimal vs naïve diversification in cryptocurrencies. *Economics Letters 171*, 93–96.
Sensoy, A. (2019). The inefficiency of bitcoin revisited: A high-frequency analysis with alternative currencies. *Finance Research Letters 28*, 68–73.
Su, C. W., Z. Z. Li, R. Tao, and D. K. Si (2018). Testing for multiple bubbles in bitcoin markets: A generalized sup ADF test. *Japan and the World Economy 46*, 56–63.
Tiwari, A. K., R. K. Jana, D. Das, and D. Roubaud (2018). Informational efficiency of bitcoin—An extension. *Economics Letters 163*, 106–109.
Troster, V., A. K. Tiwari, M. Shahbaz, and D. N. Macedo (2018). Bitcoin returns and risk: A general GARCH and GAS analysis. *Finance Research Letters*.
Urquhart, A. (2016). The inefficiency of bitcoin. *Economics Letters 148*, 80–82.
Urquhart, A. (2017). Price clustering in bitcoin. *Economics letters 159*, 145–148.
Urquhart, A., and H. Zhang (2019). Is bitcoin a hedge or safe haven for currencies? An intraday analysis. *International Review of Financial Analysis 63*, 49–57.
Vidal-Tomás, D., and A. Ibañez (2018). Semi-strong efficiency of bitcoin. *Finance Research Letters 27*, 259–265.
Wei, W. C. (2018). Liquidity and market efficiency in cryptocurrencies. *Economics Letters 168*, 21–24.
Yermack, D. (2015). Is bitcoin a real currency? An economic appraisal. In *Handbook of digital currency*, 31–43. Academic Press.
Yi, S., Z. Xu, and G. J. Wang (2018). Volatility connectedness in the cryptocurrency market: Is bitcoin a dominant cryptocurrency? *International Review of Financial Analysis 60*, 98–114.
Zargar, F. N., and D. Kumar (2019). Informational inefficiency of bitcoin: A study based on high-frequency data. *Research in International Business and Finance 47*, 344–353.

Elie Bouri, Rangan Gupta, Chi Keung Marco Lau, and
David Roubaud

The predictability between Bitcoin and US technology stock returns: Granger causality in mean, variance, and quantile

In this chapter, we test for Granger causality in mean, variance, and quantile between Bitcoin prices and various US stock indices belonging to the overall stock market and the sector of information technology and its various industries. Using daily data covering the period 18 August 2011 to 15 April 2019, results from the application of the test of Chen (2016) show the following. Unsurprisingly, there is evidence of a relationship between Bitcoin and US tech stock indices. Specifically, there is clear evidence of predictability between Bitcoin and US tech stocks, which seems to vary across quantiles. US stocks Granger cause Bitcoin return, but this is not the case for other stock indices. Generally, Granger causality from one market to another is insignificant in both mean and variance. However, when one market is in its bear state, the other become more volatile. Furthermore, there is evidence of casualties when one market is in its bear market state, while the other is in its bear or bull market state. Our findings suggest the need to use unconventional methods such as the Granger causality in moments of Chen (2016), otherwise, it might be wrongly apparent that Bitcoin and US (tech) stock indices are independent.

1 Introduction

Bitcoin continues to dominate the cryptocurrency market, with a market share exceeding 50% of the total market value of all cryptocurrencies. As a decentralized payment system, Bitcoin is backed by the blockchain technology which represents a public ledger containing all Bitcoin transactions. In fact, the blockchain technology allows for the validation of Bitcoin transactions by solving complex algorithmic puzzles. The new transactions are added to the ledger in a so-called mining process through which Bitcoins are produced and acquired as a reward for solving the crypto puzzles. Given that specialized and powerful computers are needed to conduct the computational work, there is a potential association between Bitcoin prices and the share prices of tech companies that manufacture computer hardware and software.

Although several studies examine the association between Bitcoin returns and volatility and various macro-economic and financial variables,[1] there is still a lack of

1 They apply various methods and generally show the absence or presence of a weak evidence of predictability. For more details on this literature, the reader can refer to Corbet et al. (2019).

https://doi.org/10.1515/9783110660807-005

empirical evidence regarding the relationship between Bitcoin returns and the returns of the information technology stock sector and its various industries. Therefore, in this chapter, we add to the embryonic literature dealing with the association between Bitcoin and information technology stock markets. Specifically, we use daily data covering the period 18 August 2011 to 15 April 2019, and follow the interesting approach of Chen (2016), which allows for testing Granger causality in moments. This approach allows not only for examining Granger causality for mean and variance but also for quantiles and moments. In fact, the approach of Chen (2016) enables the testing of Granger causality from the upper (lower) tails of one distribution to the lower (upper) tails of another distribution, which cannot be done using existing approaches (e. g., Hong, 2001; Balcilar et al., 2019).[2] Such a feature is important given the importance of revealing evidence of tail risk spillovers across assets (Soylu and Güloğlu, 2019).

Our contributions are on several fronts. Firstly, we add to Symitsi and Chalvatzis (2018) who do not capture the heterogeneity of relationships between Bitcoin returns and volatility, the return and volatility of technology stocks or the return and volatility spillovers in the various tails of the distribution. In fact, our analyses show evidence of Granger causalities that differ across quantiles and between the mean and the variance, which supports our choice of Granger causality tests in moments of Chen (2016). Secondly, we focus on US equity indices given the US stock market is the largest and most developed. It also contains very sophisticated investors from around the globe, and is the hub of leading and innovative technology companies. In addition to an aggregate stock index, in our case the S&P500, we use not only the information technology sector index but also indices representing the various industries within the information technology sector. This is based on the rationale that the Bitcoin ecosystem might relate differently to various tech companies belonging to computer hardware, computer software, semiconductors, and internet companies. Our results show evidence of heterogeneity in the Granger causality results across most of the indices under study, which justifies our reliance on aggregate, sector and industry level data.

The rest of the chapter is given in four sections. Section 2 reviews the literature. Section 3 explains the methodology. Section 4 describes the data and presents the results. Section 5 concludes.

2 Literature review

Predicting asset returns has always been an appealing but a challenging task for both investors and finance researchers. It has been extensively studied in the academic literature covering conventional assets such as equities, bonds (Keim and Stambaugh,

2 As indicated by Soylu and Güloğlu (2019), the Granger causality tests in moments of Chen (2016) outperform other related tests such as the tests of Hong (2001) and Balcilar et al. (2019).

1986; Liu et al., 2019; Xu et al., 2019), commodities (Zhang et al., 2019), and currencies (Baku, 2019), using various macroeconomic and financial variables as potential determinants of returns and volatility. Interestingly, recent studies indicate that predictability is not homogenous across the quantiles of the return distribution, in both of its first and second moments (e. g., Balcilar et al., 2019).

As Bitcoin has emerged as a leading digital asset, many studies consider the predictability of Bitcoin returns and volatility using various research methods and a rich set of variables. Kristoufek (2013) reports evidence of a significant association between Bitcoin prices and Bitcoin attention as proxied by search queries on Google Trends and Wikipedia. This evidence was later confirmed by Dastgir et al. (2019) who use a copula approach. Other studies associate Bitcoin returns with geopolitical risk (Aysan et al., 2019) and economic policy uncertainty (Demir et al., 2018; Yu et al., 2019) as potential predictors of Bitcoin returns or Bitcoin volatility. Other studies find evidence of a significant association between Bitcoin returns and trading volume (Balcilar et al., 2017; Bouri et al., 2019b), whereas no significant association is noticed between Bitcoin price volatility and trading volume. Interestingly, these two studies highlight the importance of studying the nexus between Bitcoin returns (volatility) and trading volume via quantile-based methods that allow for examining the whole return distribution. Another strand of research focuses on Bitcoin price predictability and the presence of long memory to make inferences regarding market efficiency. This research generally applies statistical tests of random walk in prices (e. g., Urquhart, 2016) and volatility persistence (e. g., Bouri et al., 2019a). The results generally suggest evidence of inefficiency, suggesting the ability of predicting Bitcoin prices and Bitcoin volatility. Other studies examine the association between Bitcoin price volatility and several macro-economic and financial variables (e. g., Walther et al., 2019), although Bitcoin price volatility is extremely high and persistent (Bouri et al., 2019a). Furthermore, many studies indicate that Bitcoin returns are detached from the global financial system, suggesting the suitability of Bitcoin for diversifying the downside risk of stock market returns at global, regional, and country levels. For example, Bouri et al. (2017a) apply dynamic correlation analysis augmented with quantile-based regression and report evidence that Bitcoin is useful for reducing stock market risk. Similar results are reported by both Ji et al. (2018) and Corbet et al. (2018), although they use different methods.[3] Bouri et al. (2017b) highlight the valuable role of Bitcoin for energy commodities. Shahzad et al. (2019) find that Bitcoin is an effective diversifier for G7 stock markets, although gold seems to offer higher diversification benefits. Klein et al. (2018) show that Bitcoin differs from gold in regard to equity portfolio diversification, indicating its inability to act as a hedge during stress periods. Furthermore, Bouri et al. (2018) apply a quantile-based approach and find evidence that aggregate commodity and gold prices are predictors of Bitcoin prices. They also highlight the heterogeneity

3 Ji et al. (2018) use a graph theory whereas Corbet et al. (2018) apply connectedness measures.

in the relationship across the various quantiles of the return distribution, which somewhat concords with the findings of Balcilar et al. (2017) and Bouri et al. (2019b) regarding trading volume. Interestingly, Symitsi and Chalvatzis (2018) consider the return and volatility spillovers between the market of Bitcoin and the markets of energy and technology companies. They indicate return and volatility spillovers from the technology sector index to Bitcoin prices. However, their reliance on the BEKK GARCH model makes their analyses restricted because of its sole focus on mean-based spillovers.

As shown in the above brief review of previous studies, the academic literature focusing on the relationship between Bitcoin returns and volatility and the returns and volatility of stock market indices is not well developed. Notably, it lacks evidence regarding the relationship between Bitcoin and information technology stocks, accounting for the potential heterogeneity of the return distribution across the various quantiles.

The importance of applying a tail risk approach in the Bitcoin market is highlighted by previous studies (see, among others, Balcilar et al., 2017; Feng et al., 2018; Zhang et al., 2018; Bouri et al., 2019b; Shahzad et al., 2019). This suggests the suitability of applying a quantile-based approach that allows for assessing the predictability of Bitcoin returns and volatility in specific upper, middle, and lower quantiles based on the various quantiles of tech stock returns, and vice-versa. We therefore apply the approach of Chen (2016), which enables testing of Granger causality in mean, variance, and quantile, while considering aggregate, sector, and industry stock level data from the US.

3 The test of Granger causality in moments

First, let us denote a stationary series of continuous random variables by $\{y_{it}\}$ while $Y_{i,t-1}$ is a set of information that is generated from $y_{i,t-k}$ such that for all, $k > 0$ and $i = 1, 2$. Further, let us denote $Y_{t-1} = (Y_{1,t-1}, Y_{2,t-1})$ and specify $F_i(\cdot \mid Y_{i,t-1})$ and $F_i(\cdot \mid Y_{t-1})$ to be the respective conditional distributions of two processes, i. e.: $y_u \mid Y_{i,t-1}$ and $y_u \mid Y_{t-1}$, where $i = 1, 2$. It follows logically that if $Y_{2,t-1}$ does not provide any relevant information in forecasting $F_i(\cdot \mid Y_{i,t-1})$ in such a way as equation (1), then as explained by Granger (1980), it will suffice to infer that, in distribution, y_{2t} does not Granger cause y_{1t}, otherwise y_{2t} Granger causes y_{1t}.

$$F_i(\cdot \mid Y_{i,t-1}) = F_i(\cdot \mid Y_{t-1}) \tag{1}$$

Second, within the context of hypothesis testing, the respective null hypotheses in mean, variance and quantiles that y_{2t} does not Granger cause y_{1t} are thus formulated:

No causality in mean:

$$E[\theta(y_{1t}) \mid Y_{t-1}] = E[\theta(y_{1t}) \mid Y_{t-1}] \tag{2}$$

No causality in variance:

$$E[\theta_2(y_{1t} - E[\theta_1(y_{1t}) \mid Y_{(1,t-1)}]) \mid Y_{(1,t-1)}] = \text{var}[y_{1t} \mid Y_{(1,t-1)}] \tag{3}$$

No causality in quantiles:

$$E[\theta_q(y_{1t})|Y_{1,t-1}] = E[I(Q_{1t}(\tau_1) < y_t \leq Q_{1t}(\tau_2)) \mid Y_{1,t-1}] \tag{4}$$

From equations (2) through (4), the moment functions $\theta(\cdot)$ include, but are not limited to, the following:

$$\theta_1(y) := y \tag{5}$$

$$\theta_2(y) := y^2 \tag{6}$$

$$\theta_q(y) := I(Q_{it}(\tau_1) < y \leq Q_{it}(\tau_1)) \tag{7}$$

$y \in \mathbb{R}$, $\tau_1 < \tau_2$ and $Q_{it}(\tau)$ denote τ-quantile of $F_i(\cdot \mid Y_{i,t-1})$ and $\tau \in [0,1]$

Using the G statistic as presented in equation (8), the hypotheses stated above can be tested, thus:

$$G = P(S\hat{\rho})'(S\hat{V}^{-1}\hat{\Omega}\hat{V}^{-1}S')(S\hat{\rho}) \sim X_q^2 \tag{8}$$

where:

By computation, $P = T - R$ for some $0 < R < T$, and T is the sample size, $\hat{\Omega}$ represents the variance covariance matrix, S is the qxn weight matrix for $q \leq n$. The sample cross-correlations between $\hat{\Theta}_{1t}^{c}$ and $\hat{\Theta}_{2,t-k}^{c}$ for lag k can be expressed as:

$$\hat{\rho}_k := \frac{1}{P-k} \sum_{t=R+1+k}^{T} \left(\frac{\hat{\Theta}_{1t}^{c}}{\overline{\sigma}_1}\right)\left(\frac{\hat{\Theta}_{2,t-1}^{c}}{\overline{\sigma}_2}\right) \tag{9}$$

$$\hat{\rho} := (\hat{\rho}_1, \hat{\rho}_2, \ldots \hat{\rho}_{it})' \quad \text{and} \quad V := (\overline{\sigma}_1\overline{\sigma}_2) \times I_n \quad k = 1, \ldots n,\ n < P$$

In this expression, $\Theta_{it}^{(\cdot)}$ symbolises the transformed error term ε_{it} for $i = 1, 2$. In a more precise way, it is given as:

$$\text{Mean:} \quad \Theta_{it}^{(1)} = \varepsilon_{it} \tag{10}$$

$$\text{Variance:} \quad \Theta_{it}^{(1)} = \varepsilon_{it}^2 - 1 \tag{11}$$

$$\text{Quantile:} \quad \Theta_{it}^{(q)} = I(Q_{\varepsilon,it}(\tau_1 \mid \beta_1) < \varepsilon_{it} \leq Q_{\varepsilon,it}(\tau_2 \mid \beta_1)) - (\tau_2 - \tau_1) \tag{12}$$

By denoting $\Theta_{it} := \Theta_{it}(\varphi_i)$ to be $\Theta_{it}^{(1)}, \Theta_{it}^{(2)}, \Theta_{it}^{(q)}$ or any alternative zero-mean transformed error term depending on the parameter vector φ, it is possible to write the expressions obtained as the following:

$$\Theta_{i,0t} := \Theta_{it}(\varphi_{i0}), \quad \Theta_{i,0t}^{c} := \Theta_{i,0t} - E[\Theta_{i,0t}], \quad \sigma_i^2 := E[(\Theta_{i,0t}^{c})^2], \quad \hat{\Theta}_{it} := (\hat{\varphi}_{it}),$$

$$\overline{\Theta}_i := P^{-1} \sum_{i=R+1}^{T} \hat{\Theta}_{it}, \quad \Theta_{it}^{(c)} := \hat{\Theta}_{it} - \overline{\Theta}_i \quad \text{and} \quad \overline{\sigma}_i^2 := P^{-1} \sum_{i=R+1}^{T} (\Theta_{it}^{(c)})^2 \tag{13}$$

It should be stated that while following Chen (2016), the parameter vector φ in this study is obtained from EGARCH and GARCH models for the Bitcoin reruns. This is to account for the asymmetry associated with stock returns, since $(\Theta_{1t}, \Theta_{2t})$ can assume different functional forms. To test for Granger causality in mean (i. e. $\Theta_{1t} = \Theta_{it}^{(1)}$), variance (i. e. $\Theta_{1t} = \Theta_{it}^{(2)}$) and quantile (i. e. $\Theta_{1t} = \Theta_{it}^{(q)}$), the G test can be applied.

4 Empirical results

4.1 Data

We use daily data covering Bitcoin price and the stock index of the S&P500 Composite, S&P500 Information Technology, S&P500 Internet Services & Information, S&P500 Semiconductors, S&P500 Software & Services, and S&P500 Technology Hardware & Equipment. All data are collected from DataStream, where Bitcoin price against the US dollar is from Bitstamp – the leading crypto exchange. We denote p_t^s and p_t^b as stock index and Bitcoin price on the tth trading date. The original data is transformed to return series as its log differenced data: $y_{st} = 100 \times (\ln(y_t^s) - \ln(y_{t-1}^s))$ is the return for stock index; and $y_{bt} = 100 \times (\ln(y_t^s) - \ln(y_{t-1}^s))$ is the return the return for Bitcoin. Our first aim is to test whether and how $\{y_{ct}\}$ Granger causes $\{y_{bt}\}$ in mean and in variance by setting $(\Theta_{1t}, \Theta_{2t}) = (\Theta_{1t}^{(1)}, \Theta_{2t}^{(1)})$ and $(\Theta_{1t}^{(2)}, \Theta_{2t}^{(2)})$ respectively. The second aim is to examine whether the predictability between Bitcoin return and stock return could happen in higher moments, therefore we also test one of the following moments Θ_{it}, $= \Theta_{it}^{(q1)}, \Theta_{it}^{(q2)}, \Theta_{it}^{(q3)}, \Theta_{it}^{(q4)}, \Theta_{it}^{(q5)}$ for both $i = 1, 2$, and these $\Theta_{it}^{(q)'s}$ are defined by $(0, 0.2)$, $(0.2, 0.4)$, $(0.4, 0.6)$, $(0.6, 0.8)$, and $(0.8, 1)$ respectively. In this way, we test the null hypothesis of no Granger causality in most parts of the distributions and test in various cases of $(\Theta_{1t}, \Theta_{2t})'^s$. For simplicity, we denote $i = c, t$, in, se, so, and h to represent price index of S&P500 Composite, S&P500 Information Technology, S&P500 Internet Services & Information, S&P500 Semiconductors, S&P500 Software & Services, and S&P500 Technology Hardware & Equipment, respectively. The sampling period for all data is from 18 August 2011 to 15 April 2019 with $R = 1{,}214$ and $P = 783$ for the fixed-sampling-scheme-based out-of-sample analysis.[4] Table 1 presents descriptive statistics for return series on Bitcoin and stock indices. We can see that all return series have excess kurtosis and negative skewness indicating that they are leptokurtic and skewed to the left or to the right. In addition, based on the Jarque-Bera normality (1987) test, all return series exhibit non-normality. Unreported results from conventional unit root tests show that all return series are stationary at the 1% level of significance.

4 Notably, only common daily observations between Bitcoin and the stock index are considered in the analysis.

Table 1: Summary statistics.

	Bitcoin	S&P500 Composite	S&P500 Information Technology	S&P500 Internet Services & Information	S&P500 Semiconductors	S&P500 Software & Services	S&P500 Technology Hardware & Equipment
Mean	0.00307	0.00046	0.00065	0.00084	0.00062	0.00070	0.00057
Median	0.00257	0.00028	0.00073	0.0002	0.00073	0.00049	0.00058
Maximum	0.48477	0.04840	0.05873	0.09625	0.05600	0.05875	0.06046
Minimum	−0.66394	−0.04184	−0.05200	−0.07146	−0.06893	−0.05216	−0.08202
Std. Dev.	0.05920	0.00861	0.01070	0.01329	0.01359	0.01075	0.01228
Skewness	−0.98342	−0.2846	−0.26856	0.29659	−0.29239	−0.22347	−0.30264
Kurtosis	23.1742	6.37717	5.88486	8.74535	5.36065	5.89078	6.07137
Jarque-Bera	34187.84	975.9845	716.5022	2775.911	492.1477	711.9625	815.418
Probability	0.00000	0.00000	0.00000	0.00000	0.00000	0.0000	0.00000
Observations	1997	1997	1997	1997	1997	1997	1997

Note: The table presents the summary statistics of daily returns over the period August 2011 to 15 April 2019.

4.2 Chen's Granger causality in moment test results

The Chen's G statistic, as mentioned above, is applicable for testing causality in mean, variance and quantile q by setting: $(\Theta_{1t}, \Theta_{2t}) = (\Theta_{1t}^{(1)}, \Theta_{2t}^{(1)}), (\Theta_{1t}^{(2)}, \Theta_{2t}^{(2)})$ and $\Theta_{1t} = \Theta_{1t}^{(q)}$, respectively. For the out-sample period, Tables 2 to 7 presents the results of Chen's (2016) causality test between Bitcoin and the various stock indices. In each table, Panel A shows the Granger causality from the stock index to Bitcoin, while Panel B shows the results for Granger causality from Bitcoin to the stock index. Several interesting results are summarized below, based on the 5% significance of the test statistic.

Panel A of Table 2 shows the Granger causality test results from S&P500 Composite index return to Bitcoin return. We first examine whether and how $\{y_{ct}\}$ Granger causes $\{y_{bt}\}$ in mean and in variance by setting $(\Theta_{1t}, \Theta_{2t}) = (\Theta_{1t}^{(1)}, \Theta_{2t}^{(1)})$ and $(\Theta_{1t}^{(2)}, \Theta_{2t}^{(2)})$, respectively. Results show that the G test statistic is significant for $(y_{1t}, y_{2t}) = (y_{bt}, y_{ct})$ in the out-sample context with $n = 1$. Therefore, we conclude that the S&P500 composite stock return weakly Granger causes Bitcoin return in its mean only. Panel B of Table 2 shows that the G test statistic is significant for $(y_{1t}, y_{2t}) = (y_{ct}, y_{bt})$ in the out-sample context, by focusing on $\Theta_{1t} = \Theta_{1t}^{(q2)}$ or, $\Theta_{1t}^{(q4)}$, the test statistics $\Theta_{2t} = \Theta_{2t}^{(1)}$ or, $\Theta_{2t}^{(2)}$ are significant. Specifically, there is evidence that the mean of Bitcoin return Granger causes the right tail of S&P500 Composite return with $n = 5, 10$. However, the variance of Bitcoin return Granger causes the left tail of S&P500 Composite return with $n = 1, 5$.

Secondly, we focus on the higher moment causality, and find from the significance of test statistics that Bitcoin return Granger causes S&P500 Composite return at a higher moment. For example, given $(\Theta_{1t}, \Theta_{2t}) = (\Theta_{1t}^{(1)}, \Theta_{2t}^{(q4)}), (\Theta_{1t}^{(q1)}, \Theta_{2t}^{(q4)})$ or $(\Theta_{1t}^{(q5)}, \Theta_{2t}^{(q4)})$, the G test statistic is significant for $(y_{1t}, y_{2t}) = (y_{bt}, y_{ct})$ suggesting that the stock return, especially the right tail of the stock return distribution Granger causes both the left and right tail of the Bitcoin return when $n = 1, 5$. Furthermore, the test statistic is also significant for $(y_{1t}, y_{2t}) = (y_{ct}, y_{bt})$ when $(\Theta_{1t}, \Theta_{2t}) = (\Theta_{1t}^{(q1)}, \Theta_{2t}^{(q3)})$, $(\Theta_{1t}^{(q2)}, \Theta_{2t}^{(q3)})$ or $(\Theta_{1t}^{(q5)}, \Theta_{2t}^{(q5)})$, suggesting that the right tail of the Bitcoin return distribution Granger causes both the left and right tail of the stock return when $n = 1, 10$.

Panel A of Table 3 shows the causality test results from S&P500 Information Technology stock return to Bitcoin return. We first examine whether and how $\{y_{tt}\}$ Granger causes $\{y_{bt}\}$ in mean and in variance by setting $(\Theta_{1t}, \Theta_{2t}) = (\Theta_{1t}^{(1)}, \Theta_{2t}^{(1)})$ and $(\Theta_{1t}^{(2)}, \Theta_{2t}^{(2)})$ respectively. The results indicate that the technology stock return only weakly Granger causes Bitcoin return in mean. Panel A of Table 3 shows that the G test statistic is significant for $(y_{1t}, y_{2t}) = (y_{bt}, y_{tt})$ when $(\Theta_{1t}, \Theta_{2t}) = (\Theta_{1t}^{(q4)}, \Theta_{2t}^{(1)})$ or $(\Theta_{1t}^{(q5)}, \Theta_{2t}^{(q4)})$, suggesting that the mean of technology stock return Granger causes the right tail of Bitcoin return when $n = 5$. Also, the right tail of technology stock return distribution Granger causes the right tail of Bitcoin return when $n = 5$.

Panel B of Table 3 shows the causality test results from Bitcoin return to Information Technology stock return. We first examine whether and how $\{y_{bt}\}$ Granger causes $\{y_{tt}\}$ in mean and in variance by setting $(\Theta_{1t}, \Theta_{2t}) = (\Theta_{1t}^{(1)}, \Theta_{2t}^{(1)})$ and $(\Theta_{1t}^{(2)}, \Theta_{2t}^{(2)})$, respectively. The results show that Bitcoin return only weakly Granger causes the technology

Table 2: Casualty-in-Moments Test for the S&P 500 Composite.

	N	$\phi_{1t}^{(1)}$	$\phi_{1t}^{(2)}$	$\phi_{1t}^{(q1)}$	$\phi_{1t}^{(q2)}$	$\phi_{1t}^{(q3)}$	$\phi_{1t}^{(q4)}$	$\phi_{1t}^{(q5)}$
Panel A: S&P500 Composite return $\nrightarrow$ Bitcoin return								
	1	3.742**	2.524	3.1*	0.109	0.010	0.369	0.862
$\phi_{2t}^{(1)}$	5	7.777	5.240	6.518	0.326	3.865	4.032	5.754
	10	11.761	9.800	10.164	9.543	7.026	10.485	8.587
	1	0.146	1.118	0.000	5.44**	0.188	1.750	3.054*
$\phi_{2t}^{(2)}$	5	3.458	1.851	4.727	6.287	3.201	6.991	7.344
	10	4.961	3.565	4.657	16.233*	5.278	13.062	15.947
	1	0.950	0.351	0.704	0.248	0.031	0.641	0.705
$\phi_{2t}^{(q1)}$	5	2.076	3.167	2.070	2.015	2.459	1.544	1.429
	10	6.118	5.914	7.696	13.197	2.939	9.616	6.909
	1	3.358*	0.821	3.176*	2.718*	0.359	0.197	0.759
$\phi_{2t}^{(q2)}$	5	10.809*	5.565	7.861	3.542	1.980	2.597	6.181
	10	15.174	8.684	14.975	6.174	3.366	15.044	11.585
	1	1.316	0.365	0.414	3.711*	0.920	1.366	3.008*
$\phi_{2t}^{(q3)}$	5	3.793	1.858	3.451	3.496	1.220	3.319	5.707
	10	10.675	6.982	9.120	7.452	2.454	12.878	7.579
	1	16.535***	0.517	7.789***	0.136	0.736	0.884	11.235***
$\phi_{2t}^{(q4)}$	5	17.916***	1.831	10.787**	6.560	6.409	5.119	13.305**
	10	20.412**	6.587	11.722	12.850	8.384	9.968	15.351
	1	0.321	3.184*	0.003	1.650	1.043	0.464	0.819
$\phi_{2t}^{(q5)}$	5	7.145	5.195	3.457	6.133	7.878	4.686	5.636
	10	14.406	9.244	5.453	12.483	16.106*	6.819	13.737
Panel B: Bitcoin return $\nrightarrow$ S&P500 Composite return								
	1	1.647	0.017	0.588	0.241	0.553	0.829	0.365
$\phi_{2t}^{(1)}$	5	6.690	4.147	7.191	4.336	8.433	16.624***	2.446
	10	11.182	11.922	8.956	17.118*	11.798	21.461**	8.234
	1	0.446	0.366	2.049	4.216**	0.224	2.125	0.005
$\phi_{2t}^{(2)}$	5	5.729	3.802	4.152	13.136**	4.115	7.417	2.065
	10	11.810	7.653	9.242	14.232	11.984	9.829	5.474
	1	0.273	0.023	1.359	0.630	0.203	1.557	0.003
$\phi_{2t}^{(q1)}$	5	10.696*	3.188	11.231**	6.936	4.422	9.952*	4.321
	10	14.100	15.761	16.87*	10.179	10.137	16.123*	7.581
	1	0.441	0.620	0.059	0.137	1.147	0.630	0.003
$\phi_{2t}^{(q2)}$	5	1.813	10.57*	3.372	6.103	6.041	3.320	0.180
	10	7.849	11.958	7.402	12.443	9.675	9.518	5.079
	1	0.202	0.000	5.563**	1.314	0.003	1.316	0.098
$\phi_{2t}^{(q3)}$	5	6.954	3.110	10.128*	10.633*	1.076	2.059	5.342
	10	12.130	9.312	15.666	22.465**	13.412	17.681*	7.069
	1	0.265	1.650	0.122	1.663	1.332	0.069	0.883
$\phi_{2t}^{(q4)}$	5	2.956	2.972	5.618	6.503	7.631	5.038	6.989
	10	6.521	8.412	8.946	11.709	10.481	14.756	11.097
	1	1.272	0.003	0.859	3.347*	0.331	0.044	0.980
$\phi_{2t}^{(q5)}$	5	1.489	5.591	3.834	5.185	2.782	7.223	8.807
	10	11.305	8.400	6.390	14.484	16.216*	12.351	18.863**

Note: $\phi_{it}^{(1)}$ is the first moment, $\phi_{it}^{(2)}$ is the second moment, $\phi_{it}^{(q1)}$ is the quantile of $(0, 0.2)$, $\phi_{it}^{(q2)}$ is the quantile of $(0.2, 0.4)$, $\phi_{it}^{(q3)}$ is the quantile of $(0.4, 0.6)$, $\phi_{it}^{(q4)}$ is the quantile of $(0.6, 0.8)$, and $\phi_{it}^{(q5)}$ is the quantile of $(0.8, 1)$.

***, **, and * represents significance at the 1 percent, 5 percent, and 10 percent significant level respectively.

Table 3: Casualty-in-Moments Test for S&P500 Information Technology.

	N	$\phi_{1t}^{(1)}$	$\phi_{1t}^{(2)}$	$\phi_{1t}^{(q1)}$	$\phi_{1t}^{(q2)}$	$\phi_{1t}^{(q3)}$	$\phi_{1t}^{(q4)}$	$\phi_{1t}^{(q5)}$
Panel A: S&P500 Information Technology return $\nrightarrow$ Bitcoin return								
	1	1.670	0.574	0.119	1.181	0.002	0.577	0.070
$\phi_{2t}^{(1)}$	5	8.340	0.753	5.916	1.571	8.221	16.866***	1.381
	10	11.384	9.920	9.294	3.831	11.757	17.865*	4.983
	1	1.334	0.130	1.742	2.431	0.278	0.059	0.976
$\phi_{2t}^{(2)}$	5	5.575	7.913	4.816	8.728	6.512	4.092	4.263
	10	9.763	12.634	7.425	12.996	12.467	7.606	10.715
	1	1.081	1.431	0.177	0.164	0.000	0.168	0.262
$\phi_{2t}^{(q1)}$	5	8.344	3.688	5.402	0.982	7.172	8.561	4.345
	10	11.530	10.054	9.791	13.153	10.098	11.045	7.097
	1	0.660	0.078	0.249	0.000	2.311	0.003	2.894*
$\phi_{2t}^{(q2)}$	5	4.432	3.158	2.973	2.837	5.300	3.821	5.801
	10	8.769	10.766	5.250	13.875	9.085	10.288	8.956
	1	0.243	0.343	1.132	1.154	1.221	1.352	0.129
$\phi_{2t}^{(q3)}$	5	1.696	7.237	4.625	2.852	7.781	4.199	1.742
	10	10.803	12.566	9.486	5.691	16.048*	8.139	8.586
	1	0.139	0.078	0.429	1.098	0.338	1.653	2.115
$\phi_{2t}^{(q4)}$	5	2.780	4.582	3.692	1.658	2.060	4.098	11.355**
	10	4.405	8.071	6.850	4.622	4.071	4.825	12.282
	1	0.668	0.504	0.117	0.074	0.645	0.186	0.304
$\phi_{2t}^{(q5)}$	5	3.288	6.454	2.899	1.418	8.882	6.015	2.938
	10	5.958	13.865	7.273	5.528	13.926	7.520	14.897
Panel B: Bitcoin return $\nrightarrow$ Information Technology return								
	1	0.885	4.182**	2.788*	1.566	0.207	0.535	0.976
$\phi_{2t}^{(1)}$	5	3.198	7.838	5.317	3.766	2.285	3.551	2.205
	10	6.122	10.350	8.957	9.766	4.393	3.539	4.210
	1	1.518	1.025	1.171	0.103	1.721	1.187	1.221
$\phi_{2t}^{(2)}$	5	3.101	7.648	5.223	4.186	5.785	4.067	7.094
	10	10.327	13.663	9.025	7.209	14.582	11.682	12.340
	1	0.488	0.155	0.006	1.084	0.076	0.090	1.248
$\phi_{2t}^{(q1)}$	5	2.917	8.808	1.452	2.626	0.972	1.091	3.339
	10	7.892	12.129	5.909	16.543*	2.890	7.926	8.533
	1	1.088	0.167	1.965	5.967**	0.555	0.025	0.652
$\phi_{2t}^{(q2)}$	5	11.905**	3.286	12.354**	7.237	1.459	7.535	4.462
	10	15.801	9.694	17.564*	8.638	8.364	14.018	10.452
	1	0.421	0.420	0.168	0.339	0.015	0.256	0.752
$\phi_{2t}^{(q3)}$	5	1.866	1.357	4.134	3.478	4.499	2.584	2.295
	10	8.163	7.815	8.747	6.369	6.500	4.479	9.562
	1	2.577	0.176	0.001	1.026	0.316	0.797	3.827**
$\phi_{2t}^{(q4)}$	5	8.271	3.243	4.361	2.273	4.126	4.888	7.657
	10	10.320	5.080	9.285	8.509	5.714	12.991	9.937
	1	1.345	6.759***	1.935	1.052	0.543	0.163	0.309
$\phi_{2t}^{(q5)}$	5	3.367	10.529*	3.103	3.280	7.318	16.995***	2.359
	10	6.141	11.211	6.801	8.441	11.844	17.798*	5.354

Note: See notes to Table 2.

stock return in various cases. Panel B of Table 3 shows that the G test statistic is significant for $(y_{1t}, y_{2t}) = (y_{tt}, y_{bt})$ when $(\Theta_{1t}, \Theta_{2t}) = (\Theta_{1t}^{(2)}, \Theta_{2t}^{(1)})$, $(\Theta_{1t}^{(1)}, \Theta_{2t}^{(q2)})$, $(\Theta_{1t}^{(2)}, \Theta_{2t}^{(q5)})$, $(\Theta_{1t}^{(q1)}, \Theta_{2t}^{(q2)})$, $(\Theta_{1t}^{(q2)}, \Theta_{2t}^{(q2)})$, $(\Theta_{1t}^{(q4)}, \Theta_{2t}^{(q5)})$ or $(\Theta_{1t}^{(q5)}, \Theta_{2t}^{(q4)})$, implying that Bitcoin return Granger causes all parts of technology stock return distribution when $n = 1, 5$.

Panel A of Table 4 shows the causality test results from Internet S&P500 Services & Information stock return to Bitcoin return. We first examine whether and how $\{y_{it}\}$ Granger causes $\{y_{bt}\}$ in mean and in variance by setting $(\Theta_{1t}, \Theta_{2t}) = (\Theta_{1t}^{(1)}, \Theta_{2t}^{(1)})$ and $(\Theta_{1t}^{(2)}, \Theta_{2t}^{(2)})$, respectively. The results indicate that the internet stock return only weakly Granger causes Bitcoin return in variance. Panel A of Table 4 shows that the G test statistic is significant for $(y_{1t}, y_{2t}) = (y_{bt}, y_{it})$ when $(\Theta_{1t}, \Theta_{2t}) = (\Theta_{1t}^{(q2)}, \Theta_{2t}^{(2)})$, suggesting that the variance of internet stock return Granger causes the left tail of Bitcoin return when $n = 1, 5, 10$. Panel A of Table 4 shows that the G test statistic is significant for $(y_{1t}, y_{2t}) = (y_{bt}, y_{it})$ when $(\Theta_{1t}, \Theta_{2t}) = (\Theta_{1t}^{(1)}, \Theta_{2t}^{(q2)})$, $(\Theta_{1t}^{(q1)}, \Theta_{2t}^{(q2)})$, $(\Theta_{1t}^{(q1)}, \Theta_{2t}^{(q4)})$ or $(\Theta_{1t}^{(q5)}, \Theta_{2t}^{(q3)})$, implying that internet return Granger causes the Bitcoin stock return of extreme distribution (i. e. $q1$ and $q5$).

Panel B of Table 4 shows the causality test results from Bitcoin return to internet stock return. We first examine whether and how $\{y_{bt}\}$ Granger causes $\{y_{it}\}$ in mean and in variance by setting $(\Theta_{1t}, \Theta_{2t}) = (\Theta_{1t}^{(1)}, \Theta_{2t}^{(1)})$ and $(\Theta_{1t}^{(2)}, \Theta_{2t}^{(2)})$ respectively. It appears that Bitcoin return only weakly Granger causes the internet stock return in various cases. Panel B of Table 3 shows that the G test statistic is significant for $(y_{1t}, y_{2t}) = (y_{tt}, y_{bt})$ when $(\Theta_{1t}, \Theta_{2t}) = (\Theta_{1t}^{(2)}, \Theta_{2t}^{(1)})$, $(\Theta_{1t}^{(2)}, \Theta_{2t}^{(q5)})$, $(\Theta_{1t}^{(q1)}, \Theta_{2t}^{(q4)})$, $(\Theta_{1t}^{(q1)}, \Theta_{2t}^{(q5)})$, $(\Theta_{1t}^{(q3)}, \Theta_{2t}^{(q4)})$ or $(\Theta_{1t}^{(1)}, \Theta_{2t}^{(q2)})$, implying that Bitcoin return Granger causes the variance and both the left and right tail distributions of internet stock return.

Panel A of Table 5 shows the causality test results from S&P500 Semiconductors stock return to Bitcoin return. Panel A of Table 5 shows that the G test statistic is significant for $(y_{1t}, y_{2t}) = (y_{bt}, y_{set})$ when $(\Theta_{1t}, \Theta_{2t}) = (\Theta_{1t}^{(q3)}, \Theta_{2t}^{(1)})$, $(\Theta_{1t}^{(q4)}, \Theta_{2t}^{(1)})$, $(\Theta_{1t}^{(q?)}, \Theta_{2t}^{(2)})$, $(\Theta_{1t}^{(q3)}, \Theta_{2t}^{(q1)})$, $(\Theta_{1t}^{(q3)}, \Theta_{2t}^{(q2)})$ or $(\Theta_{1t}^{(q1)}, \Theta_{2t}^{(q3)})$, implying that semiconductor return Granger causes the Bitcoin stock return of all parts of the distribution. Especially, the mean of semiconductor return Granger causes the right tail of Bitcoin return, and the variance of semiconductor return Granger causes the left tail of Bitcoin return. Moreover, the left tail of semiconductor return Granger causes the right tail of Bitcoin return, while the right tail of semiconductor return Granger causes the left tail of Bitcoin return.

Panel B of Table 5 shows the causality test results from Bitcoin return to semiconductor stock return. We can see that there is no evidence of Granger causality from Bitcoin return to the semiconductor return in mean and variance. Panel B of Table 5 shows that the G test statistic is significant for $(y_{1t}, y_{2t}) = (y_{set}, y_{bt})$ when $(\Theta_{1t}, \Theta_{2t}) = (\Theta_{1t}^{(1)}, \Theta_{2t}^{(q4)})$, $(\Theta_{1t}^{(2)}, \Theta_{2t}^{(q5)})$ or $(\Theta_{1t}^{(q1)}, \Theta_{2t}^{(q2)})$, implying that Bitcoin return Granger causes the mean and variance of semiconductor stock return, as well as the semiconductor stock return left distribution.

Panel A of Table 6 shows the causality test results from S&P500 Software & Services stock return to Bitcoin return. Panel A of Table 5 shows that the G test statis-

Table 4: Casualty-in-Moments Test for S&P500 Internet Services & Information.

	N	$\Phi_{1t}^{(1)}$	$\Phi_{1t}^{(2)}$	$\Phi_{1t}^{(q1)}$	$\Phi_{1t}^{(q2)}$	$\Phi_{1t}^{(q3)}$	$\Phi_{1t}^{(q4)}$	$\Phi_{1t}^{(q5)}$
Panel A: S&P500 Internet Services & Information return ↛ Bitcoin return								
$\Phi_{2t}^{(1)}$	1	1.345	0.781	0.221	0.098	0.214	0.144	0.948
	5	10.168*	2.564	8.938	2.133	6.371	7.050	2.441
	10	14.761	7.070	15.555	5.558	16.01*	6.687	4.784
$\Phi_{2t}^{(2)}$	1	0.388	0.702	0.171	4.554**	7.376***	1.455	0.713
	5	3.227	6.069	3.780	15.908***	13.202**	3.205	4.080
	10	14.539	10.905	13.597	19.184**	15.083	12.258	15.371
$\Phi_{2t}^{(q1)}$	1	2.479	1.320	0.246	0.003	0.070	0.512	0.110
	5	9.993*	5.613	6.129	2.466	1.706	4.316	2.037
	10	15.181	7.794	13.334	3.516	6.218	8.641	4.674
$\Phi_{2t}^{(q2)}$	1	7.109***	0.494	4.443**	0.342	0.010	0.369	3.129*
	5	12.76**	3.189	6.845	3.557	2.135	5.383	3.593
	10	14.565	7.667	14.260	8.420	5.775	9.646	10.966
$\Phi_{2t}^{(q3)}$	1	3.727*	0.040	0.010	0.641	0.428	0.004	3.262*
	5	7.043	5.163	1.660	2.520	4.775	0.754	11.624**
	10	16.533*	7.494	7.574	11.833	9.384	10.574	19.255**
$\Phi_{2t}^{(q4)}$	1	0.392	1.114	0.001	0.810	1.643	0.370	0.090
	5	10.989*	6.195	11.18**	2.513	5.513	6.154	9.295*
	10	16.445*	10.462	17.459*	3.382	14.319	11.742	13.825
$\Phi_{2t}^{(q5)}$	1	1.173	0.780	1.159	1.932	0.506	0.246	0.073
	5	1.884	5.441	4.633	3.398	6.444	3.704	1.863
	10	8.547	8.932	7.923	9.910	16.081*	8.263	6.311
Panel B: Bitcoin return ↛ S&P500 Internet Services & Information return								
$\Phi_{2t}^{(1)}$	1	0.308	4.146**	0.986	1.270	0.444	1.330	1.375
	5	4.465	6.654	6.813	3.676	6.358	5.701	2.562
	10	5.822	8.426	7.694	11.442	15.462	7.630	7.368
$\Phi_{2t}^{(2)}$	1	1.771	2.043	2.583	0.182	1.351	0.800	0.003
	5	5.337	7.844	7.223	4.888	7.397	2.707	4.695
	10	11.026	14.645	9.764	12.938	8.958	8.006	13.670
$\Phi_{2t}^{(q1)}$	1	0.079	2.157	0.320	0.237	0.636	0.629	0.607
	5	2.669	7.836	4.356	0.480	6.430	6.251	1.074
	10	9.131	9.432	7.419	7.326	15.929	11.965	9.923
$\Phi_{2t}^{(q2)}$	1	1.624	1.592	2.152	1.025	0.084	0.263	0.261
	5	14.259**	3.144	10.527*	2.910	5.307	4.250	8.190
	10	19.189**	6.716	16.981*	11.702	18.615**	11.158	16.785*
$\Phi_{2t}^{(q3)}$	1	0.999	0.368	0.137	0.385	0.118	0.737	1.102
	5	3.463	2.540	0.531	1.344	1.163	3.542	3.192
	10	11.051	6.801	4.747	4.688	9.056	6.877	10.189
$\Phi_{2t}^{(q4)}$	1	0.536	0.166	0.226	0.800	4.367**	1.051	1.544
	5	3.677	4.150	11.262**	6.218	4.487	8.313	3.646
	10	6.284	13.640	10.624	9.140	5.270	17.015*	7.261
$\Phi_{2t}^{(q5)}$	1	1.828	5.732**	5.407**	1.199	0.036	1.347	0.436
	5	4.942	9.022	7.598	5.204	4.772	4.210	7.834
	10	5.468	11.401	10.189	15.134	9.323	10.204	12.668

Note: See notes to Table 2.

Table 5: Casualty-in-Moments Test for S&P500 Semiconductors.

	N	$\Phi_{1t}^{(1)}$	$\Phi_{1t}^{(2)}$	$\Phi_{1t}^{(q1)}$	$\Phi_{1t}^{(q2)}$	$\Phi_{1t}^{(q3)}$	$\Phi_{1t}^{(q4)}$	$\Phi_{1t}^{(q5)}$
Panel A S&P500 Semiconductors return $\nrightarrow$ Bitcoin return								
	1	0.636	0.757	0.001	0.982	0.406	0.051	0.008
$\Phi_{2t}^{(1)}$	5	10.651*	2.782	5.071	1.500	12.922**	16.088***	0.443
	10	16.731*	7.298	10.861	5.987	14.012	16.673*	5.928
	1	1.303	0.005	0.553	1.648	0.830	0.062	1.628
$\Phi_{2t}^{(2)}$	5	3.279	2.900	2.102	11.324**	8.847	5.606	3.874
	10	10.456	10.941	9.333	16.698*	12.224	10.215	8.071
	1	1.226	0.711	0.054	1.218	4.564**	0.401	0.622
$\Phi_{2t}^{(q1)}$	5	5.453	1.084	4.857	2.760	13.565**	1.922	1.119
	10	16.931*	4.407	11.130	11.077	19.149**	5.421	10.746
	1	0.209	1.029	0.510	1.163	5.11**	0.890	1.348
$\Phi_{2t}^{(q2)}$	5	7.823	6.888	7.461	2.096	6.332	3.492	6.905
	10	11.987	10.551	10.718	6.082	8.105	5.464	7.786
	1	3.376*	2.842*	4.371*	0.019	0.380	2.469	0.611
$\Phi_{2t}^{(q3)}$	5	9.774*	5.860	7.672	3.059	2.496	9.327	6.102
	10	14.497	8.509	11.445	5.224	5.662	18.154	10.142
	1	0.943	0.101	0.525	4.779	0.610	2.048	2.430
$\Phi_{2t}^{(q4)}$	5	1.466	9.653*	6.345	6.478	5.493	7.351	10.996*
	10	7.017	13.93	12.476	11.955	11.849	11.327	14.691
	1	0.012	0.830	0.432	0.397	0.338	0.778	0.004
$\Phi_{2t}^{(q5)}$	5	5.947	4.759	2.465	6.135	3.937	11.239	3.000
	10	9.329	8.127	7.659	8.247	8.377	14.190	7.752
Panel B: Bitcoin return $\nrightarrow$ S&P500 Semiconductors return								
	1	1.230	4.04**	2.72*	0.640	0.001	0.102	0.040
$\Phi_{2t}^{(1)}$	5	3.668	7.459	6.865	2.319	2.817	3.697	2.682
	10	6.411	11.169	15.055	8.851	3.681	8.017	8.155
	1	1.416	0.029	2.735*	0.162	0.265	2.031	1.217
$\Phi_{2t}^{(2)}$	5	4.448	10.885*	5.019	4.789	4.090	4.891	7.191
	10	9.715	15.944	9.709	9.842	9.277	8.688	17.485*
	1	0.411	1.127	0.198	0.409	0.048	2.377	0.001
$\Phi_{2t}^{(q1)}$	5	2.202	5.456	1.625	4.950	2.449	3.772	1.208
	10	5.569	8.744	8.720	13.189	6.791	7.953	2.282
	1	2.361	0.000	4.079**	0.397	1.555	0.113	0.852
$\Phi_{2t}^{(q2)}$	5	8.666	4.011	7.697	2.742	4.036	1.662	4.368
	10	13.680	4.625	10.916	7.801	15.022	8.348	10.388
	1	0.699	0.015	0.139	0.339	1.738	0.376	1.315
$\Phi_{2t}^{(q3)}$	5	2.318	5.181	2.275	2.583	6.175	5.125	4.351
	10	8.081	12.010	6.614	10.389	13.034	10.627	7.277
	1	4.279**	0.169	2.328	0.260	1.630	0.093	2.212
$\Phi_{2t}^{(q4)}$	5	8.639	2.969	4.258	2.127	8.325	1.763	8.478
	10	11.008	5.982	5.069	14.503	10.610	11.013	9.631
	1	1.605	3.963**	1.502	0.000	0.259	0.028	0.162
$\Phi_{2t}^{(q5)}$	5	3.858	5.615	1.942	2.964	1.420	1.988	1.144
	10	4.701	7.447	5.360	7.426	9.304	3.261	9.292

Note: See notes to Table 2.

Table 6: Casualty-in-Moments Test for S&P500 Software & Services.

	N	$\Phi_{1t}^{(1)}$	$\Phi_{1t}^{(2)}$	$\Phi_{1t}^{(q1)}$	$\Phi_{1t}^{(q2)}$	$\Phi_{1t}^{(q3)}$	$\Phi_{1t}^{(q4)}$	$\Phi_{1t}^{(q5)}$
Panel A S&P500 Software & Services return ↛ Bitcoin return								
$\Phi_{2t}^{(1)}$	1	2.089	0.565	0.204	0.542	0.030	0.226	0.052
	5	7.218	0.969	6.653	1.034	6.622	13.194	1.535
	10	12.179	12.990	12.361	2.515	11.421	13.892**	4.321
$\Phi_{2t}^{(2)}$	1	1.280	0.181	2.155	3.296*	1.455	0.189	0.013
	5	4.070	8.585	6.918	10.152*	7.068	7.429	2.950
	10	10.526	13.803	10.949	15.290	13.299	11.723	9.877
$\Phi_{2t}^{(q1)}$	1	2.083	1.251	0.929	0.496	0.019	0.015	0.183
	5	14.537**	4.396	8.839	2.513	5.069	6.216	7.248
	10	15.683	10.325	12.526	8.021	10.039	6.601	8.393
$\Phi_{2t}^{(q2)}$	1	0.076	0.510	0.214	1.393	1.897	0.085	0.552
	5	0.485	4.092	6.614	7.635	6.987	5.027	2.666
	10	10.657	7.481	11.015	15.075	14.569	15.974	4.146
$\Phi_{2t}^{(q3)}$	1	0.005	0.471	1.644	1.631	1.403	1.691	0.036
	5	5.505	6.179	11.684**	8.807	9.276*	5.208	2.053
	10	16.382*	11.659	22.08**	13.321	14.303	7.984	11.353
$\Phi_{2t}^{(q4)}$	1	0.514	0.005	1.133	0.170	0.141	3.937**	0.149
	5	3.323	3.779	1.528	4.975	5.477	5.120	3.982
	10	11.712	8.611	6.669	7.363	11.407	6.312	8.596
$\Phi_{2t}^{(q5)}$	1	1.448	0.488	0.149	0.076	0.212	0.145	0.050
	5	1.771	7.075	1.692	1.199	4.800	6.935	1.136
	10	6.436	12.939	8.926	2.919	8.011	9.654	6.807
Panel B: Bitcoin return ↛ S&P500 Software & Services return								
$\Phi_{2t}^{(1)}$	1	0.341	3.889	2.161	0.903	0.121	0.150	0.233
	5	4.386	7.474	10.784*	5.475	7.055	3.301	1.290
	10	6.821	11.643	13.796	7.591	11.214	4.408	4.990
$\Phi_{2t}^{(2)}$	1	1.855	1.532	1.006	0.324	1.300	0.578	0.006
	5	2.947	5.784	3.730	3.682	3.301	6.098	5.053
	10	8.036	12.382	6.736	6.144	15.407	10.153	13.25
$\Phi_{2t}^{(q1)}$	1	0.122	0.314	0.407	0.210	0.139	0.055	0.150
	5	3.506	9.852*	7.251	5.091	2.140	3.370	2.420
	10	9.351	13.417	16.172*	14.622	6.151	6.852	9.019
$\Phi_{2t}^{(q2)}$	1	1.650	0.279	1.544	0.398	0.010	0.055	0.139
	5	12.817**	3.863	7.648	4.761	1.895	6.808	10.629*
	10	16.011*	9.882	12.782	13.161	8.019	15.223	12.234
$\Phi_{2t}^{(q3)}$	1	0.330	0.623	0.267	0.340	0.177	2.371	1.623
	5	2.035	1.165	1.897	5.494	4.516	4.548	4.448
	10	10.452	6.680	6.977	8.703	5.645	7.047	14.360
$\Phi_{2t}^{(q4)}$	1	1.998	0.001	0.535	0.764	2.479	0.055	1.861
	5	8.108	2.653	11.091**	6.202	3.389	5.516	4.647
	10	11.238	6.036	13.794	9.592	5.498	17.029*	8.993
$\Phi_{2t}^{(q5)}$	1	1.400	6.421**	5.836**	0.558	1.953	1.506	0.328
	5	3.215	10.663*	9.666*	6.728	8.232	15.802***	4.607
	10	5.452	11.689	12.996	8.850	10.154	17.437*	7.678

Note: See notes to Table 2.

tic is significant for $(y_{1t}, y_{2t}) = (y_{bt}, y_{sot})$ when $(\Theta_{1t}, \Theta_{2t}) = (\Theta_{1t}^{(q4)}, \Theta_{2t}^{(1)})$, $(\Theta_{1t}^{(1)}, \Theta_{2t}^{(q1)})$, $(\Theta_{1t}^{(q1)}, \Theta_{2t}^{(q3)})$ or $(\Theta_{1t}^{(q4)}, \Theta_{2t}^{(q4)})$, implying that software return Granger causes the mean of Bitcoin stock return and extreme parts of the distribution. Especially, the mean of software return Granger causes the right tail of Bitcoin return, and the left tail of software return Granger causes the mean of Bitcoin return, while the right tail of software return Granger causes both the left and right tails of Bitcoin return.

Panel B of Table 6 shows the causality test results from Bitcoin return to software stock return. We can see that there is no evidence of Granger causality from Bitcoin return to the software return in mean or variance. The G test statistic is significant for $(y_{1t}, y_{2t}) = (y_{sot}, y_{bt})$ when $(\Theta_{1t}, \Theta_{2t}) = (\Theta_{1t}^{(1)}, \Theta_{2t}^{(q2)})$, $(\Theta_{1t}^{(2)}, \Theta_{2t}^{(q5)})$, $(\Theta_{1t}^{(q1)}, \Theta_{2t}^{(q4)})$, $(\Theta_{1t}^{(q1)}, \Theta_{2t}^{(q5)})$ or $(\Theta_{1t}^{(q4)}, \Theta_{2t}^{(q5)})$, implying that Bitcoin return Granger causes the mean and variance of software stock return, as well as the software stock return left and right distributions.

Panel A of Table 7 shows the causality test results from S&P500 Technology Hardware & Equipment return to Bitcoin return. The results show that the G test statistic is significant for $(y_{1t}, y_{2t}) = (y_{bt}, y_{ht})$ when $(\Theta_{1t}, \Theta_{2t}) = (\Theta_{1t}^{(1)}, \Theta_{2t}^{(2)})$, $(\Theta_{1t}^{(2)}, \Theta_{2t}^{(q4)})$, $(\Theta_{1t}^{(q1)}, \Theta_{2t}^{(q4)})$, $(\Theta_{1t}^{(q2)}, \Theta_{2t}^{(2)})$, $(\Theta_{1t}^{(q2)}, \Theta_{2t}^{(q3)})$, $(\Theta_{1t}^{(q2)}, \Theta_{2t}^{(q5)})$, $(\Theta_{1t}^{(q3)}, \Theta_{2t}^{(q2)})$, $(\Theta_{1t}^{(q3)}, \Theta_{2t}^{(q3)})$, $(\Theta_{1t}^{(q3)}, \Theta_{2t}^{(q4)})$, $(\Theta_{1t}^{(q4)}, \Theta_{2t}^{(2)})$, $(\Theta_{1t}^{(q4)}, \Theta_{2t}^{(q3)})$, $(\Theta_{1t}^{(q4)}, \Theta_{2t}^{(q4)})$, $(\Theta_{1t}^{(q5)}, \Theta_{2t}^{(2)})$, $(\Theta_{1t}^{(q5)}, \Theta_{2t}^{(q3)})$ or $(\Theta_{1t}^{(q5)}, \Theta_{2t}^{(q4)})$, implying that hardware return Granger causes the mean and variance of Bitcoin stock return and all parts of its distribution.

Panel B of Table 7 shows the causality test results from Bitcoin return to hardware stock return. The results indicate that there is no evidence of Granger causality from Bitcoin return to hardware return in mean or variance. It is clear that the G test statistic is significant for $(y_{1t}, y_{2t}) = (y_{ht}, y_{bt})$ when $(\Theta_{1t}, \Theta_{2t}) = (\Theta_{1t}^{(1)}, \Theta_{2t}^{(q3)})$, $(\Theta_{1t}^{(1)}, \Theta_{2t}^{(q4)})$, $(\Theta_{1t}^{(1)}, \Theta_{2t}^{(q5)})$ or $(\Theta_{1t}^{(q4)}, \Theta_{2t}^{(q3)})$, implying that the right tail distribution of Bitcoin return Granger causes the mean of hardware stock return. Furthermore, the right tail distribution of Bitcoin return Granger causes the hardware stock return right distribution.

To conclude there are several important observations regarding the causality between Bitcoin return and stock return. Starting with the return of the S&P500 Composite stock index, which Granger causes the mean of Bitcoin return only. In general, there is slightly stronger evidence that stock return causes Bitcoin return, but this is not the case for the other stock indices. It is interesting to observe that both the mean and the right tail distribution of stock return Granger cause Bitcoin return, while this is not the case for the opposite. Notably the mean return of Bitcoin Granger causes the right tail distribution of stock return, but this is not the case for the opposite. The above observation implies that causality is more likely to occur when both markets are in their bear states. Regarding the other stock market indices, asymmetric causality evidence is found for all markets, except S&P500 Software & Services. There is stronger evidence of causality flow from stock markets to the Bitcoin market (i. e. S&P500 Software & Services return, S&P500 Internet Services & Information return, S&P500 Semiconductors return, and S&P500 Technology Hardware & Equipment re-

Table 7: Casualty-in-Moments Test for S&P500 Technology Hardware & Equipment.

	N	$\phi_{1t}^{(1)}$	$\phi_{1t}^{(2)}$	$\phi_{1t}^{(q1)}$	$\phi_{1t}^{(q2)}$	$\phi_{1t}^{(q3)}$	$\phi_{1t}^{(q4)}$	$\phi_{1t}^{(q5)}$
Panel A S&P500 Technology Hardware & Equipment return ↛ Bitcoin return								
	1	1.563	0.150	0.906	0.001	0.001	1.108	0.000
$\phi_{2t}^{(1)}$	5	4.813	3.765	2.403	7.432	2.392	4.550	2.566
	10	13.393	7.106	5.943	10.815	5.769	6.649	11.262
	1	0.081	0.223	0.063	10***	0.828	0.530	1.441
$\phi_{2t}^{(2)}$	5	5.806	7.758	3.852	10.612*	7.915	2.428	2.921
	10	25.995***	15.486	9.847	20.203**	17.872*	18.929**	21.547**
	1	0.586	0.244	1.116	2.155	1.245	0.170	1.209
$\phi_{2t}^{(q1)}$	5	3.367	9.321*	2.302	7.479	3.357	7.939	7.406
	10	13.171	11.616	9.503	12.593	5.839	10.596	11.552
	1	1.778	0.166	1.906	1.861	2.551	1.499	1.603
$\phi_{2t}^{(q2)}$	5	6.082	6.509	7.055	9.194	12.461**	6.162	6.872
	10	12.068	9.951	16.053*	16.422*	22.306**	11.613	12.921
	1	0.139	0.064	0.943	3.849**	4.818**	0.056	4.325**
$\phi_{2t}^{(q3)}$	5	4.335	10.34*	5.411	5.112	7.385	9.176	12.769**
	10	9.219	13.699	13.042	12.734	9.763	21.482**	17.521*
	1	0.995	4.383**	4.854**	1.128	4.998**	2.965*	1.228
$\phi_{2t}^{(q4)}$	5	3.909	4.502	4.808	8.257	10.317*	12.946**	10.364*
	10	7.468	9.946	12.848	15.438	13.767	14.07	18.416**
	1	2.247	0.014	0.001	4.649**	1.396	1.135	1.859
$\phi_{2t}^{(q5)}$	5	6.279	10.419*	8.618	10.016*	8.400	5.018	6.151
	10	12.258	14.615	10.838	18.248*	15.955	15.126	13.63
Panel B: Bitcoin return ↛ S&P500 Technology Hardware & Equipment return								
	1	0.196	0.055	0.352	0.070	0.166	0.056	1.019
$\phi_{2t}^{(1)}$	5	5.272	4.634	2.235	0.373	1.763	1.239	3.343
	10	11.076	9.617	5.479	1.580	3.403	1.250	3.971
	1	0.574	0.814	0.380	0.001	0.114	0.016	0.297
$\phi_{2t}^{(2)}$	5	4.553	7.022	1.452	0.018	5.094	0.122	2.565
	10	12.054	9.744	3.510	0.158	6.434	0.222	3.654
	1	0.697	0.575	0.351	0.094	0.923	0.004	2.490
$\phi_{2t}^{(q1)}$	5	3.242	8.144	0.972	0.566	1.656	0.780	9.036
	10	12.179	9.408	6.924	1.342	3.053	1.573	12.235
	1	0.392	0.104	0.000	0.169	0.020	0.300	0.155
$\phi_{2t}^{(q2)}$	5	3.096	10.946*	5.742	0.576	1.280	1.196	0.918
	10	6.761	15.289	9.203	0.916	2.353	1.362	2.937
	1	2.518	14.442***	0.005	0.097	0.672	0.002	4.755**
$\phi_{2t}^{(q3)}$	5	3.392	14.099**	0.787	0.464	1.548	1.078	6.926
	10	10.211	17.963*	3.868	0.752	4.213	1.851	16.679*
	1	0.340	0.758	0.122	0.068	0.082	0.267	0.022
$\phi_{2t}^{(q4)}$	5	3.803	13.257**	2.908	0.481	2.686	1.108	7.768
	10	11.643	16.322*	6.558	0.847	7.371	1.261	16.742*
	1	0.030	0.011	0.186	0.185	0.003	0.623	0.199
$\phi_{2t}^{(q5)}$	5	9.249	13.041**	8.694	0.699	3.844	1.517	6.968
	10	11.667	16.678*	12.628	1.650	7.019	1.097	9.815

Note: See notes to Table 2.

turn). Of all the markets, the S&P500 Technology Hardware & Equipment shows the most obvious asymmetric causality between its return and Bitcoin return. However, S&P500 Information Technology is the only index to see significant information flow from Bitcoin return to its return.

There are some other interesting observations. Firstly, there is no evidence of causality from the mean return of one market to the mean return of another. This implies that causality seldom occurs when both markets are in their normal states. Secondly, there is no evidence of causality from the variance of the return of one market to the variance of the return of another. The two observations above reassure us that Chen's Granger causality in moment test is needed. Thirdly, in most cases when causality happens, it is from the right tail distribution of one market to the variance of another, which implies that when one market is in its bear market state, it makes the other become more volatile. Lastly, most cases of casualty occur when one market is at its bear market, while the other is in its bear or bull market state.

5 Conclusion

It is known that Bitcoin's survival depends on mass behaviour collaboration and the blockchain technology through which transactions are confirmed and added and Bitcoins are mined. In such a technologically backed payment system, potential associations between the markets of Bitcoin and tech companies are not surprising, especially in the US, the hub of the largest stock market and innovative technology. In this chapter, we use the Granger causality in moments approach of Chen (2016) on daily data covering Bitcoin and US tech stock indices. Unsurprisingly, the results show evidence of a relationship between Bitcoin and US tech stock indices. Specifically, there is clear evidence of predictability between Bitcoin and US tech stocks, which seems to vary across quantiles. US stock returns Granger cause Bitcoin return, but this is not the case for other stock indices. Generally, Granger causality from one market to another is insignificant in both mean and variance. However, there is evidence of significant causality in at least two cases: firstly, when one market is in its bear market state, while the other is in a high volatility state, and secondly, when one market is at its bear market, while the other is in a bear or bull market state.

While the results extend our understanding of the relationship between Bitcoin and US tech stock returns, they are comparable to Symitsi and Chalvatzis (2018). However, they are more nuanced, suggesting the need to examine the approach of Chen (2016) to reveal relationships across the various quantiles of the return distribution. Otherwise, it might wrongly be apparent that Bitcoin and US tech stock indices are independent.

These results are mainly important for investors and portfolio managers, without ignoring their importance to policymakers. Investors and portfolio managers can build on the results to better predict the return and volatility of Bitcoin based on the US equity aggregate, sector, and industry indices (and vice versa), which can help them refine their investment decisions. For policymakers, evidence of reported predictability is informative as it is contradictory to market efficiency. This is somewhat in line with Urquhart (2016).

Future studies could consider using higher frequency data, to make inferences regarding Granger causalities between Bitcoin and tech stocks, while extending the analyses to Asian markets where Bitcoin represents a very hot digital asset.

Bibliography

Aysan, A. F., E. Demir, G. Gozgor, and C. K. M. Lau (2019). Effects of the geopolitical risks on bitcoin returns and volatility. *Research in International Business and Finance 47*, 511–518.

Baku, E. (2019). Exchange rate predictability in emerging markets. *International Economics 157*, 1–22.

Balcilar, M., E. Bouri, R. Gupta, and D. Roubaud (2017). Can volume predict bitcoin returns and volatility? A quantiles-based approach. *Economic Modelling 64*, 74–81.

Balcilar, M., R. Gupta, W. J. Kim, and C. Kyei (2019). The role of economic policy uncertainties in predicting stock returns and their volatility for Hong Kong. *Malaysia and South Korea. International Review of Economics & Finance 59*, 150–163.

Bouri, E., R. Gupta, A. Lahiani, and M. Shahbaz (2018). Testing for asymmetric nonlinear short- and long-run relationships between bitcoin, aggregate commodity and gold prices. *Resources Policy 57*, 224–235.

Bouri, E., P. Molnár, G. Azzi, D. Roubaud, and L. I. Hagfors (2017a). on the hedge and safe haven properties of bitcoin: Is it really more than a diversifier? *Finance Research Letters 20*, 192–198.

Bouri, E., N. Jalkh, P. Molnár, and D. Roubaud (2017b). Bitcoin for energy commodities before and after the December 2013 crash: Diversifier, hedge or safe haven? *Applied Economics 49*(50), 5063–5073.

Bouri, E., L. A. Gil-Alana, R. Gupta, and D. Roubaud (2019a). Modelling long memory volatility in the bitcoin market: Evidence of persistence and structural breaks. *International Journal of Finance & Economics 24*(1), 412–426.

Bouri, E., C. K. M. Lau, B. Lucey, and D. Roubaud (2019b). Trading volume and the predictability of return and volatility in the cryptocurrency market. *Finance Research Letters 29*, 340–346.

Chen, Y. T. (2016). Testing for Granger causality in moments. *Oxford Bulletin of Economics and Statistics 78*(2), 265–288.

Corbet, S., B. Lucey, A. Urquhart, and L. Yarovaya (2019). Cryptocurrencies as a financial asset: A systematic analysis. *International Review of Financial Analysis 62*, 182–199.

Corbet, S., A. Meegan, C. Larkin, B. Lucey, and L. Yarovaya (2018). Exploring the dynamic relationships between cryptocurrencies and other financial assets. *Economics Letters 165*, 28–34.

Dastgir, S., E. Demir, G. Downing, G. Gozgor, and C. K. M. Lau (2019). The causal relationship between bitcoin attention and bitcoin returns: Evidence from the Copula-based Granger causality test. *Finance Research Letters 28*, 160–164.

Demir, E., G. Gozgor, C. K. M. Lau, and S. A. Vigne (2018). Does economic policy uncertainty predict the bitcoin returns? An empirical investigation. *Finance Research Letters 26*, 145–149.

Feng, W., Y. Wang, and Z. Zhang (2018). Can cryptocurrencies be a safe haven: A tail risk perspective analysis. *Applied Economics 50*(44), 4745–4762.

Granger, C. W. (1980). Testing for causality: A personal viewpoint. *Journal of Economic Dynamics and control 2*, 329–352.

Hong, Y. (2001). A test for volatility spillover with application to exchange rates. *Journal of Econometrics 103*(1–2), 183–224.

Jarque, C., and A. Bera (1987). A test for normality of observations and regression residuals. *International Statistical Review 55*, 163–172.

Ji, Q., E. Bouri, R. Gupta, and D. Roubaud (2018). Network causality structures among bitcoin and other financial assets: A directed acyclic graph approach. *The Quarterly Review of Economics and Finance 70*, 203–213.

Keim, D. B., and R. F. Stambaugh (1986). Predicting returns in the stock and bond markets. *Journal of financial Economics 17*(2), 357–390.

Klein, T., H. P. Thu, and T. Walther (2018). Bitcoin is not the new gold—A comparison of volatility, correlation, and portfolio performance. *International Review of Financial Analysis 59*, 105–116.

Kristoufek, L. (2013). BitCoin meets Google trends and Wikipedia: Quantifying the relationship between phenomena of the Internet era. *Scientific reports 3*, 3415.

Liu, X., B. Yang, Z. Cai, and L. Peng (2019). A unified test for predictability of asset returns regardless of properties of predicting variables. *Journal of Econometrics 208*(1), 141–159.

Shahzad, S. J. H., E. Bouri, D. Roubaud, and L. Kristoufek (2019). Safe haven, hedge and diversification for G7 stock markets: Gold versus Bitcoin. *Economic Modelling*. https://doi.org/10.1016/j.econmod.2019.07.023.

Soylu, P. K., and B. Güloğlu (2019). Financial contagion and flight to quality between emerging markets and us bond market. *The North American Journal of Economics and Finance 50*, 100992.

Symitsi, E., and K. J. Chalvatzis (2018). Return, volatility and shock spillovers of bitcoin with energy and technology companies. *Economics Letters 170*, 127–130.

Urquhart, A. (2016). The inefficiency of bitcoin. *Economics Letters 148*, 80–82.

Walther, T., T. Klein, and E. Bouri (2019). Exogenous drivers of bitcoin and cryptocurrency volatility—A mixed data sampling approach to forecasting. *Journal of International Financial Markets, Institutions and Money*. https://doi.org/10.1016/j.intfin.2019.101133.

Xu, Q., Z. Bo, C. Jiang, and Y. Liu (2019). Does Google search index really help predicting stock market volatility? Evidence from a modified mixed data sampling model on volatility. *Knowledge-Based Systems 166*, 170–185.

Yu, M., R. Gao, X. Su, X. Jin, H. Zhang, and J. Song (2019). Forecasting bitcoin volatility: The role of leverage effect and uncertainty. *Physica A: Statistical Mechanics and its Applications 533*(1), 120707.

Zhang, W., P. Wang, X. Li, and D. Shen (2018). Some stylized facts of the cryptocurrency market. *Applied Economics 50*(55), 5950–5965.

Zhang, Y., S. Ding, and E. M. Scheffel (2019). A key determinant of commodity price co-movement: The role of daily market liquidity. *Economic Modelling 81*, 170–180.

Jiri Svec, Sean Foley, and Angelo Aspris

Market structure of cryptocurrencies

Cryptocurrencies are an electronic medium of exchange that can be traded by different trading groups via digital currency exchanges. A growing list of altcoins has seen a proliferation of cryptocurrency exchanges emerge over the last decade as regulations in many countries around the world struggle to comprehend with appropriate investor protection rules. Although there is no central authority to register these exchanges, it is estimated that there are currently up to five hundred exchanges in circulation, characterised by varying platforms, geographical reach, and compliance with regulatory frameworks. Cryptocurrency markets share many similar characteristics with both foreign exchange and equity markets such as limit order books and matching algorithms, and exchanges that can be both centralised or decentralised. As these markets are still in their infancy, what shape or form they will take in future will depend on a combination of acceptance from consumers, the investment community, as well as worldwide regulators.

1 Using cryptocurrency for trade

All transactions on the Bitcoin (and other) blockchains are publicly recorded. This allows all users to determine the balance of all wallets in existence. However, blockchains are only useful for transferring units of cryptocurrency between users. When a user wants to exchange his/her cryptocurrency for an asset – say a Pizza, the movement of the bitcoin from the consumer to the pizzeria will be visible, however the delivery of the pizza will not be recorded. Similarly, in the sale of bitcoin for cash, the bitcoin transfer will be recorded but there will be no record of the fiat-currency price paid, nor the actual delivery of the fiat currency.

Yermack (2015) and Baur et al. (2018) and Foley et al. (2019) show that most cryptocurrency transactions currently are between speculative investors, and only a small proportion are used for purchases of goods and services. As a result, they behave more like speculative investments than currencies. Even from a legal and taxation perspective, in many jurisdictions cryptocurrencies are classified as tokens, virtual assets or commodities rather than currencies (whether it be digital, cyber or electronic).[1]

1 Library of congress, https://www.loc.gov/law/help/cryptocurrency/world-survey.php

https://doi.org/10.1515/9783110660807-006

2 Establishing an exchange

As cryptocurrencies became tradeable assets, numerous markets developed, beginning with the now infamous (and defunct) "Mt Gox". The decentralized nature of cryptocurrencies necessitated that exchanges take on the role of 'custodian'. In order to sell bitcoin on an exchange, one needs to deposit bitcoins to an address whose private key is controlled by the exchange. This address is usually called a 'hot wallet', and is directly connected to the Internet. It is analogous to the amount of cash held by a teller at the bank: the balance is not infinite but is useful for daily deposits and withdrawals. Once the balance in the *hot wallet* becomes too large, most exchanges move their cryptocurrency supplies into a 'cold wallet' – this is typically an account held offline which requires multiple individuals to access (multisig) – analogous to a bank vault which requires three different keys to unlock.

Exchanges control all cryptocurrencies held within their system. Deposits and withdrawals of cryptocurrency to/from the exchange will appear on the public blockchain. However, once held by the exchange, it is up to the exchange to keep track of which bitcoins belong to which user.

3 Trading and fees

The market structure of cryptocurrencies resembles modern equity markets with continuous trading via a limit order book without intermediaries. Traders can either execute immediately with a market order or wait for a better execution price with a limit order. Limit orders are stored in the limit order book and are executed according to price-time priority. Order driven markets without a designated market maker primarily rely on Endogenous Liquidity Providers (ELPs) to supply liquidity because it is profitable. Since ELPs have no obligations to maintain markets, they can withdraw when liquidity provision becomes risky or unprofitable, adversely impacting market quality (Anand and Venkataraman, 2016). To increase the participation of ELPs in the market, most cryptocurrency exchanges use the maker-taker model to differentiate between orders that provide liquidity and orders that remove liquidity. The maker-taker model reduces undesirable trading behaviour by charging a higher fee to traders that demand immediacy and lower fees (or no fees) to ELPs for providing liquidity to the market. The typical fee for average sized transactions ranges between 10 and 30 basis points (bps) for traders that consume liquidity and between 0 and 15 bps for market makers, depending on the cryptocurrency traded. Fees are generally calculated on the value (USD equivalent) executed in the last 30 days.

3.1 Where do trades get reported?

Given movements are only recorded on the blockchain when cryptocurrencies are deposited/withdrawn from the exchange, users who deposit fiat currency, buy bitcoin, hold them within the exchange, and then sell them at the same exchange later for a profit, will not generate any record on the blockchain. In fact, trades themselves within an exchange will not be recorded at all, except by the exchange. Many exchanges make this transaction level data public, however this is entirely separate from the blockchain itself. Like Bloomberg for equities, organisations such as cryptocompare.com and tardis.dev provide historical and real-time access to data on exchange-level transactions.

3.2 What happens if the exchange gets hacked?

Depositing crypto-assets with an exchange exposes individuals to significant counterparty default risk. Put simply, if an exchange goes bankrupt or is hacked, there are few recourses available to investors. The 'trust less' nature of cryptocurrencies means that there is no way to cancel or recover lost crypto assets. As the popularity, and price, of cryptocurrencies has grown, so too has their allure as targets of cybercriminals. Numerous exchanges have been hacked in the last few years – some of the more notable hacks are listed below, and represent some of the largest names in cryptocurrency trading globally:

- 2011 – Mt. Gox – 2,643 bitcoin stolen by an auditor.
- 2012 – Bitfloor – 24,000 bitcoin stolen from backup servers via unencrypted private keys.
- 2013 – Vicurex – 1,454 bitcoin stolen by attackers, leading to exchange bankruptcy.
- 2014 – Mt. Gox – 850,000 bitcoin stolen by attackers, leading to exchange bankruptcy.
- 2015 – Bitstamp – 19,000 bitcoin stolen via a phishing attack on employees.
- 2016 – Bitfinex – 120,000 bitcoin stolen via their payment processor, BitGo.
- 2018 – QuadrigaCX – $190 million of crypto assets lost during suspicious death of CEO.
- 2019 – Binance – 7,000 bitcoin stolen by a phishing scam.

As users' concerns about hacks has risen, a number of responses have been undertaken by exchanges themselves. For example, customers affected by the 2016 Bitfinex hack were provided with "BFX" tokens in lieu of their stolen bitcoins. These represented an "I owe you" of bitcoin from Bitfinex to its users. Within 244 days, all hacked bitcoins were repaid. Often, exchanges will go bankrupt, leaving their users as unsecured creditors. In 2017, an innovation known as "Decentralized Exchanges" were launched on the Ethereum platform, removing the custody of the crypto assets from the exchange to the user.

Concerns about the robustness of the market infrastructure, account security, high volatility and low liquidity combined with limited regulation reduces the appeal of cryptocurrencies to highly-regulated institutional investors and consequently, they have been largely absent from this market thus far.

4 Types of exchanges

There are literally hundreds of crypto exchanges globally. As of 2019, Coinmarketcap.com lists transaction volumes for over 285 exchanges. The majority of these exchanges are described as "centralised" in that there is a single, trusted counterparty that is responsible for operating the limit order book, accepting deposits/withdrawals in fiat and cryptocurrencies, complying with "Know Your Customer" (KYC) regulations, and acting as a custodian for the assets deposited inside the market. In contrast, "Decentralized Exchanges" (DEXs) do not maintain custody of any assets themselves, are typically not operated by any individual and cannot go bankrupt nor be hacked.

4.1 Centralized vs decentralized exchanges

Typical exchanges (for example, Binance, Bitfinex, Poloniex, Kraken, Bitstamp) are centralized, and operate in ways which would be familiar to participants of traditional stock exchanges such as NYSE and NASDAQ. Each exchange chooses which crypto assets to trade (i. e. Bitcoin, Ethereum, Litecoin) as well as which currency pairs to create markets in (i. e. Euro/Bitcoin, USD/Bitcoin, Ethereum/Bitcoin). Users can deposit crypto assets and/or fiat currencies, and trade these assets in a centralized limit order book. Whilst these markets are all technically operated independently in isolation of one another, arbitrage will tend to keep these markets synchronised, similar to the global FOREX markets (see, Makarov and Schoar, 2019).

These markets tend to follow price-time priority, with varying levels of price granularity, often up to 8 decimal places (Dyhrberg et al., 2018). This allows for very high precision pricing, and ensures the orders of traders willing to trade at better prices execute first.

The advent of smart contracts on the Ethereum network (as well as the large number of initial coin offerings conducted on the Ethereum platform using ERC20 tokens) allowed limit orders (the fundamental necessity for limit order markets) to be coded into self-contained contracts. A smart contract can be encoded such that it offers to provide N units of an ERC20 currency in return for E units of Ethereum. A user can then send a 'market' order, delivering E units of Ethereum and automatically receiving N units of ERC20. Such a contract is entirely analogous to a limit order.

An aggregation of such orders could form a virtual 'limit order book'. For example, an offer to provide 10 XYZ in return for 1 Ethereum would be preferred to an offer to provide 9 XYZ, but would be inferior to an offer to provide 11 XYZ.

In order to function effectively as a marketplace, users of a DEX would need to observe all available orders, rank them by their price priority, and then choose which orders to interact with. The first DEXs (i. e. OasisDex and EtherDelta) used *fully on-chain* execution. This means that all order entries, executions and cancellations were processed by the Ethereum blockchain itself. As such, the speed of matching was constrained to the blocktime of Ethereum (currently 14 seconds). Figure 1 below documents the operation of a fully on-chain DEX.

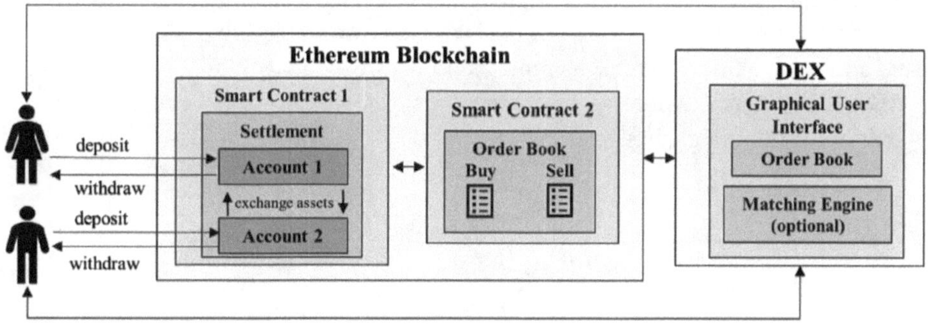

Figure 1: The operation of a fully on-chain decentralized exchange.

It rapidly became evident that relying on the Ethereum network (and paying fees) to enter, amend or cancel an order would significantly constrain the growth of DEXs. This led to the creation of *Hybrid Exchanges*, such as IDEX and 0×, where a centralized organisation collated all order entries, amendments and cancellations off-chain (similar to a centralized exchange) but custody and clearing (after matches were confirmed) were undertaken on the Ethereum blockchain. Centralizing the limit order book facilitated much faster confirmation of transactions and reduced the cost constraint of needing to pay miners to update stale limit orders. However, it did introduce a single, central point of failure and/or censorship. Figure 2 below documents the operation of a DEX with an off-chain order book utilising on-chain settlement.

4.2 Advantages of DEXs

DEXs offer users many potential advantages over traditional exchanges. These include: no counterparty default risk since the exchange never takes custody of your token; no KYC regulations since (similar to torrents) there are no centralized parties on whom to enforce any regulation; the ability to list virtually any token immediately;

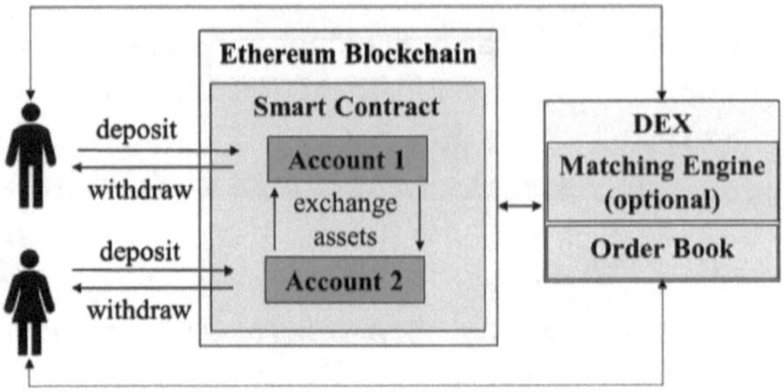

Figure 2: The operation of an off-chain decentralized exchange.

and the ability to remain free of any government based censorship in a truly decentralized environment. For these reasons, DEXs have attracted increasing numbers of users and transaction volumes, as reported in Figure 3 below. Whilst trading activity in DEXs is growing, the number of transactions executed in these venues is dwarfed by that of centralised exchanges.

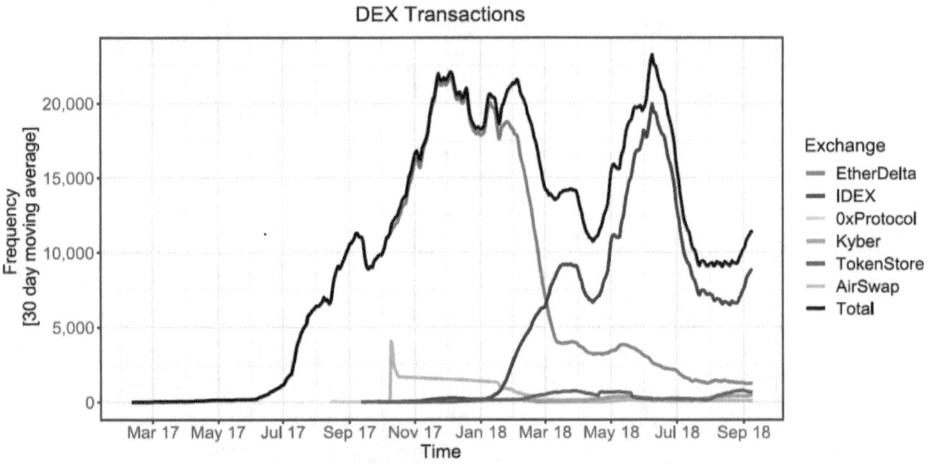

Figure 3: Transaction volumes on decentralized exchanges.

4.3 Disadvantages of DEXs

Whilst the nature of DEXs is changing rapidly, there are currently many limitations of DEXs which hinder their widespread adoption. These include: a public transaction ledger which allows all users to see the addresses associated with all transactions, an inability to trade tokens outside of the (currently Ethereum based) smart contract environment (e. g. fiat currencies and Bitcoins cannot be traded); slow speed of transactions due to a reliance on the underlying blockchain; as well as low levels of liquidity and basic order type functionality due the reliance on smart contracts. Another disadvantage of DEXs is that they do not strictly enforce price time priority. This, combined with the complexity and high precision (many decimal points) of cryptocurrency trades mean mistakes can be very costly – missing one decimal place can result in an arbitrage opportunity with a factor of 10× or more. This has resulted in a variety of mispricings appearing on all DEXs, costing participants significant profits.

4.4 Investability of cryptocurrencies

The value of cryptocurrencies has risen rapidly in recent years. When it briefly touched 20,000 USD in December 2017, Bitcoin alone was valued at more than 300 billion USD. But how investable are cryptocurrencies? Dyhrberg et al. (2018) examine this issue by estimating the transaction costs and intraday trading patterns of the Bitcoin/USD exchange rate across the Gdax, Gemini and Kraken cryptocurrency exchanges. In contrast to quote-driven markets, where effective spreads are generally smaller than quoted spreads as some trades take place within the spread, traders in fully electronic order-driven cryptocurrency markets cannot trade inside the quotes. Furthermore, trades frequently do not execute at the best prices as quoted depths are very small and order quantity frequently exceeds the best posted depth. Consequently, traders are forced to walk up the limit order book and effective spreads are frequently larger than quoted spreads. Dyhrberg et al. (2018) find that quoted spread across the three cryptocurrency exchanges ranges from 0.54 to 7.80 while effective spread ranges from 5.60 to 22.51 bps. This is significantly narrower than the average quoted (effective) spread of 37.2 (23.9) bps of stocks on the NYSE (Boehmer et al., 2005), 32 (27) bps on the Australian Stock Exchange (Aitken et al., 2017), 25.9 (25.0) bps on the centralized electronic order book of Euronext, and 70.5 (40.2) bps on the hybrid order-driven segment of the LSE (Gajewski and Gresse, 2007). In fact, Bitcoin spreads are comparable to the one hundred most liquid stocks on the NYSE which display an average quoted (effective) spread of 10.9 (7.3) bps (Boehmer et al., 2005).

Figure 4 presents the intraday variations in liquidity, spread and volatility observed in the Bitcoin market on U.S. exchanges. As cryptocurrency markets trade continuously, the graph is more consistent with intraday patterns generally found in the foreign exchange markets and does not depict the typical U-shape bid-ask spread and volatility associated with trader behaviour in the equity markets.

Figure 4 shows the trading activity dips early in the morning (U.S. time) as the European markets open and then rises to peak as the U.S. markets begin trading. Trading then declines through the U.S. market close and subsequently drops off as the Asian market close. Volatility follows the same pattern but the peak and troughs are not as pronounced, while quoted and effective spreads display an inverse relationship with

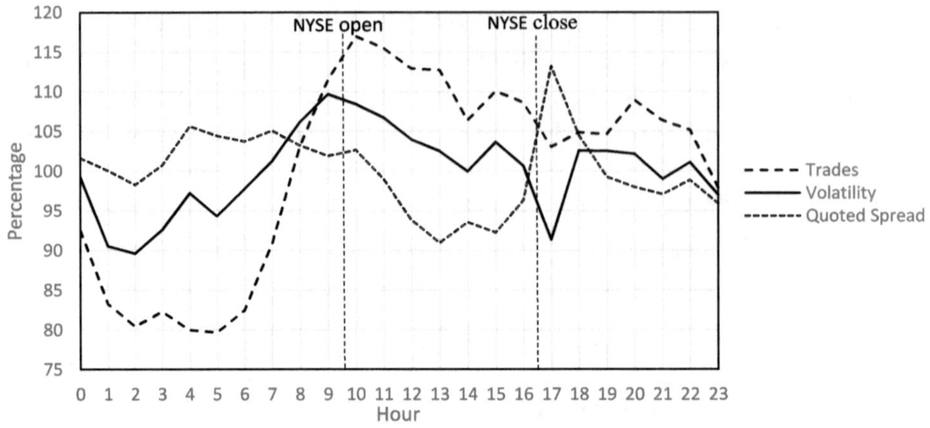

Figure 4: Intraday variation in volume, quoted spread and volatility for the Bitcoin/USD exchange rate between 7th September, 2017 and 10th May, 2018 averaged across Gemini, Gdax and Kraken cryptocurrency exchanges. All variables are hourly averages, scaled by the variable average (Dyhrberg et al., 2019).

liquidity and volatility. This distinct intraday pattern shows that trades on U.S. cryptocurrency exchanges originate mostly during the day which is consistent with orders being executed by retail investors. Interestingly, weekend generate a similar pattern, which contrasts with the subdued trading activity typically observed in the foreign exchange market.

To better gauge the investability of cryptocurrencies, Figure 5 shows the proportion of time the bid or ask side is able to absorb different sized liquidity shocks across six currency pairs between Bitcoin (XBT), Ethereum (ETH), Ethereum classic (ETC), Litecoin (LTC) and USD. The figure shows that investors can generally trade between 500 USD and 1,000 USD within the best ten price levels of the order book. However, there is generally insufficient depth for larger institutional sized transactions. XBT/USD currency pair offers the best prospects of executing a larger order.

4.5 Cryptocurrency derivatives

In December 2017, the Chicago Mercantile Exchange (CME) and the Chicago Board Options Exchange (CBOE) paved the way for the nascent cryptocurrency financial futures, launching their respective cash-settled bitcoin futures trading contract. The launch of a financial futures contract was intended to provide institutional investors, investments funds, miners, and retail investors with a regulated and centralized marketplace to speculate on the price and volatility of Bitcoin.[2] Users would also benefit

2 Around the same time CMEs rival, Cboe Global Markets also introduced Bitcoin futures under the ticker "XBT". However, these were discontinued in March 2019 due to a lack of demand. Bakkt is an-

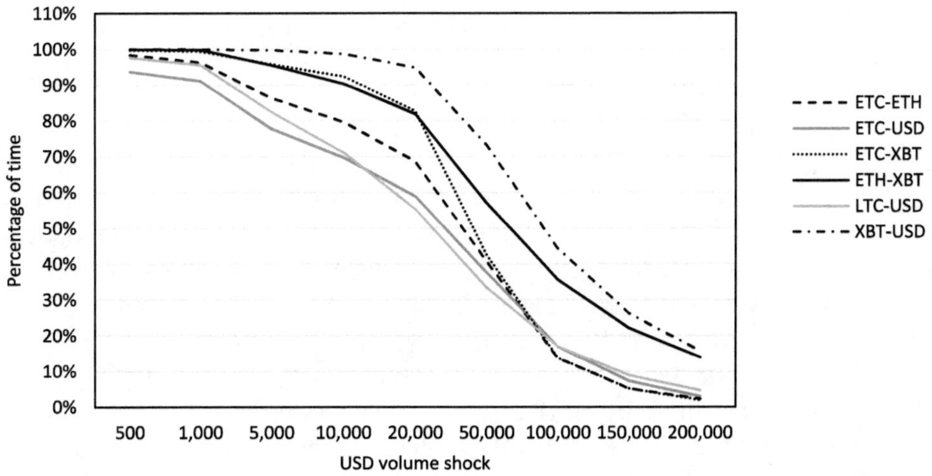

Figure 5: The proportion of time investors can trade cryptocurrencies within the best ten levels of the order book across different trade sizes (from 1st August to 5th October, 2017). All currency pairs are converted into USD.

from the risk management opportunities afforded by financial derivatives from spot currency price movements. The introduction of Bitcoin futures on CME was seen by many observers as a significant step towards the legitimization of digital currencies, potentially elevating cryptocurrencies to a recognized emerging asset class.

The CME Bitcoin futures are based on the CME CF Bitcoin Reference Rate (BRR) as of 4:00 pm London Time. The reference price aggregates executed order flow at global cryptocurrency spot exchanges, including Bitfinex, Bitstamp, Coinbase, Genesis Global Trading, itBit, and Kraken during a specific calculation window prior to its publication.[3] The price and size of each relevant transaction is recorded and added to a list which is partitioned into 12, 5-minute equally-weighted time intervals between 3:00 and 4:00 pm. For each partition, a volume-weighted median trade price is calculated across these constituent exchanges and the BRR is then determined by taking an equally-weighted average of the volume-weighted medians of all partitions.[4] The BRR was designed by CME Group and Crypto Facilities Ltd (CF),[5] around the IOSCO

---

other bitcoin futures contract launched by the Intercontinental Exchange (ICE) in 2018 where buyers receive physical Bitcoin delivery on the day of their trade.

3 Although these constituent exchanges and platforms are unregulated, each has proactively instituted Know-Your-Customer (KYC) and Anti-Money Laundering (AML) policies.

4 For greater detail around pricing of these benchmarks see https://www.cryptofacilities.com/cms/storage/resources/cme-cf-reference-rate-methodology.pdf

5 CF Benchmarks is authorized by the U.K.s Financial Conduct Authority (FCA) and recognized as a Benchmark Administrator under the European Benchmarks Regulation (EU BMR).

Principles for Financial Benchmarks[6] and is a daily reference rate of the USD price of one bitcoin. The choice of this benchmark is geared toward resilience and replicability in the underlying spot market.

Like many of its other financial derivatives, Bitcoin futures trade on CMEs Globex platform (and ex-pit via Clearport) between Sunday and Friday from 5:00 pm to 4:00 pm with a 60-minute break each day. The market is supported by a market-maker program to ensure sufficient liquidity for its participants. The fees for trading Bitcoin are priced at a significant premium to Equity Index futures (approximately 3× higher).[7] Margin requirements for Bitcoin futures are also significantly more onerous than for other instruments. The maintenance margin for Bitcoin futures is currently around 37% (compared to 4% for E-mini S&P 500 futures), where the Initial Margin for hedgers (speculators) is 100% (110%) of the maintenance margin. These requirements are subject to change and the CME retains the right to impose exposure limits or additional capital requirements. This trading and clearing are regulated by the Commodity Futures Trading Commission (CFTC).

Since its launch in 2017, the CME has seen over 20 futures expiration settlements, with over 3,300 individual accounts trading approximately 7,000 CME Bitcoin futures contracts each day. The contract unit is for 5 bitcoins with a minimum price fluctuation of 25 USD per contract. As of September 2019, the value of a single BTC contract was approximately 50,000 USD.

Corbet et al. (2018) examine the relationship between Bitcoin futures and spot prices, finding that the underlying leads the futures contract in terms of price discovery. They suggest that both the financial instrument and market structure may play a role in this surprising relationship, commenting that the absence of a large cohort of institutional investors may impede its contribution to price discovery. An examination of the Commodity Futures Trading Commission (CFTC) Commitments of Traders (COT) report reveals that "Leveraged Funds" and "Other Reportables" dominate open interest in BTC futures with institutional investors (asset managers) holding only small interests. As of September, 2019, Asset Manager (Institutional) percent of open interest for long and short positions measured only 6.3% and 4.8%, respectively. Leveraged funds are defined in Traders in Financial Futures (TFF) as traders that may be engaged in managing and conducting proprietary futures trading and trading on behalf of speculative clients.[8] Other reportables, meanwhile are traders that are not

6 In 2013, IOSCO recommended principles for administrators of financial market benchmarks that have been widely accepted as representing best practices by regulators: see International Organization of Securities Commission, "Principles for Financial Benchmarks: Final Report" (July 2013). https://www.iosco.org/library/pubdocs/pdf/IOSCOPD415.pdf

7 Through to May 31, 2018, the CME provided a 50% discount to all market participants for Globex spread transactions.

8 The COT report separates traders in financial futures and options markets into four main categories: Dealer/Intermediary; Asset Manager/Institutional; Leveraged Funds; and Other Reportables. The TFF placed in a dealer, asset manager, or leveraged fund category and mainly consist of retail traders with fewer than 25 bitcoin contracts. The relatively high representation of traders with small positions in CFTC reportable data distinguishes it from other more prominent financial market contracts and suggests that it may be a factor in the lack of price discovery in this market.

Given the success of Bitcoin futures, in September 2019, CME Group announced that it would offer options on its Bitcoin futures contracts starting in the first quarter of 2020 pending a regulatory review. The options aimed to provide clients with additional tools for precision hedging and trading.

5 Cryptocurrency specific trading issues

5.1 Undercutting

While the physical trading on cryptocurrency exchanges is comparable to trading on other equity exchanges, relative tick size, the minimum allowable trading price increment expressed as a percentage of the price is much smaller than on equity exchanges. Tick size selection is one of the most important decisions made by an exchange to influence overall market quality. Tick size determines the cost to gain price priority over a standing limit order and dictates the minimum bid-ask spread, a major component of trading cost. As the price of cryptocurrencies rose, and Bitcoin in particular, the relative spread became increasingly small and unconstrained. On most cryptocurrency exchanges is it either one cent (for example, Bitstamp and Coinbase) or ten cents (Bitfinex) which leads to a relative tick size of as low as 0.01 bps when one bitcoin trades around 10,000 USD.

With such a small trading increment, it is relatively inexpensive for traders to improve limit orders by a negligible amount to gain priority, as illustrated in Figure 6. This 'undercutting' behaviour dis-incentivizes traders to supply liquidity and encourages them to cross the spread to get executed, leading to lower depth at best quotes and deteriorations in quoted spread.

Buti et al. (2019) develop a theoretical model of the public limit order book to analyze the effects of a tick size on market quality and show that market quality for spread unconstrained securities can be improved with a tick size increase. Several exchanges have recognised that small tick sizes can lead to excessive undercutting behaviour

report provides a weekly breakdown of each Tuesday's open interest for markets in which 20 or more traders hold positions equal to or above reporting levels established by the CFTC. The trader categories are obtained via Form 40 which is required under CFTC Regulation 18.04 to be completed by reportable traders. Among the reported details in the TFF report are spreading (open interest by long and short positions) and the number of traders in each category.

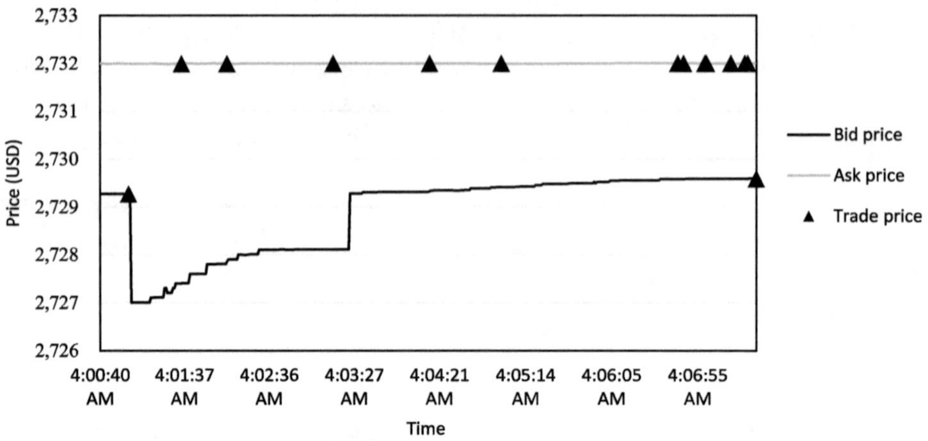

Figure 6: The bid and ask quote and trade prices for BTC-USD on August 2nd 2017 from 4:00 am to 4:07 am (Dyhrberg et al., 2019).

and have begun to increase tick sizes for many of the currency pairs to improve market quality.[9] The following excerpt from a Kraken press release in 2017 highlights the impact of rising cryptocurrency prices on the prevalence of undercutting.

> *Reducing the price precision will help reduce extraneous activity in the order books as traders continually jump in front of each other by a very small fraction. We have received many requests from clients for this reduction and it will help reduce load on the trade engine with more efficient order books.*
> (Kraken Press Release, August 26, 2017)

Dyhrberg et al. (2019) confirm that a wider tick size on Kraken changes traders' behaviour, significantly reduces undercutting, and leads to an overall improvement in market quality. Figure 7 shows the relative quoted spread and the relative tick size in bps (log scale) for the constituents of the S&P 500 index and the currency pairs on Kraken pre and post the tick size increases in August/September 2017.

5.2 Short selling constraints

The ability to short a security by allowing rational arbitrageurs to borrow without constraints is seen in finance theory as a necessary condition for efficient capital markets. It is associated with price discovery and increased market liquidity and yet it is a feature that is not built into the blockchain. Users cannot spend cryptocurrencies they do

9 For example, both Kraken and BitMex have increased their tick size in 2017.

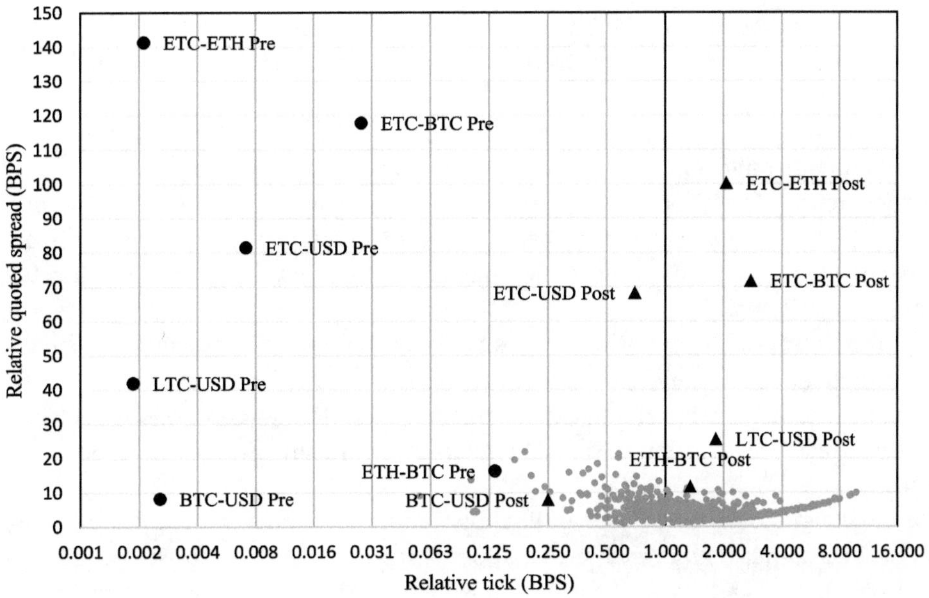

Figure 7: Comparison of relative tick sizes and relative quoted spreads across Kraken and S&P500 stocks (Dyhrberg et al., 2019).

not have; however, this does not preclude users from taking financial positions related to the value of this currency.

> *I would short it if there was an easy way to do it*[10]
> Bill Gates, Microsoft co-founder

Prior to the establishment of Bitcoin futures listed on the Cboe and CME, users wanting to bet against Bitcoin (or other altcoins) or engage in some form of risk management were limited to just a few platforms. Amongst the most popular for shorting were Bitfinex and Poloniex. In a short sale, the seller enters into a regular spot sale of the digital currency except that the transaction is settled by delivering cryptocurrency that was borrowed. In this regard shorting cryptocurrencies is similar to shorting listed securities – short sellers must locate the currency to borrow it. Cryptocurrencies can be borrowed on an exchange (e. g. Bitfinex or Poloniex) through peer-to-peer functionality, meaning that borrowers are borrowing from other participants, who will receive a rebate in the form of interest income. The rebate will depend on the term of the loan and the rate will exhibit variation over time. The cryptocurrency borrower may seek offers or make a bid to borrow digital tokens and are not permitted to exceed certain leverage thresholds. Bitcoin borrowers on Bitfinex, for example, are not permitted to

10 https://www.cnbc.com/2018/05/07/bill-gates-i-would-short-bitcoin-if-i-could.html

borrow more than 70% of the bitcoins sold in a short sale. The fiat proceeds of any short sale serve as collateral for the borrowing of the bitcoins until those bitcoins are repaid.

Given the prohibitively onerous margin requirements for retail traders to short Bitcoin (and other altcoins), alternative shorting options, for example, CFDs (contracts for difference) have been established by a range of brokers including, Plus500 and eToro. CFDs function in a manner that is similar to futures contracts, in that investors can bet on an underlying asset without having to own it physically, thereby allowing for short positions.

The North American Derivatives Exchange (Nadex) is a U.S.-based regulated exchange that offers binary options and spreads to investors.[11] Option spreads can be used to limit risk while gaining exposure to both the short and long side of Bitcoin. The contracts are settled in USD and therefore do not require ownership of the physical.

Looking to overcome issues of liquidity (particularly amongst specific altcoins) in the peer-to-peer crypto exchange platforms, repo markets have recently been canvased with crypto assets. A repo can be thought of as a loan secured against collateral, except the collateral is not pledged, it is sold and repurchased at maturity. By providing crypto asset holders with an ability to lend in this environment, professional market participants could borrow for the purposes of taking or covering short positions. A current example of a platform providing this service is Oxygen.[12]

Finally, prediction markets also provide a possible approach to short cryptocurrencies. These markets allow investors to create an event to make a wager based on the outcome. For example, predicting that Bitcoin will decline by a certain percentage sets a wager that other parties can participate in by taking the other side. These wagers are conducted in an unregulated market and thus pose significant risks.

5.3 Front running

Unlike stock markets, all transactions on the blockchain are public, including the wallet address of the user. This may seem harmless at first, however it exposes large orders to the risk of being front run. Imagine a trader holds 100 million USD of Bitcoin, and decides to sell. In order to do so, the trader first needs to transfer the large stack of bitcoins to an exchange. Such a transaction will show up on the blockchain, and monitoring sites such as WhaleAlert.io may broadcast this transaction to the world at large. This may not be an issue if the trader is able to execute large orders immediately. However, due to the trust-less nature of cryptocurrencies, exchanges typically

11 Nadex is regulated by the Commodity Futures Trading Commission.
12 https://oxygen.trade/

'lock' deposits for 30-60 minutes to protect themselves from double spend attacks. This means that keen observers, noticing a large influx of bitcoins, may infer the depositor intends on selling. If this sale is large enough to have a significant price impact, the observer may themselves sell the asset deposited in order to 'front run' the depositor, making profit from the eventual price impact of the large order. Analytics like these enabled researchers to identify that there may be a connection between the USD Tether and the pumping of the bitcoin price on the associated Bitfinex exchange (see Griffin and Shams, 2018).

5.4 Griefing

Stock markets central matching engines process orders in pure price-time priority. These engines are now calibrated to separate orders to an incredibly fine measurement of time – typically to the picosecond (one trillionth of a second). However, many DEXs utilise the 'clock time' of the Ethereum network (14 seconds), which can cause problems.

Specifically, imagine a situation in which a user posts an order on a DEX which is mispriced, which gives rise to potential arbitrage. In order to exploit this opportunity, a user needs to submit a 'market' order to the DEX, exhausting the attractive liquidity. The issue is that this order will not be confirmed until the next Ethereum block is mined. As miners process transactions in order of fee priority, an arbitrageur can offer a high fee to interact with a profitable arbitrage opportunity. Daian et al. (2019) identify thousands of such opportunities, and document 'bidding wars' with the miners to take advantage of these situations.

When one user sees an arbitrage opportunity in a DEX, they submit a market order with a fee – say \$1. This order is only executed once incorporated by a miner into a transaction. Before the market order is executed, a second arbitrageur may also spot this opportunity, and offer a \$2 fee to the miner. When a miner eventually solves the cryptographic puzzle, they will collect fees from both users, but only the user with the

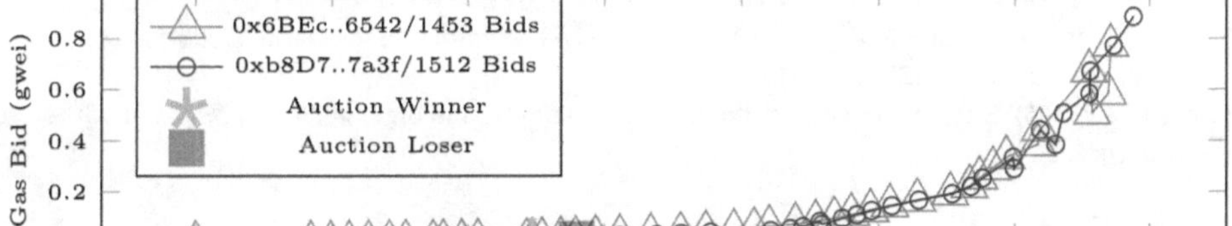

Figure 8: A bidding war between two arbitrageurs attempting to submit a market order to the Ethereum blockchain (Daian et al., 2019).

highest fee will have their order executed. The 'losing' bidder will pay the fee to attempt to interact with a smart contract which has already been exhausted of liquidity.

Such conduct is called "Griefing" and is documented by Daian et al. (2019). Figure 8 below extracted from their paper demonstrates a 'bidding war' between two arbitrageurs attempting to submit a market order to the Ethereum blockchain, bidding in the fee they are willing to pay the miner to prioritise their order.

Bibliography

Aitken, M., H. Chen, and S. Foley (2017). The impact of fragmentation, exchange fees and liquidity provision on market quality. *Journal of Empirical Finance 41*, 140–160.

Anand, A., and K. Venkataraman (2016). Market conditions, fragility, and the economics of market making. *Journal of Financial Economics 121*, 327–349.

Baur, D. G., K. Hong, and A. D. Lee (2018). Bitcoin: Medium of exchange or speculative assets? *Journal of International Financial Markets, Institutions and Money 54*, 177–189.

Boehmer, E., G. Saar, and L. Yu (2005). Lifting the veil: An analysis of pre-trade transparency at the NYSE. *Journal of Finance 60*, 783–815.

Buti, S., B. Rindi, Y. Wen, and I. M. Werner (2019). Tick size, trading strategies and market quality. Available at: https://papers.ssrn.com/sol3/papers.cfm?abstract_id=3330807.

Corbet, S., B. Lucey, M. Peat, and S. Vigne (2018). Bitcoin futures – What use are they? *Economics Letters 172*, 23–27.

Daian, P., S. Goldfeder, T. Kell, Y. Li, X. Zhao, I. Bentov, L. Breidenbach, and A. Juels (2019). Flash Boys 2.0: Frontrunning, transaction reordering, and consensus instability in decentralized exchanges. Available at: https://arxiv.org/pdf/1904.05234.pdf.

Dyhrberg, A., S. Foley, and J. Svec (2018). How investible is bitcoin? Analyzing the liquidity and transaction costs of bitcoin markets. *Economics Letters 17*, 140–143.

Dyhrberg, A., S. Foley, and J. Svec (2019). The impact of tick sizes on trader behavior: Evidence from cryptocurrency exchanges. Available at: https://papers.ssrn.com/sol3/papers.cfm?abstract_id=3194932.

Foley, S., J. R. Karlsen, and T. J. Putniņš (2019). Sex, drugs, and bitcoin: How much illegal activity is financed through cryptocurrencies? *The Review of Financial Studies 32*, 1798–1853.

Gajewski, J-F., and C. Gresse (2007). Centralized order books versus hybrid order books: A paired comparison of trading costs on NSC (Euronext Paris) and SETS (London Stock Exchange). *Journal of Banking and Finance 31*, 2906–2924.

Griffin, J. M., and A. Shams (2018). Is bitcoin really un-tethered? Available at SSRN: https://ssrn.com/abstract=3195066 or http://dx.doi.org/10.2139/ssrn.3195066.

Makarov, I., and A. Schoar (2019). Trading and arbitrage in cryptocurrency markets. *Journal of Financial Economics 135*, 293–319.

Yermack, D. (2015). Bitcoin, innovation, financial instruments, and big data. In *Handbook of digital currency*. 31–43.

Shaen Corbet and Douglas J. Cumming

The Wild West of ICOs

1 Introduction

As with any juvenile and rapidly expanding financial product, we must be aware of the potential for illicit and ethically-challenging decision-making while the boundaries for regulation continue to be designed. The very creation of cryptocurrencies has somewhat challenged regulators. Cryptocurrencies have provided an exceptionally easy platform that can be used for cross-border trade, but they can easily generate illicit activity. Companies and governments alike can utilise these products for somewhat 'questionable' practices. Three specific key concerns have been identified in recent literature: 1) the use of cryptocurrencies by governments to circumvent internationally-binding sanctions and controls; 2) the announcement of companies of their broad intentions to enter the cryptocurrency market, with little or no intention of following through on their commitments; and 3) the simplistic nature through which investor theft has continued to escalate within the scope of unregulated ICOs. These situations necessitate broad consideration by regulators and policy-makers before the markets for cryptocurrencies can be truly identified to have evolved to levels similar to that of other types of traditional markets.

There have been a number of ethically-challenged issues that have arisen since the establishment of Bitcoin and other growing cryptocurrencies and digital asset types. Regulatory bodies and policy-makers alike have observed the growth of cryptocurrencies with a certain amount of scepticism based on the growing potential for illegality and malpractice through the use of cryptocurrencies. Some regulatory authorities, including the International Monetary Fund, have expressed their satisfaction with the product's development and the benefits that are contained within its continued growth, however, the Securities and Exchange Commission (SEC) amongst other international authorities have explicitly warned of the potential market manipulation techniques and ability to utilise fraudulent methods to defraud and steal from unwilling and unsuspecting investors.

The rest of this chapter is as follows. Section 2 presents a thorough review of the literature relating to the development and issues relating to ICOs and criminality in cryptocurrencies. Section 3 presents a review of the irregularities that have occurred in ICO markets, with emphasis on criminality, the use of ICOs by sovereign states and corporates and other examples of questionable ICOs. Section 4 presents and overview as to how the regulation has changed over time, while Section 5 concludes.

https://doi.org/10.1515/9783110660807-007

2 Previous literature

Research based on ICOs has developed substantially since 2018, focusing on a broad number of areas such as underlying technology, financing and governance. It is notable that a developing strand of research has began to focus on issues such as illicit usage of ICOs and the developing role that cybercriminality has begun to play at the point at which cryptocurrencies begin their existence. Adhami et al. (2018) analysed the determinants of the success 253 ICOs to find that the probability success is higher if the code source is made available, when a token presale is organized, and when tokens allow contributors to access a specific service (or to share profits). While Hashemi Joo et al. (2019) identify that ICOs have generated billions of dollars of funding to startups and projects worldwide in less than two years, many successful ICOs yielded extremely high returns to investors. While the ICO is a revolutionary vehicle for business funding, it has raised concerns among users as well as potential investors about its risk and lack of regulation. The future of this innovative funding method highly depends on further development and placement of appropriate regulatory supervision, better understanding of risk and benefits and attaining the confidence of users. Deng et al. (2018) focused on the September 2017 decision to ban ICOs in Chine, noting that the decision could hamper revolutionary technological developments and dampen the growth of this potentially beneficial market. The authors provide a non-exhaustive classification of the legal status of ICOs, including the pre-sale of products or services, offering of shares, issue of debentures, issue of derivatives, collective investment schemes and crowdfunding, as well as a possible regulatory reform of the current ICO ban in China. It is concluded that ICOs could be best regarded as pre-sale of products or services, whereas, the other five types of ICOs are highly likely to be considered as financial securities and thus should be subject to securities laws. O'Dair and Owen (2019) went as far as to investigate as to how new music ventures might obtain alternative entrepreneurial finance through token sales or ICOs, presenting evidence as to the breadth that this new developing market can reach. Fisch (2019) assessed the determinants of the amount raised in 423 ICOs while drawing on signalling theory to show that technical white papers and high-quality source codes increase the amount raised, while patents are not associated with increased amounts of funding. The results indicate that some of the underlying mechanisms in ICOs resemble those found in prior research into entrepreneurial finance, while others are unique to the ICO context. Felix and von Eije (2019) found that the average level of under-pricing of ICOs of 123% in the US and 97% in the other countries. The results for the US ICOs are significantly higher than for US IPOs on average and also higher than US IPOs at the beginning of the dot.com bubble. The authors also study the determinants of ICO under-pricing. Further, companies that use a large issue size or a pre-ICO (a sale of cryptocurrencies before the ICO) leave less money on the table.

Cohney et al. (2019) found that many ICOs failed even to promise that they would protect investors against insider self-dealing and that a significant fraction of issuers retained centralised control through previously undisclosed code permitting modification of the entities' governing structures. Barone and Masciandaro (2019) analyse separate money laundering techniques including the use of cryptocurrency to shed light on their relative role as an effective device for the criminal organisations to clean their illegal revenues. This research is developed further in the work of Corbet et al. (2019) who develop on the specific methods of illegality that have become a central issue in the developing cryptocurrency markets. Among the most alarming issues in recent years include that which have substantially damaged market integrity and identified the presence of potential fraud and criminal behaviour within the broad market system (Gandal et al. (2018); Griffins and Shams (2018)). Such issues have become ever more alarming due to the multiple identified interactions between both product (Corbet et al. (2018); Katsiampa et al. (2019); Corbet and Katsiampa (2018); Corbet et al. (2020); Celeste et al. (2019); Akhtaruzzaman et al. (2019)) and derivative types (Corbet et al. (2018)). Further, Corbet et al. (2019) investigate the effectiveness of technical trading rules in cryptocurrency markets and provide significant support for the moving average strategies, with emphasis on the variable-length moving average rule performs the best with buy signals generating higher returns than sell signals.

Nguyen et al. (2019) found that the negative impact of an Initial Public Offering (IPO) on existing stock prices can also be observed in the cryptocurrency market, where altcoin introductions are found through the use of Autoregressive-Distributed-Lag (ARDL) estimations, to reduce Bitcoin returns by 0.7%. This result is found to be particularly pertinent as the average and median daily returns of Bitcoin are 0.6% and 0.3%, respectively. Lahajnar and Rozanec (2018) analysed a number of factors, which directly or indirectly influence the successful implementation of ICO projects, and the researchers extracted the most important among them (model parameters). Huang et al. (2019) found using 915 ICOs issued in 187 countries between January 2017 and March 2018 that ICOs take place more frequently in countries with developed financial systems, public equity markets, and advanced digital technologies. The availability of investment-based crowdfunding platforms is also positively associated with the emergence of ICOs, while debt and private equity markets do not provide similar effects. Further, countries with ICO-friendly regulations have more ICOs, whereas tax regimes are not clearly related to ICOs. Chen (2019) focus on signals released in multiple channels in different ICO stages to investigate the relations between signal processing and information asymmetry. The authors find differing results throughout the different stages analysed, first indicating that in the crowd sale stage, high credible and easy-interpretable signals have significant influences on token sales. In the listing stage, low credible and easy-interpretable signals have significant effects on token trading. High credible and hard-interpretable signals, which deliver project fundamental information, lose their functions in both stages, causing information asymmetry in ICOs. Further, investor comments on social media, which is a multiple-way communication channel, play the role of information surveillance for ventures' voluntary disclosures.

3 Some brief examples of cryptocurrency and ICO irregularities

The very creation of cryptocurrencies has somewhat challenged regulators. Nakamoto (2008), while attempting to change the face of finance and fiat currency as we know it, challenged the views of many based on the viability of the cryptocurrencies at large. However, in the decade since the creation of Bitcoin, there have been a number of opportunistic manoeuvres that we must consider. Cryptocurrencies have provided an exceptionally easy platform that can be used for cross-border trade and generally illicit activity. Further, while pricing dynamics continue to be challenged as possessing a substantial bubble Corbet et al. (2018), companies and governments alike can utilise these products for 'questionable' practices. Three key concerns have been identified: 1) the use of fake ICOs to steal unsuspecting investor funds; 2) the use of cryptocurrencies by governments to circumvent internationally-binding sanctions and controls; and 3) the announcement of companies of their broad intentions to enter the cryptocurrency market, however, with little or no intention of following through on their commitments. Both of these situations contain substantial asymmetric information and moral hazards that necessitate broad consideration by regulators and policy-makers. In this section, we discuss each issue in detail.

3.1 Questionable motives, criminality and ICO disappearance

A controversial area of Initial Coin Offerings (ICOs) concerns financial regulators and businesses highlighting the importance of full and fair disclosure of corporate intention to incorporate blockchain technology. While ICOs can help companies to reduce the costs of raising capital, the lack of transparency and very limited information available for investors in the white papers might affect the corporate performance in the long run. The absence of a unified regulatory framework creates multiple speculation opportunities for all market players. At corporate level, the decision to adopt cryptocurrency or blockchain technology can change the corporate identity of the firm, for example, from a more conventional identity to that of a Fintech company, and attract a new group of investors. However, those intentions to adopt blockchain often stays at the stage of writing a white paper, making corporate announcements, or even simply changing the name of corporation, and not going further to actually launching the stated cryptocurrency or building the proposed platform. Thus corporations may try to take advantage of the euphoric and speculative investment motives and ride a wave on the cryptocurrency bubble. The explosive behaviour of the cryptocurrency markets can be compared with Dot.com bubble and related corporate name changes (Cooper et al. (2001)).

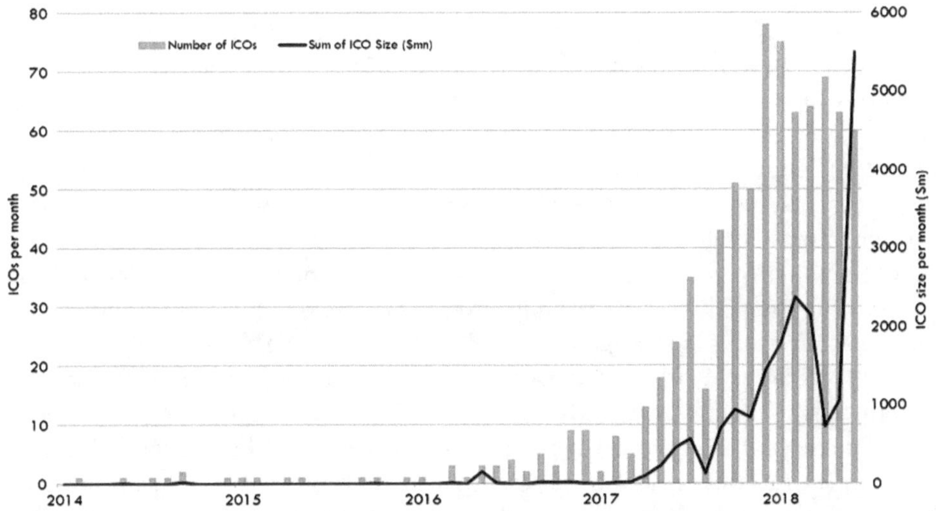

Figure 1: Number and monetary value of initial coin offerings, 2014–2018.

Note: Data was available between 1 January 2014 and 31 July 2018. Data was obtained from www.coindesk.com. The above bars represents the number of ICOs initiated per month while the black line represents their size as measured in US$ millions.

One of the largest signals that there exist the presence of irrational exuberance in cryptocurrency markets is denoted within not only the number of Initial Coin Offerings (ICOs) in recent years (see Figure 1), but indeed the source of these coin offerings. A substantial number of corporate entities have made announcements with regards to their intentions to enter the cryptocurrency sphere, for a host of differing reasons. This has raised alarm due to the inherent dangers associated with asymmetric information and moral hazard. As with any new financial product, we must be aware of the potential for illicit and ethically-challenging decision-making as the boundaries of regulation are designed. The very creation of cryptocurrencies has somewhat challenged regulators. Cryptocurrencies have provided an exceptionally easy platform that can be used for cross-border trade and generally illicit activity. Companies and governments alike can utilise these products for 'questionable' practices. Two key concerns have been identified: 1) the use of cryptocurrencies by governments to circumvent internationally-binding sanctions and controls; and 2) the announcement of companies of their broad intentions to enter the cryptocurrency market, however, with little or no intention of following through on their commitments. Both of these situations necessitate broad consideration by regulators and policy-makers. Regulatory bodies and policy-makers alike have observed the growth of cryptocurrencies with a certain amount of scepticism, based on this growing potential for illegality and malpractice. Foley et al. (2019) estimate that around $76 billion of illegal activity per year involve

Bitcoin (46% of Bitcoin transactions). This is estimated to be in the same region of the U.S. and European markets for illegal drugs, and is identified as 'black e-commerce'.

However, at the core of the main issue with ICOs is simply that of direct theft, which has occurred on multiple occasions, including the most simplistic of financial crime, where the host of the ICO simply disappears. Unfortunately, this type of scam has become far too common in recent times. Amongst the most well-known is that of Pincoin, representing one of the largest ICO scam in history. Together with Ifan, another blockchain company, 32,000 investors were duped out of the equivalent of $660 million. The company had promised its investors a 40% monthly returns on their investment, luring unsuspecting investors with claims that the ICO was to be overseen by PIN Foundation. Further, Modern Tech promised an 8% reward to every investor for bringing in another investor, indicative of a classic multi-level-marketing scheme with the benefit of hindsight. Titanium was another example of a textbook ICO case of fraud. The ICO was based on a social media marketing blitz that allegedly deceived investors with purely fictional claims of business prospects. Charges were then filed against Michael Alan Stollery, a self-described blockchain evangelist, who is reported to have lied about business relationships with the Federal Reserve and dozens of well-known firms, including PayPal, Verizon, Boeing, and The Walt Disney Company. The complaint alleges that Titanium's website contained fabricated testimonials from corporate customers. As evidence of the sharp perceptions and actions of regulatory authorities, the Titanium ICO was stopped before it was finished.

In 2016, over $30 million dollars were seized by Chinese authorities investigating the OneCoin operation in the country. The company claimed to be officially licensed in Vietnam, but this was later refuted by the country's government. More than five countries have warned investors of the risks involved for those choosing to invest in the company, including Thailand, Croatia, Bulgaria, Finland and Norway. In 2017, another example of substantial ICO fraud was that of Confido, who had collected 1235 Ethereum, at the time valued at approximately $375,000 before the price of tokens became tradable and their value subsequently skyrocketed. At one point, the price of one CFD token rose approximately that of twenty times the amount of the initial ICO price. This price jump made Confido one of the best-performing ICOs ever in terms of short-term token price rise, and the tiny project possessed a market cap of $10 million in a very short amount of time. However, a number of market monitors had raised suspicions based on the lack of credibility and the continued anonymity of those responsible. Thereafter, a message on Confido's subreddit said that the company is having unspecified legal problems which will delay development 'until a resolution is found.' Shortly after, the value of CFD had collapsed to $0.03 and all associated had become non-responsive.

BitConnect closed down its crypto-lending platform in January 2018 following the issuance of cease-and-desist orders from Texas and North Carolina securities regulators, which claimed the company was engaging in an unregistered securities sale through its initial coin offering (ICO). Users exchanged Bitcoin for BitConnect

Coin (BCC) on the BitConnect platform which had launched in January 2017, and were promised substantial returns on their investments. There were broad accusations and signs that there existed a broad ponzi scheme referral system. BitConnect's BCC token plunged more than 90 percent, falling from over $400 to less than $20 in the first weeks of 2018. A number of users have since launched a class action lawsuit against BitConnect to recoup lost funds.

Further, in a quite astonishing case in 2018, in a creditor protection filing from the Nova Scotia Supreme court, QuadrigaCX passed on 9 December 2018, leading to a liquidity crisis at the exchange. CEO Gerald Cotten had died of complications with Crohn's disease 'while travelling in India, where he was opening an orphanage to provide a home and safe refuge for children in need.' The company had said that Cotten was the sole person with passwords to access the exchange's 'cold storage,' where the vast majority of its client holdings were held. QuadrigaCX filed for creditor protection in compliance with the Companies' Creditors Arrangement Act (CCAA). The exchange only has CA$375,000 in cash, while it owed approximately CA$260 million to its users. The exchange kept most its assets in offline storage systems called cold wallets, which are secured by digital security keys in order to protect them from hacking and theft. Cotten was solely responsible for the wallets and corresponding keys, which the company has been trying to find after his passing.[1] The company's auditors raised substantial, ongoing suspicions when they wrote in a 2019 report that they had 'been unable to locate any traditional books and records, including accounting records documenting Quadriga's financial results and operations following 2016'.

In April 2019, the founder of German-based startup Savedroid has allegedly disappeared after raising a reported $50 million through both an ICO and private funding. It was later reported that Savedroid's CEO posted a video to YouTube claiming that the apparent exit scam was actually a PR stunt the company pulled off to advocate for 'high quality ICO standards.' This type of behaviour again presents further evidence of the non-standard incidents that have been repeatedly occurring in the market for ICOs, generating substantial erosion of trust while verifying continued suspicion on behalf of regulators and market participants alike.

3.2 Facebook and Project Libra

One of the largest ICO-related announcements in recent times surrounded that of Project Libra, which is a proposed digital currency by that of Facebook with an estimated launch date during 2020. The project, currency and transactions are to be man-

1 However, it was widely reported that Cotten mostly worked from his computer at home, which is encrypted. Cotten's wife, Jennifer Robertson, reportedly stated in an affidavit, 'I do not know the password or recovery key. Despite repeated and diligent searches, I have not been able to find them written down anywhere.'

aged and cryptographically entrusted to the Libra Association, which was founded by Facebook's subsidiary Calibra and a number of other companies across payment, technology, telecommunication, online marketplace, venture capital and nonprofits. It was first rumoured in May 2019 that Facebook had been secretly planning to release a cryptocurrency, with names reported such as GlobalCoin and Facebook Coin. The new coin is not proposed to be decentralised, thereby firmly relying on trust in the Libra Association as a lender of last resort. The company also announced a new digital wallet called Calibra, which will be operated by Facebook as a separate subsidiary and provide users with a way to store and spend Libra. Facebook provided an image of Calibra's design, including a three-wave symbol that serves as the Libra's equivalent of a dollar sign. The currency's blockchain, which is open source, will be programmed in a new language developed by Facebook called Move. Facebook will invite third parties to build smart contracts and other blockchain-based services. The proposed idea to leverage upon the already global Facebook network, utilising a token which would be backed by financial assets including currencies and US Treasury securities in an attempt to mitigate issues with volatility, with substantial financial support to be provided by a variety of companies that have already offered their support to the idea. The Libra Association will thereby create new Libra currency units based on demand while previous currency units will be retired as they are redeemed for conventional currency. In the related white paper, it was proposed that the reconciliation of transactions will be performed at each service partner, and the blockchain's distributed ledger will be used for reconciliation between service partners which would theoretically prevent an association member extracting and analysing the distributed ledger. In a May 2002 report in the Wall Street Journal, it was widely reported that there were a number of additional business models and benefits that Facebook was considering to be central to the creation of Libra, including: 1) a plan to launch a full payments network while the company had been reportedly in discussions with payment networks Visa and Mastercard, payments processors such as giant First Data as well as large e-commerce merchants to support the launch; 2) that Facebook had been the ability to generate up to $1 billion in investments collectively from associated firms to provide collateral to bolster and back the stablecoin that will be associated with the new payments network; 3) the new coin will exist as the currency of the payments system in order to eliminate credit card fees for merchants as well as to avoid the volatility of other cryptocurrencies like Bitcoin and Ether; and 4) the new coin could potentially be tied to Facebook's core advertisement engine, thereby rewarding users for viewing advertisements and then purchasing goods, similar to how loyalty points rewards work.

The announcement of Libra's coincided with unprecedented scrutiny from regulators surrounding Facebook's actions and behaviours across multiple fronts in recent years. The company has spent much time since 2017 battling to regain user trust after multiple privacy scandals, thereby experiencing much scepticism when Project Libra was initially announced. Since Libra's unveiling, the project has received quite a negative reception from some policymakers. The United States Federal Reserve Chairman Jerome Powell signalled much scepticism about Facebook's plans for Libra, stating that he did not 'think that the project can go forward' and that it was of the utmost importance that there be 'broad satisfaction with the way the company has addressed money laundering' during testimony before the House Financial Services Committee. Regulators had possessed 'serious concerns' with the project in its entirety when gauging its potential from the previous announcements. It has also not been identified as to whether money has actually changed hands from members who had expressed interest in the Libra association as some of the companies who agreed to lend their names to the project avoided making strong public statements in support of it. This very fact reflected significant uncertainty about how Libra will actually work and even if it is possible to launch a network like this within the bounds of international law, potentially explaining the reluctance for some companies to offer support. At the core of this project, Facebook is trying to build a payment system that combines the best characteristics of blockchain and conventional networks. But the result may wind up just being a contradictory and jurisdictional, regulatory and legislative disaster. Amongst one of the key issues is whether Libra will actually provide meaningful privacy to its users, particularly as Facebook's plan incorporates delegating responsibility of the company's network to its subsidiary Calibra, where Facebook executives have stated that Calibra will not share account holder's purchase information with Facebook without authorisation. After the multiple privacy issues that have occurred in recent times, this is highly unlikely to lead to a positive response from users.

The European response has been far more damning. In September 2019, French finance minister Bruno Le Maire stated that the nation will not allow the development of the cryptocurrency in Europe as it is a threat to the monetary sovereignty of nations. He also spoke about the potential for abuse of marketing dominance and systemic financial risks as reasons for not allowing cryptocurrency in Europe. He announced that the French government refused to authorise the development 'on the European soil'. He continued to state that 'the monetary sovereignty of states is at stake. Any failure in the functioning of this currency, in the management of its reserves could create considerable financial disorders'. One of the major fears around the Libra is that it replaces the national currency in states where the currency is weak or experiencing a strong devaluation. There are also substantial fears that cryptocurrency escapes control over the financing of terrorism. In early August 2019, a joint statement by several regulators in charge of personal data protection, in the US, Europe, the UK, Canada and Australia, summoned the social network to give guarantees in this area. The EU's competition authority subsequently begun investigating Libra, fearing 'possible impediments to competition'. From a political standpoint, the United States House Committee on Financial Services Committee asked Facebook to halt the development and launch of Libra, citing a list of recent scandals and that 'the cryptocurrency market currently lacks a clear regulatory framework'. Further, the US House Committee on Financial Services

Democrats later sent a letter to Facebook asking the company to stop development of Libra, citing concerns of privacy, national security, trading, and monetary policy. In one of the most damning attacks on the planned cryptocurrency, Jerome Powell, chair of the Federal Reserve, testified before Congress on 10 July 2019 that the Federal Reserve had 'serious concerns' as to how Libra would deal with 'money laundering, consumer protection and financial stability'. It would be very much considered that the project, even after substantial development will face considerable opposition at all stages prior to establishment and throughout the process international regulatory alignment.

3.3 Venezuela and the Petro

In mid-December 2018, the Venezuelan economy is estimated by the IMF to have exceeded 1,000,000% price inflation, otherwise identified as hyperinflation, combined with a premium of approximately 2,500% between its official currency, the bolivar, and a black-market exchange rate that has been thriving under the influence of those with access to the official rate at source. Throughout 2018, the Venezuelan government under the leadership of President Nicolas Maduro have established a number of routes through which they could reduce the burden of economic collapse. Primarily, a new sovereign bolivar (bolivar soberano) was identified to replace the old bolivar (bolivar fuerte) at a conversion rate of 100,000:1, indicating that 100,000 old bolivars was the equivalent of US$1.5 cent.[2] Other countries with high levels of inflation, like Zimbabwe and Ecuador, have escaped by adopting the dollar, which would most likely be politically unacceptable for Mr Maduro's regime. Zimbabwe pegged their economy to the US dollar when citizens refused to accept payments in the local currency. In Venezuela, which deprives people of access to dollars more effectively than did Zimbabwe (noting that the Zimbabwean economy underwent four rounds of redenomination and the printing of the $100 trillion bill before resorting to building a new currency), people could switch from the bolivar to the Petro.

This innovative product aimed at restructuring the Venezuelan economy was launched in February 2018 through the Petro, indicative of a cryptocurrency that would be supported 'by oil assets and issued by the Venezuelan State as a spearhead for the development of an independent, transparent and open digital economy open to direct participation of citizens'. The associated product white-paper[3] states that

2 We must note that the greatest level of hyperinflation was identified in Hungary, where the daily inflation rate reached 207% in July of 1946, leading to a currency reform on August 1, 1946. The Pengo was replaced by the Forint, and the conversion rate was 400 octillion Pengo to one Forint.

3 Available at: https://www.petro.gob.ve/

> *Venezuelan oil assets will be used to promote the adoption of crypto assets and technologies based on the country's block-chain. ... The Venezuelan population will have at their reach a technology that will allow them having a valuable reserve and robust means of payment to stimulate savings and contribute to the country's development. Petro will be an instrument for Venezuela's economic stability and financial independence, coupled with an ambitious and global vision for the creation of a freer, more balanced and fairer international financial system.*

The base price of the Petro was denoted at one barrel of oil. The link to oil is no more convincing. The Petro is not yet itself exchangeable for oil. It is simply backed by a government's guarantee that it is backed by oil. The very creation, advertisement and distribution of such a currency during a period of exceptional economic strife generated substantial concern about the credibility of this ground-breaking sovereign asset. The Petro's pre-sale to investors began on 20 February 2018, where 38.4 million tokens were made available until 19 March 2018. The Venezuelan government stated that US$3.3 billion was raised through the sale but this has yet to be independently verified. We must also note that one of the very characteristics of a cryptocurrency is that it be free of government intervention, explicitly decentralised from central bank authority.

The introduction of the Petro is quite similar to the German government's decision to introduce the Rentenmark to stem the growth of hyperinflation during the 1920s. The Rentemark was made stable through the backing of property used for agriculture and business, tangible products through which the German population could hold as security to underpin the value of the Papiermark. This is one of the key differences when observing the Petro and it's underlying fulcrum. Without explicit backing, this product is simply driven by unsupported market sentiment, offering little for a population desperate for economic stability. Although not the first Venezuelan cryptocurrency, products such as Bolivarcoin, Onixcoin, Rilcoin and Perlacoin have preceded Petro, however, each have had little purchase internationally. When initially announced in December 2017 by President Maduro, one major concern was identified in this new cryptocurrency's ability to circumvent US sanctions that had been implemented on the Venezuelan economy and their ability to access international financing. Officials of Iran and Russia have said their governments might be interested in issuing cryptocurrencies. The Marshall Islands announced that it would issue one, called the sovereign, that it will accept as legal tender. The Marshall Islands is a dollarised economy; a second currency would give it at least the illusion of greater control over its money. Iran and Russia are subject to American sanctions. The one common theme throughout these envisaged planned cryptocurrencies is a non-standard relationship between these countries and the economy of the United States. The US Department of the Treasury have explicitly warned that investor's partaking in the initial coin offering of Petro would be in breach of such sanctions that have been imposed on countries such as Venezuela.

The ethical underpinning that supports the generation of the Petro is somewhat opaque. A number of rating agencies, international economists and news agencies have all stated that this product is nothing more than a scam and a product to circumvent restrictions while providing false hope to a desperate population. The project has been identified as missing critical information, from the description of the mechanism to its technology and supposed oil-backing. The underlying technology supporting the product has been broadly challenged and has throughout 2018 changed substantially from that information provided in the Petro's original white-paper. The principal platform for the coin is NEM, where accounts are anonymous, but can disclose their identities in the description of their coins if they wish. The Venezuelan government issued 82.4 million tokens from an NEM account in March 2018 described as preliminary coins. The product has continued to evolve as a product who's underlying structure remains fluid, but this is not a unique selling point, in fact, it would raise fears that there is a strong theme of desperation from economic collapse at the foundations of the necessity for this outlier sovereign product designed specifically to 'petrolise' salaries and prices. The Petro has also continued to obtain support from a number of international exchanges. Hong Kong-based Bitfinex, one of the world's largest exchanges by volume, in March said it never intended to list the Petro due to its 'limited utility.' The only exchange that has publicly discussed plans to list the Petro is India's Coinsecure. As of late 2018, the product remains un-traded. The technology behind the coin is said to be in development while nobody has been able to make use of the Petro despite claims of substantial investment at the time of the ICO. Further, a number of international journalist who have contacted the Venezuelan government for comment remain unanswered while the Superintendence's website is unresponsive. In August 2018, President Maduro announced that salaries, pensions and the exchange rate for the bolivar would be pegged to the Petro, thereby underpinning the economy to the simplistic assumption that one barrel of oil (priced at approximately $66 at the time that this peg had taken place, backed with crude oil reserves located in a 380-square-kilometre area surrounding Atapirire[4]) is equivalent to one Petro. This statement and the precarious nature of this sovereign cryptocurrency presented a strong signal of the desperation that had now taken over, that a government would simply rest their economic future (although already bleak) on an exceptionally high-risk, high-volatility, untested, unverified and most likely illegal product.

3.4 KodakCoin and other examples of corporate manoeuvres

On the 9 of January 2018, camera manufacturer Kodak announced that it was entering the cryptocurrency market through the creation of KODAKOne, described as

4 To date, there is no evidence of oil accumulation at this site.

a revolutionary new image rights management and protection platform secured in the blockchain. Kodak announced that its development seamlessly registers, manages and monetises creative assets for the photographic community (Corbet et al. (2019)). It would be used to underpin the assured buying and selling of rights-cleared and protected digital assets while ensuring transparency. The announcement had a significant sharp impact on volatility (which peaked at over 60% per day) with shares increasing from over $3 per share to over $12 in less than one week. This was associated with an increase in market sentiment and research using terms such as 'Kodak' and 'KODAKCoin'. Kodak CEO Jeff Clarke said in a press statement, 'For many in the technology industry, 'blockchain' and 'cryptocurrency' are hot buzzwords, but for photographers who've long struggled to assert control over their work and how it's used, these buzzwords are the keys to solving what felt like an unsolvable problem.' In theory, photographers will be able to upload their images to a platform called KodakOne, create a blockchain-based license for each image, and use web-crawling software to scour the Internet looking for copyright violations. Instead of using dollars, photographers can have clients pay them in KODAKCoins. However, there are many analysts and market-commentators alike that continue to identify Kodak's strategy as a technique to capitalise on the current cryptocurrency frenzy or is it indeed a valid evolutionary characteristic of blockchain.

The results provided by Corbet et al. (2019) indicate a substantial and sustained increase in return volatility in the period after the announcement of Kodak's intention to create a cryptocurrency. Such announcements can potentially take advantage of the euphoric and speculative investment motives that have been inflating what some consider to be a significant bubble in cryptocurrency markets. Announcements without strong supporting evidence can present an channel through which speculative contagion can flow from cryptocurrency markets to equity markets. The definition provided by the US Securities and Exchange Commission for a 'pump-and-dump' specifically comes to mind, that often occur on the Internet where it is common to see messages posted that urge readers to buy a stock quickly or to sell before the price goes down, or a telemarketer will call using the same sort of pitch. Often the promoters will claim to have 'inside' information about an impending development or to use an 'infallible' combination of economic and stock market data to pick stocks. In reality, they may be company insiders or paid promoters who stand to gain by selling their shares after the stock price is 'pumped' up by the buying frenzy they create. Once these fraudsters 'dump' their shares and stop hyping the stock, the price typically falls, and investors lose their money. These 'sudden' cryptocurrency announcements have also attracted the attention of regulators. Jay Clayton, the chairman of the Securities and Exchange Commission (SEC), said that the agency was 'looking closely at the disclosures of public companies that shift their business models to capitalise on the perceived promise of distributed ledger technology.' However, Kodak then decided to delay the ICO of KODAKCoin in an attempt to verify accredited status of approximately 40,000 potential investors. The SEC requires that an individual accredited investor has a net worth that exceeds $1 million, or an annual income of at least $200,000, along with other conditions. The company claims it needs 'several weeks' to verify the 'accredited investors' status of those who applied to invest in the ICO. Potential investors from outside the US would then be considered in accordance with their local jurisdictions. But one key point that can be taken from the case of Kodak is that it's price, two months later, remained elevated by almost 100% of that from early January 2018. Even without the implementation of an ICO, the announcement of a cryptocurrency related plan has potentially incorporated any cryptocurrency speculation into the share price of a publicly traded company. This is a point of concern for regulators and policy-makers alike.

While Kodak provide an example of a company that has attempted to incorporate cryptocurrency into their non-cryptocurrency-related business practices, there have also been a number of companies that have gone one-step further and attempted to change their names to identify as a cryptocurrency-related company. This is even more astonishing as some of these companies for the most-part had no prior interaction with any form of IT or technological development. In a detailed analysis investigating both the financial market effects and the theoretical grounding or indeed ethical support surrounding such decisions, Akyildirim et al. (2019) found that thirty-one companies are identified to have partaken in 'crypto-exuberant' naming behaviour. In 2015 and 2016, there are only two companies, NXChain and First Bitcoin Capital that change their names, previous known as AgriVest Americas and Grand Paracaraima Gold respectively. In 2017, there are twelve companies who then change their names, and eleven in 2018. When comparing the companies who had partaken in crypto-exuberant company announcements, those who have utilised cryptocurrency and blockchain when naming are found to have on average higher returns, yet more volatile returns with mean returns of –0.0081% and a standard deviation of 5.1575%. Further, such companies exhibit far more substantial extreme returns (where evidence is provided of one-day price decreases of 52.8% and increases of 57.7% when compared to –15.9% and 16.9% in non-cryptocurrency companies respectively), further associated with skewness and kurtosis in excess of three times that of other non-cryptocurrency-based company names. Such a result indicates that companies that partake in the use of cryptocurrency-based naming practices are found to be substantially riskier shares to purchase when compared to other companies that have changed their corporate name for other types of reasons.

Quite incredibly, there have also been two companies who have actually changed their name twice, in both cases from a non-crypto-exuberant name to a crypto-exuberant name and then back again. In August 2018, Focused Capital II Corp announced its intention on the TSX Venture Exchange to change its name to Fortress Blockchain Corp, clearly positioning its corporate identity to be further associated with the growing blockchain and cryptocurrency markets. During this transaction, the company issued 71.2 million common shares and signalled its intention to begin trading on the TSXV under the ticker 'FORT'. In a largely unanticipated move, in

April 2019, Fortress Blockchain then applied to the TSX Venture Exchange to change its name to Fortress Technologies Inc while continuing to use the same ticker. This situation is the only identified case within the dataset of a company retracting on its decision to partake in crypto-exuberant behaviour. However, Long Island Iced Tea Corp. remains as one of the most famous companies to employ a crypto-exuberant naming strategy when changing their corporate identity to Long Blockchain Corp in 2017. The stock price then sharply increased almost 300% stating that it was 'shifting its primary corporate focus' from tea to distributed-ledger technology. In 2019, it has been announced through warrants in the United States that the FBI is looking for evidence of insider trading and securities fraud connected to Long Island Iced Tea stock, where two men related to a separate company, were arrested for securities fraud. There have also been broad accusations about the presence of a 'pump-and-dump' scheme, where promoters buy a cheap stock, start hyping it to investors with eye-catching claims, then sell their own holdings during the resulting mania, hopefully securing a profit before the stock comes crashing down. Based on a number of text messages that the FBI have since uncovered, they are interested in a person known as 'Eric W' in a series of messages, where the accused person owned approximately 15% of the shares in Long Island Iced Tea at the time that the company's name was changed. There is further investigation into the use of an investor relations program to develop hype around the company during this time. Riot Blockchain has also been investigated throughout 2018 and 2019 by the SEC. It had previously changed its name from Bioptix, where its previous business practices was based on the development of veterinary products patent and developing new ways to test for disease.

4 How has the regulation of ICOs changed over time?

While clearly portraying evidence of the multiple issues that the market for ICOs have experienced in recent times, including that of moral hazard, adverse selection, insider trading and market manipulation amongst others, and the very fact that participants have been continuously proven to have acted out outside existing regulatory frameworks, have caused much distrust within the broad ICO market. In many cases there was an absence of due diligence, standardised financial reporting, prospectuses containing the main risk factors of the company and its businesses and broad corporate governance. Instead, many fund providers to these projects released whitepapers with poor information, in some cases omitting the name of the company or its address, however, focusing on marketing techniques, even in some cases using celebrities in an almost tactical capacity to distract investors. The first responses from national regulators around the world focused on warnings and guidance while providing thorough investigations with reports and outright bans (such as that seen in China in September 2017). Most regulators would agree that although ICOs are currently not governed by specific regulations, the broad practices of many ICOs might already fall under existing legal and jurisdictional coverage. Recently, it has been discussed that some ICOs might actually be contained within the scope of regulation focused on Initial Public Offerings (IPOs), private placement of securities, crowdfunding or even collective investment schemes.

The development and growing sophistication of international regulatory scrutiny has somewhat alarmed cryptocurrency entrepreneurs. In the past, the rapidly expanding ICO landscape resembled a free for all, where the most talented and knowledgeable appear to have been taking funds from the most vulnerable who were seeking quick profit. The negative media coverage on cryptocurrency criminality has most certainly attracted the attention of regulatory authorities. The effect of increased scrutiny by authorities has been to multiply regulatory barriers for entrepreneurs aspiring to begin an ICO. However, this has generated some confusion. There has been considerable controversy over the status of utility tokens, which require fewer disclosure forms and checks from the SEC and which are favoured by most startups opting for an ICO. The SEC were seen to have adequately forewarned cryptocurrency startups when asserted that most ICO tokens would require greater disclosure, the first time that the commission had clarified its stance regarding ICOs. The increased level of regulation for a security token sale appears to have made ICOs costlier while taking more time as compared to an ICO for utility tokens, where the average cost is estimated to be between $1 million and $3 million for a security token sale. Private sales to accredited investors also shift costs of conducting a public ICO. Entrepreneurs have increasingly begun issuing a bonus (or discount) on their tokens to private investors.

When the SEC released the 'Framework for Investment Contract Analysis of Digital Assets' in April 2019, many in the cryptocurrency community were unhappy with the broad definition which the SEC applied to securities, which left little room for true utility tokens. Initial Exchange Offerings (IEOs) have been another area in which regulators and cryptocurrency innovators have recently developed contrasting opinions. The largest concerns for the users of cryptocurrencies has been the security as a multitude of hacking events have generated many negative reverberations throughout the industry. It is against this backdrop that more regulatory oversight has become necessary.

Regulators must also continue to monitor the growth of online casinos, who have somewhat recently revolutionised the world of gambling through the use of cryptocurrency in online casinos. It is now possible to gamble using Bitcoin amongst other cryptocurrencies, which had been found to improve the security of your gambling experience. More online casinos have started accepting cryptocurrency in a bid to attract younger players, which further provides an anonymous playing experience and improve the transaction processes. This also generates widespread issues with regards to the taxation and cross-border monitoring of fund flows and has been identified one of the trends that has contributed to the immense growth of the online gambling industry.

5 Concluding comments

In this chapter, we provide a thorough account of the key issues that have engulfed the ICO market in recent years, somewhat stifling the growth of illicit cryptocurrency auctions, but further failing to eliminate the issue completely. A central theme throughout these listed issues and examples surrounds substantial damage to credibility within the market. We have observed cases of theft at the level of the exchange, within the whitepapers that have been provided, through the usage of celebrities to support marketing tactics, through the illegal cross-jurisdictional transfer of funds and indeed, the most simplest form of theft, where the ICO counter-party quite simply disappears with the accumulated assets of investors. While cryptocurrency-enthusiasts continue to promote the positive attributes that support the potential growth of this new investment asset, the same proponents cannot ignore that this entire sector has been rampant with levels and styles of fraudulent behaviour that is quite difficult to find in other international markets of similar scale and scope. But there have been significant positive developments in terms of the future scope of international regulation and the potential to eliminate fraudulent behaviour. It is essential that during the continued growth of the sector for cryptocurrencies that regulation, including a broad international set of standards, be developed and maintained to grow at pace with the market for cryptocurrencies. It is essential that regulations must compare effectively with the sophistication of the market that they attempt to monitor. Until the broad gap between regulation and the capacity for cryptocurrency market misuse is diminished, there will continue to be substantial and frequent loss of investor assets through mechanisms that represent those usually observed in an exceptionally juvenile market.

Bibliography

Adhami, S., G. Giudici, and S. Martinazzi (2018). Why do businesses go crypto? an empirical analysis of initial coin offerings. *Journal of Economics and Business 100*, 64–75.

Akhtaruzzaman, M., A. Sensoy, and S. Corbet (2019). The influence of bitcoin on portfolio diversification and design. *Finance Research Letters*.

Akyildirim, E., S. Corbet, A. Sensoy, and L. Yarovaya (2019). How has the intention to incorporate blockchain technology affected information asymmetry and the transparency of corporations? Available at SSRN.

Barone, R. and D. Masciandaro (2019). Cryptocurrency or usury? crime and alternative money laundering techniques. *European Journal of Law and Economics 47*(2), 233–254.

Celeste, V., S. Corbet, and C. Gurdgiev (2019). Fractal dynamics and wavelet analysis: Deep volatility and return properties of bitcoin, ethereum and ripple. *Quarterly Review of Economics and Finance*.

Chen, K. (2019). Information asymmetry in initial coin offerings (ICOs): Investigating the effects of multiple channel signals. *Electronic Commerce Research and Applications 36*.

Cohney, S., D. Hoffman, J. Sklaroff, and D. Wishnick (2019). Coin-operated capitalism. *Columbia Law Review 119*(3), 591–676.

Cooper, M., O. Dimitrov, and P. Rau (2001). A Rose.com by any other name. *Journal of Finance 56*, 2371–2387.

Corbet, S., V. Eraslan, B. Lucey, and A. Sensoy (2019). The effectiveness of technical trading rules in cryptocurrency markets. *Finance Research Letters 31*, 32–37.

Corbet, S. and P. Katsiampa (2018). Asymmetric mean reversion of bitcoin price returns. *International Review of Financial Analysis* https://doi.org/10.1016/j.irfa.2018.10.004.

Corbet, S., C. Larkin, B. Lucey, A. Meegan, and L. Yarovaya (2020). Cryptocurrency reaction to fomc announcements: Evidence of heterogeneity based on blockchain stack position. *Journal of Financial Stability* 46.

Corbet, S., C. Larkin, B. Lucey, and L. Yarovaya (2019). KodakCoin: a blockchain revolution or exploiting a potential cryptocurrency bubble? *Applied Economics Letters*, 1–7.

Corbet, S., B. Lucey, M. Peat, and S. Vigne (2018). Bitcoin futures – what use are they? *Economics Letters 172*, 23–27.

Corbet, S., B. Lucey, A. Urquhart, and L. Yarovaya (2019). Cryptocurrencies as a financial asset: A systematic analysis. *International Review of Financial Analysis 62*, 182–199.

Corbet, S., B. Lucey, and L. Yarovaya (2018). Datestamping the Bitcoin and Ethereum bubbles. *Finance Research Letters 26*, 81–88.

Corbet, S., A. Meegan, C. Larkin, B. Lucey, and L. Yarovaya (2018). Exploring the dynamic relationships between cryptocurrencies and other financial assets. *Economics Letters 165*, 28–34.

Deng, H., R. Huang, and Q. Wu (2018). The regulation of initial coin offerings in china: Problems, prognoses and prospects. *European Business Organization Law Review 19*(3), 465–502.

Felix, T. and H. von Eije (2019). Underpricing in the cryptocurrency world: evidence from initial coin offerings. *Managerial Finance 45*(4), 563–578.

Fisch, C. (2019). Initial coin offerings (icos) to finance new ventures. *Journal of Business Venturing 34*(1), 1–22.

Foley, S., J. R. Karlsen, and T. J. Putnins (2019). Sex, drugs, and Bitcoin: How much illegal activity is financed through cryptocurrencies? *Review of Financial Studies 32*, 1789–1853.

Gandal, N., J. Hamrick, T. Moore, and T. Oberman (2018). Price manipulation in the Bitcoin ecosystem. *Journal of Monetary Economics 95*, 86–96.

Griffins, J. and A. Shams (2018). Is Bitcoin really un-Tethered. *SSRN Working Paper*.

Hashemi Joo, M., Y. Nishikawa, and K. Dandapani (2019). ICOs, the next generation of IPOs. *Managerial Finance*.

Huang, W., M. Meoli, and S. Vismara (2019). The geography of initial coin offerings. *Small Business Economics*.

Katsiampa, P., S. Corbet, and B. Lucey (2019). Volatility spillover effects in leading cryptocurrencies: A Bekk-Mgarch analysis. *Finance Research Letters 29*, 68–74.

Lahajnar, S. and A. Rozanec (2018). Initial coin offering (ICO) evaluation model. *Investment Management and Financial Innovations 15*(4), 169–182.

Nakamoto, S. (2008). *Bitcoin: A peer-to-peer electronic cash system*.

Nguyen, T., B. Nguyen, T. Nguyen, and Q. Nguyen (2019). Bitcoin return: Impacts from the introduction of new altcoins. *Research in International Business and Finance 48*, 420–425.

O'Dair, M. and R. Owen (2019). Financing new creative enterprise through blockchain technology: Opportunities and policy implications. *Strategic Change 28*(1), 9–17.

Thomas A. Hulme

The ethical and legal aspects of blockchain technology and cryptoassets

1 Introduction

Cryptoassets have been in existence since circa 2008 when Bitcoin ("BTC") was created. Since then, the law with respect to cryptoassets and smart contracts have not been tested as merely not enough consumers and businesses were dealing with them; fast-forward to the end of 2017, and the price per 1 BTC was circa $20,000.

Two years later, at the end of 2019, the cryptoasset market is now testing, particularly legal principles due to the volume of business and wealth concerning this market. Infrastructure exists to facilitate the storage and trading of cryptoassets; further, smart contracts and derivative contracts exist to allow faster transfer of wealth and to speculate on the price of any given cryptoasset. Moreover, there are hundreds if not thousands of cryptoassets, with more being created each month. The cryptoasset market has grown, and it is now at the point where businesses and consumers are unsure where they stand with respect to this new asset. In particular, what rights these new assets have and further concerns with respect to the business activities they are carrying out and the clarity to understand if they are applicable to their business. Examples of theft cases, less-than-ethical businesses practices, money laundering concerns and consumer protection concerns are all factors which have contributed to organisations such as the Financial Conduct Authority ("FCA") and Her Majesty's Revenue & Customs ("HMRC") to investigate and provide guidance. Furthermore, we are seeing more civil cases enter and proceed through the commercial courts of England and Wales, which implies the value of claim any given claimant is seeking, is substantial enough for it to warrant issuing a claim with the courts.

2 Previous literature

Literature concerning blockchain technology and cryptoassets generally speaking has increased since the rise in the price of BTC in 2017. With respect to the law, literature has been scarce, to say the least. However; there are some notable publications from particularly individuals and government bodies which have shed some light on the approach of government and the applicability of existing laws.

Leigh Sagar is a practising barrister of England and Wales and wrote a book called *The Digital Estate*, published in 2018; this book examines the law concerning (inter alia) digital assets and cryptoassets and seeks to provide clarification on the rights and practical considerations in relation to these new assets. It is very much a practice guide

https://doi.org/10.1515/9783110660807-008

for those lawyers who wish to understand more the rights and remedies associated with (inter alia) cryptoassets.

Turning to other types of literature, in November 2019 the Lawtech Delivery Panel released a statement named *Legal statement on cryptoassets and smart contracts*. The Lawtech Delivery Panel is a group arranged by The Law Society of England and Wales to explore the ongoing technological changes in the legal industry. This statement considers the key and most topical points which are legally pertinent. Those points being the law of property and the applicability of cryptoassets, and further, smart contracts. This publication was key in the progression of the legal industry dealing with these new conceptual assets, of which, characteristics have not been tested in the law previously. The Financial Conduct Authorities *Guidance on Cryptoassets* published in January 2019. This guidance was written after an initial statement published by the FCA and public consultation to the public and appropriate professionals. This guidance seeks to clarify the FCA's position with respect to finance law, specifically the Financial Services and Markets Act 2000. The guidance sets out different types of cryptoassets and applies them to the appropriate laws.

Some more academic papers have been written, reviewing the regulatory framework with respect to cryptoassets, one of which is Global Cryptoasset Regulatory Landscape Study released in May 2019 by the University of Cambridge Faculty of Law research. The paper seeks to review the regulatory measure implemented by different jurisdictions and the challenges each jurisdiction faces with respect to the actives being conducted. In 2018 Kevin Warbach wrote Trust, but Verify: Why the Blockchain Needs the Law, a publication reviewed the practical consequences of implanting blockchain technology into existing systems and the consequences that will have on the law, as a result of smart contracts, and systems and contract which do not need enforcing.

3 Blockchain technology and cryptoassets

3.1 What is blockchain

Blockchain is the name given to a piece of software, coded in a particular way. The key characteristic of a blockchain system is the implantation of an abstract process of data storage. Typically programs will store data on the running computer hard drive, or a hard drive which the computer running the program is connected with, on the Internet; the source of data is from a single hard drive. When a piece of software is created implementing blockchain systems, the data of a piece of software is stored in several hard drives, simultaneously.

Creating software in this way has a profound effect on the data; in that, once the data is within any particular system, it can not be amended or deleted. In order to distinguish between typical software and blockchain software, an example is set out below.

When one creates a document which contains words, on any particular word processing software, one can save the document as a file on the hard drive of the computer the software is installed. Alternatively, one may wish to save it on a hard drive in a data centre, or a "cloud". Further, one may wish to save the document at each of those places. Each place where the file is saved, the file can be amended or deleted. One could make an amendment of the cloud file and save it. If one wanted to continue working from that document, one would have to access the file stored on the cloud, not on the hard drive of the computer. More importantly, if the cloud then corrupts, the file is lost. If the type of data storage was blockchain based, one would need to ensure that the computer hard drive is part of the blockchain network. Once the file is saved on the computer, it will simultaneously be saved on all hard drives that are part of that particular blockchain system. If the computer was destroyed, the same file would be accessible. Further, another party would not be able to delete or amend the document.

3.2 What are cryptoassets

Cryptoassets are a strange concept. They are not tangible property which is easily identifiable and which we can physically pass to each other. They are not intellectual property ("IP") (although there will inherently be IP in the software code which creates cryptoasset through the utilisation to blockchain technology). They have been likened to currency; however, the consensus is that it is not currency (perhaps currently). Previous chapters in this book will no doubt discuss the principles of money in more significant detail and apply them to the current cryptoasset landscape. Cryptoassets are a generic name for the existence of a log created as a result of the running of a program which utilises the concept of blockchain technology. A blockchain program can be designed and used for purposes other than creating cryptoassets; however, the characteristics of cryptoassets are likely to be contained within the program.

Blockchain technology is a concept applied to the software which creates a ledger. Inputting data into the ledger containing numbers creates a ledger of a numerical account. If the software enables more than an account to exist and the theoretical transfer of numeric data from one account to another, you have two accounts in the blockchain transferring numbers. The concept of digital accounts that record numbers is not new and is currently used widely by banks. When one signs into their online banking, they will see their account with numbers, these numbers represent the monetary value which the bank owes you. There will be a ledger of sorts behind the figures one sees on a banks database. These numbers can, however, be altered manually by one who has access to the software; an account can read £100 and then for someone with access to accidentally or purposefully add an addition "0" at the end.

The account will then have £1,000 within it; this is because these numbers are just a log to make sure the bank (and we) know how much they owe us.

Returning to blockchain systems; this ledger is different from typical ledgers (such as the ones a bank would typically use) because the data is stored simultaneously on blocks. This has the effect that the data within the ledger can not unilaterally be manipulated as the software requires each block to agree and confirm any change. This creates a system where a finite amount of numbers exist in a ledger (depending on how the software is written); this brings a sense of permanence to the numbers. These numbers and entries in the ledger are used and called Cryptoassets. Similarly, the data in numbers can be replaced by other data, such as word, patents etc. and this is the permanence element of blockchain systems.

A typical Cryptoasset ledger will typically contain a set amount of numbers, (or cryptoassets). Alternatively, the program will have an additional software layer which enables users to access the open-source blockchain software to join it and become part of the blockchain; as a result, further cryptoassets can be created, or "mined".

In conclusion, a cryptoasset is a piece of data which can only be created on a blockchain system. Characteristics of a cryptoasset are (but are not limited to) that they can be accessed by using a public key (to direct one to the particular blockchain), a private key which will allow one to deal with the cryptoassets and finally, that any given cryptoasset is unique. A cryptoasset can not be copied, deleted or manipulated; it has a sense of permanence.

3.3 What are smart contracts

As an element of security is provided by way of the blockchain technology systems, smart contracts have been created. A smart contract is a piece of software which has the terms and typically the enforceability of the terms, built within the code of the piece of software. This could operate outside of the blockchain area; however, security would be an issue if blockchain wasn't used. A smart contract could be in the form of a cryptoasset which can be sent and exchanged. That cryptoasset may have the term built within it that on a particular date, it will send instructions to its own software, to create another cryptoasset and send it to whichever wallet it currently exists in.

The purpose of a smart contract is to enable two parties to interact with security and without the fear that the other party may not fulfil their obligation. The reason for that is because the obligations are held within the contract and outside of the control of either party.

4 The law

The law of England and Wales consists and is created in several different ways. Firstly, there is common law which comes from disputes being heard at court, and a particular legal principle being drawn from it. Secondly, there is legislation which is passed through parliament. Lastly, there is law which comes from the European Union ("EU"), which is either a Regulation, Directive or Decision. A Regulation is a piece of legislation which all EU members must adhere to, as it is written. A Directive is a broad set of guidelines; each member state must following and implement by their own legislation. A Decision is a law which is directed and specific member states. Although the UK is no longer a member state, they will still be subject to certain EU laws, unless they are repealed.

Blockchain technology itself is a concept and therefore, not broadly subject to any law. Therefore, this part of the chapter will only review cryptoassets.

4.1 Different types and current use of cryptoassets

Theoretically and conceptually, blockchain technology and cryptoassets could be utilised for an incredibly broad range of commercial and general purposes. Within this chapter, I will only mention what I suggest are the current uses and loosely defined types of cryptoasset. The FCA has released to sets of cryptoasset guidance and has (broadly) provided for five different types:

1. Exchange Tokens
2. Utility Tokens
3. Security Tokens
4. E-money Tokens
5. Unregulated Tokens

4.1.1 Exchange Tokens

Exchange tokens are Cryptoassets such as BTC which have a permanence to them; however, do not represent anything. They simply exist. Derivatives of BTC exist such as Litecoin ("LTC") and Bitcoin Cash ("BCH"), and they have similar qualities, although they are not the same as BTC. These tokens are unregulated by the FCA.

4.1.2 Utility Tokens

I liken Utility Tokens to a credit one can possess in a shop. They are like Exchange Tokens in a sense they do not represent anything; they can, however, be used or traded in exchange for something else. During the ICO boom, the majority of the Cryptoassets which were created were Utility Tokens. An organisation (typically a tech start-up) would create a limited number of Cryptoassets which can then be sold for other Cryptoassets or FIAT currency. The organisation would then have equity to funds its business. In the event, their product or service comes to market, those who bought the native Cryptoassets or Token of the start-up would be able to use the Token to purchase or use whatever the product or service us.

These tokens are generally unregulated by the FCA. However, these tokens may possess other qualities which make them akin to E-Money.

4.1.3 Security Tokens

Security Tokens provide a right or obligation in relation to a Specified Investments. An example of this is a Cryptoasset which represents, or mirrors the characteristics of (inter alia) a share, bond or debt contract. These Cryptoassets are regulated and fall within the Financial Services and Markets Act 2000 and fall within the remit of the FCA.

4.1.4 E-money Tokens

E-Money Tokens are such tokens which act like E-Money. E-Money is something set out in the Electronic Money Regulation ("EMR") and which is regulated by the FCA. An E-Money Token is one which meets the characteristics of E-Money:

1. electronically stored a monetary value that represents a claim on the issuer;
2. issued on receipt of funds for the purpose of making payment transactions;
3. accepted by a person other than the issuer; and
4. it is not excluded by regulation 3 of the EMRs.

Example. *I create 100 "E-Money Cryptoassets" ("EMC") of which each is worth £1.00.*

A consumer approaches me and purchases 50 EMC for £50.00. That consumer can then redeem the 50 EMC for £50.

Not only can the consumer trade 50 EMC with me, but their local shop also accepts the EMC. The consumer purchases a product from the shop for 25 EMC. The shop can then approach me and redeem the 25 EMC for £25.

An essential factor is that I, the issuer, have contracted that anyone in "possession" of the EMC can redeem it through me.

4.1.5 Unregulated Tokens

This is a broad general categorisation which includes Cryptoassets such as BTC. As long as a Cryptoasset is not regulated like the above, for the FCA, they are not regulated.

It is convenient to note at this point that just because a Cryptoasset does not fall within the definition or E-Money or is a regulated asset for the above purposes; that does not mean that it is not regulated at all. Laws will generally apply, and the above definitions are provided by the FCA and are specific to financial regulation as that has been the most common use of cryptoassets at this point in time.

One of the most poignant laws is the Proceeds of Crime Act 2002 ("POCA"), which applies to assets generally and sets out the legislative scheme for the recovery of criminal assets. As the majority of cryptoassets are untraceable to a person and they have been synonymous with illegal activity, POCA will apply to cryptoassets. This chapter will not specifically detail this piece of legislation, however.

4.2 The rights over cryptoassets

Cryptoassets have become increasingly popular and used for multiple reasons. Further, the value associated with them can be quite significant; take BTC, for example with a current price of circa $8,000. With such value being placed upon them, certainty about rights and obligations must be provided and understood. This is especially important as Cryptoassets are mostly a new form of "property"; it has the characteristics of actual property in that they are unique. However, they also have similar features of Intellectual Property, information or data.

Cryptoassets are being used to store vast amounts of wealth, transfer the wealth associated with an asset from one entity to another and used to purchase real products, such as real property, cars or a bottle of water. Therefore, if one posses a Cryptoasset and relies on an implied right, those rights must be, in fact, the legal rights one has over property if it is in fact, property.

Property in terms of law is not property as one may understand it to be. Property is a recognised term in law and has been developed in common law and legislatively. There are different classes of legal property, which result in different rights associated with those properties and also a variety of separate legislation.

The law and the courts of England and Wales are used to enforce a legal right that one has over a thing. If a piece of land belongs to a person legally, in the event another person attempts to assume a right over the said property (physically by taking possession or by way of conduct by attempting to sell the property, for example), I can apply to the courts to recognise my rights over a property. The courts will order that actions are carried out which recognise my right over the property.

If Cryptoassets are not defined as a class of property in law, in the event that one needs or wants to enforce their right over property (for example ones Cryptoasset was stolen and I want to retrieve them back) the court may not have jurisdiction to order an action to facilitate the return of the property.

4.3 Law of property

In typical situations, the classification of something being property is not a thought that would cross one's mind. If I sell a car, there is no dispute that a vehicle is a piece of personal property. If I have legal title over a vehicle and it is stolen, or I enter into a contract which I want to remind (and I have the legal right to do so), the courts have jurisdiction to deal with the car as a piece of property. They can place a freezing order over it or alternatively an order for delivery, for example.

IP is another form of property, which is intangible, however laws and infrastructure has developed to accommodate this form; such as the ability to register certain forms of IP. The rights that IP have can, therefore, be enforced through the courts; they recognise a right over the IP. If I have a registered piece of IP and someone appropriates or uses it, I can enforce my right through the courts.

The concept of property, in law, comes from the piece of legislation which is the Law of Property Act 1925 which defines property as "*anything in action, and any interest in real or personal property*". Thereafter, the nature of the rights associated with the property was considered by Lord Wilberforce in the case of National Provincial Bank v Ainsworth. Lord Wilberforce stated that a property **right** was "definable, identifiable by third parties, capable in its nature of assumption by third parties, and [must] have some degree of permanence or stability.". Common law (a type of law derived from heard cases of which legal principles arise) defines personal property as one of two categories:

1. a chose in possession; or
2. a chose in action

A chose in possession is a tangible object, such as a car. It can be seen, touched and identified.

A chose in action is a right to a possession, which can be, enforced by legal action such as a debt or the money in one's bank account.

Although the majority of Cryptoassets are definable, identifiable by third parties and has some degree of stability, they are not tangible. Further, they are not pieces of

IP (however it is possible that IP can be registered or written into the code of a cryptoasset by way of implementation on blockchain systems).

4.4 Are cryptoassets property?

If one "owns" 10 BTC, worth circa $80,000 and one were transacting with another party with the broad terms that one will purchase an object for 10 BTC. 10 BTC is transferred to another party, and they give me the possession of the object. However, on delivery of the object, it is not the object that was agreed upon. If I exchange cash (as a chose in possession) or execute a bank transfer (a chose in action), I can apply to the court to claim damages or execute a right to return the property. If BTC is not property, nor is it IP, what right or action can one bring to take possession of it?

There have been two known judgments from the courts of England and Wales which consider the question of if BTC is property. It is imperatively essential to note the distinction that this is in reference to BTC and not Cryptoassets generally.

Liam David Robertson v Persons Unknown

In this case, Robertson is a Cryptoasset investor and had accumulated circa 100 BTC. These BTC were stolen. Robertson was able to locate the BTC to a particular wallet, in control of the well-known Cryptoasset exchange and custody agent, Coinbase. Robertson was able to identify the BTC due to the fact that each BTC or divisive BTC is identifiable (unlike cash) and that on the BTC blockchain, you can trace the movement of every BTC. Robertson applied to the Commercial Court in London seeking that a freezing order is placed upon the BTC located and within the control of Coinbase so that they would not be dissipated. The basis of this application was that Bitcoin was legal property and its legal title was with Robertson. For the purpose of this application, BTC was allowed to be viewed as property.

Vorotyntseva v Money-4 Ltd (*T*/*A* Nebus.com) and others

This case was heard in 2018; however, the judgment was only published on 13 November 2019. This matter was an application for a freezing order and involved BTC and the Cryptoasset Ethereum (ETH). The order was granted as a "very preliminary order" by Justice Birss. Mr Justice (sir) Birss is a judge in the courts of England and Wales who is known to have a particularly astute understanding and knowledge of technology. It is important to note that the question of whether BTC or ETH is property was not brought up and therefore gives no further certainty to the rights over cryptoassets. A further hearing will take place in which an argument may be put forward that BTC or ETH is or is not personal property.

Not all crypto assets are the same, and many have significantly different characteristics. BTC and ETH are two particular cryptoassets, which are similar in some respect but are different in others. At this stage, it is impossible to rely upon the judgments above as it did not consider particular characteristics of the Cryptoasset. It is important moving forward that Cryptoassets should not be given a broad definition and rights assigned to them due to the nature and individuality of each Cryptoasset. BTC and ETH, for example, are created on a public blockchain and is, therefore, open-source.

There are however private blockchain systems which subsequently create Cryptoassets. These systems may not be branded as Cryptoassets; however, they are, for all intents and purposes.

Examples of these are:

1. the J. P. Morgan coin created for the purpose of internal wealth transfer; and
2. the cryptoasset used to transact within the Ripple Network.

The Ripple Network uses a system by issuing cryptoassets (which is more akin to a chose in action rather than a chose in possession) which are redeemable for an underlying asset, such as several Great British Pounds or BTC. This allows the Ripple Network to be used to transfer wealth efficiently, and the asset, which the issued Cryptoasset represents, can be redeemed by the original person that the Cryptoasset was issued, or the person to whom it has been transferred. In the circumstances such as this, more significant thought must be had into the rights and classification of the Cryptoasset used to represent the underlying asset and furthermore, the underlying asset itself, if it is a Cryptoasset.

4.5 Legal interest

To complicate matters further, there are two principles ways of ownership in English law. These two types are a Legal interest and a Beneficial (or Equitable) interest.

Legal ownership is concerning the title of the property; an easy example of this is a motor vehicle purchased and registered in England. When a motor vehicle is bought, a V55 is completed and sent to the Driver and Vehicle Licensing Agency which will then record the new owner and keeper of the motor vehicle. If however I asked a friend to purchase a car on my behalf and I give him/her the money to purchase the motor vehicle, it would be registered in his/her name. He/she will have the legal title to the motor vehicle; however, I have a beneficial interest in the vehicle, which can be enforced through the courts.

If Cryptoassets are capable of being property, the law of ownership and interest will likely apply, especially in the circumstances of private blockchain Cryptoassets which are used as an identification of a beneficial interest in an underlying property.

When considering Cryptoassets, one may think it difficult to demonstrate that one owns a Cryptoasset; there is no central register where all Cryptoassets and owners are registered. Neither are they tangible property where one can have physical possession of an object, which is prima facie evidence of legal or beneficial ownership. Cryptoassets are stored on a wallet on the blockchain; which is shared with all other participants of the blockchain; this gives the impression that one person can no own them. However, due to the intrinsic characteristics of the Cryptoassets and the fact a public and a private key is required in order for a Cryptoasset is to be dealt with, typically, possession or knowledge of a private key is prima facie evidence of ownership. However, if a private key is appropriate, it becomes challenging to identify the owner of the Cryptoasset and the courts would likely turn to the evidence of fact to determine an owner or the Cryptoasset.

Companies such as Bitcoin Suisse have created a "paper" waller. This wallet is printed and is one of a kind; it contains a QR code which will link the user to the public address. It also includes a scratch surface, which when scratched away reveals the private key to access the wallet; this is an example of how a physical note or possession is being associated with a Cryptoasset, mostly shared on a blockchain.

4.6 The Anti Money Laundering Directive & the Money Laundering Regulations

The EU passed a piece of legislation which is the Anti Money Laundering Directive ("AML"), requiring member states to implement their own law to deal with particular ant money laundering (and counter-terrorism) considerations. There have been five amendments to the AML, the most recent being implemented on 10 January 2020. The UK has implemented the AML by way of the Money Laundering Regulations ("MLRs").

The MLRs were previously with respect to particular regulated organisations which are typically targeted by those who seek to launder money, such as solicitors and those in the financial sector; however, as of the fifth AML and MLRs, cryptoasset businesses are now brought within its remit. This has the consequences that the majority of cryptoasset business must comply with the MLRs and must register with the FCA. Whether a business will fall within this remit will depend on the activities that the business undertakes, they are:

1. Cryptoasset exchange provider (including Cryptoasset Automated Teller Machine (ATM), Peer to Peer Providers, Issuing new cryptoassets, e. g. Initial Coin Offering (ICO) or Initial Exchange Offerings); and
2. Custodian Wallet Providers.

The requirements include (inter alia) having particular policies which determine the processes a business must undertake in identifying the person they are dealing with and where the funds they receive originated.

4.7 Identifiability

BTC has been likened to the rare metal, gold. This is because there is a finite resource of them and therefore deflationary in nature. There is one key difference between the two: unless the metal is a registered coin with a serial number, one piece of gold ore is indistinguishable to another (apart from its weight); one BTC, however, is easily identifiable. However, when one purchases a BTC, they purchase a number of them, not each number specifically by public key address or ledger entry.

4.8 Smart contracts

A contract is a legal agreement in law which is defined by its characteristics and requires a particular set of requirements to be fulfilled in order for it to be legally binding and enforceable. A contract needs to have an offer; the Offer needs to be accepted; consideration needs to pass between parties (each party receives something in exchange for something else), and there must be intentions to be legally bound. A contract can be defined in writing, spoken, or by way of conduct. A smart contract is a contract embedded within a piece of software typically implementing blockchain technology. The point of a Smart Contract is to code a set of obligations of which can be automatically and autonomously carried out. It is possible to do this without the implantation of Blockchain technology, however, with the implementation of Blockchain technology, for the reasons set out above, the terms of the contract are secure; they can not be amended. Therefore there is a sense of assurance and reliability that we have not seen or been able to rely on typically. A smart contract, in concept, will usually act like an "escrow agent" or the way solicitor's undertakings work. An escrow agent is typically used (outside of England and Wales) in a transaction. In contrast, a set of funds are held on behalf of both parties on either side of a transaction; to be paid on completion of a contractual obligation. This is typically used when obligations are fulfilled in tranches, or the value of the contractual obligation is relatively substantial.

By way of example:

If Party A wanted to purchase 1,000,000 widgets for the price of £1.00 per widget from Party B. This might be a substantially sized contract for each party, and there is an element of risk:

Party A will want to ensure that the widgets they are receiving are of specified quality, and Party B will want to secure payment of £1,000,000.

If Party A pays Party B £1,000,000 and then they receive the widgets, but only half of them arrive, or a part of the whole of them are not to the specified quality or description, Party A has lost £1,000,000, and they can not sell the widgets.

In order for Party A to recover damages, they will need to enforce the contract through the courts, which is a financial risk and will take time.

To ensure this doesn't happen, Party A may suggest that the funds are placed with an independent escrow agent. Once they receive the widgets of satisfactory quality, they will inform the escrow agent, and payment is made. If the widgets are not of satisfactory quality or the contract is wrong, they have not lost the £1,000,000, the widgets can be returned (if agreed), and Party A will not insure a cash flow issue for the loss.

The involvement of an escrow agent costs time and money and leaves room for human error. The ability to automate the entire process is, therefore, beneficial for both parties. This is what a Smart Contract is. The nature of Blockchain technology and the aforementioned subsequent creation of Cryptoassets (which may or may not be regarded as property and therefore rights and obligations come with them), allows for the theoretical possibility that these Smart Contracts can thereafter be sold, containing their obligations.

Inevitably, when the execution of a contract is at the mercy of a program, disputes will arise. The dispute that is in questions is if the smart contract fails to perform the obligation as it was intended, where does the fault and liability lie, to ensure the damaged party is put in a place if the smart contract had not failed? Fortunately, this question has recently been raised in a Court of Appeal case in Singapore in the case of Quoine Pte Ltd v B2C2 Ltd [2020] SGCA(I) 02. In this case, the Appellant (Quoine) was a business operating a cryptoasset exchange (the "Exchange") and would also carry out market-making activities to create liquidity. The Respondent (B2C2 Ltd) was a trader on the Exchange using an algorithmic trading software ("ATS"), created by the director of the Respondent and it worked with little human intervention. The ATS was deterministic in that it would always give the same output to the corresponding input; however, a failsafe existed whereas if the ATS could not receive data, the default position or fail-safe would activate and automatically purchase 10 BTC for 1 ETH. In 2017 the Respondent failed to appropriately update the Exchanges operating system, and as a result, the ATS made thirteen trades at the default position. These trades were circa 250 times the actual value; in essence, as a result of the failure to appropriately update the Exchange operating system, the Respondent came into a windfall and received BTC worth circa 250 times what he had paid for them. The Appellant, noting the abnormality of these trades, cancelled them. The Respondent consequently claimed breach of contract against the Appellant. In the first instance, the Respondent was successful with their claim. The Appellant then appealed the judgment, and the question of the legal principle of Mistake arose.

The pertinent factors in this appeal decision are with respect to the contract formed as a result of an automated process, or smart contract. Those particular factors are:

1. where deterministic algorithms (i. e., those that always produce the same output given the same input) are concerned, it is the programmer's state of knowledge that is relevant and to be attributed to the parties;

2. the relevant inquiry is whether, when programming the algorithm, the programmer was doing so with actual or constructive knowledge of the fact that the relevant offer would only ever be accepted by a party operating under a mistake and whether the programmer was acting to take advantage of such a mistake; and
3. the relevant time frame within which the knowledge of a programmer or the person running the algorithm should be assessed is from the point of programming up to the point that the relevant contract was formed.

4.9 Tokenisation

Tokenisation is the concept of creating a series of Cryptoassets which can be assigned to a physical object, allowing the rights over a portion of that object to be dealt with by way of Cryptoasset. An example of this concept is with respect to investments, to make such investments more accessible to the public. A painting may cost £1,000,000, and a consumer may want to invest in that painting as they suspect its value will increase. If that person does not have £1,000,000, they are unable to invest in the painting. If however the painting was principally split into 16ths and a cryptoasset is created for the sole purpose of attaching to the painting, of which only 16 Cryptoassets exist, it is possible that the painting can be stored independently. Individuals can purchase 16ths of the painting. That person would then have ownership and legal interest in the Cryptoasset and beneficial interest in one-sixteenth of the painting; that person can then independently sell their 16th interest in the painting to a buyer.

Considerations of legal property, regulation and property interest are factors which are applicable in this circumstance; however, there are very few actual examples of structures such as this.

5 Ethical considerations

Cryptoassets can be quite difficult to understand conceptually; however, to the public, they are broadly seen as either:

1. something used to illicit activities;
2. a way to get rich quick.

5.1 Anonymous currency

This perception is not unwarranted, and the rise in popularity stems from these activities. Although BTC was originally created as a way for consumers to transfer wealth without a government body, due to their anonymous nature, in that anyone could control a BTC wallet and that wallet is not associated with a name, BTC is often used to be the payment of choice to purchase illicit objects such as illegal drugs and firearms. Anyone can track the movement of any particular individual or BTC; however, associating a geographical location or person to that wallet is impossible. It isn't just BTC, but a large amount of cryptoassets created on a public blockchain share the same anonymous characteristics as BTC and therefore can also be used for the same ends. Further, the price of BTC has encouraged criminals to hack into the servers of cryptoasset business and then to transfer all the BTC or other cryptoasset held in a wallet, to a wallet held by the criminal. Again, anyone would be able to see the transfer of the cryptoassets from wallet A to wallet B; however, it is impossible to determine the owner of wallet B.

The aforementioned MRL will seek to limit anonymity with this respect by ensuring cryptoasset business have all the correct and up to date, "know your customer" information for each waller or BTC holder. If ones BTC are stolen, and they can be traced on the blockchain to a wallet which is in the possession or custody of a cryptoasset business, it is likely that the cryptoasset business will have the personal information of the person controlling the wallet, containing the stolen BTC.

5.2 Initial Coin Offerings ("ICO")

An ICO is when a business, typically a startup, or younger, would create their own cryptoasset and sell them to the mass public, in order to take on capital to develop a product or service. After the dramatic rise in the price of BTC, many opportunists saw this as a way to get rich quick. Individuals would write a "White-paper" briefly setting out an idea and in some cases with little to no detail of the end goal product. Those individuals would then market the sale of their cryptoassets (or tokens) by way of ICO. Information concerning cryptoassets was limit at the start of 2018, and if the public knew one thing about them, it was that BTC rose from $1,000 to $20,000 in the space of a year. As a result, many consumers were more than willing to send the hosts of these ICOs their hard-earned money with the hope, one of the tokens will rise in price, as did BTC.

Some of these ICOs were genuine and yielded a product or service after years of development, some of the ICOs were undertaken by naive individuals, and the rest were utterly fraudulent.

5.3 Scams

As briefly mentioned, due to the lack of general knowledge of cryptoassets, individuals prey on those consumers, willing to part with their cash. There are several types of common scams that occur in high frequency; the most typical example being:

A website that suggests if you purchase BTC with them, they will hold the BTC for you and then you will earn interest on your BTC. Once the victims pay, they will have an account which shows they own a number of BTC, which then increases every day. This gives the victim the illusion that they have in fact bought BTC and they have a growing amount which they can soon sell for FIAT currency at a huge profit. The victim will then look to withdraw the BTC, at which point the scammers seem to go quiet, then several months later the website disappears.

6 Concluding remarks

This chapter, albeit briefly, sets out an overview of the key components of the underlying blockchain technology and the characteristics which it provides, the subsequent creation of cryptoassets and the applicability of smart contracts. Further, the chapter sets out the applicable laws and challenges the law faces when dealing with complex systems and the new digital asset, cryptoassets. It is clear that existing legislation is somewhat adequate to deal with cryptoassets and smart contracts, as are some principles of law, however, there are circumstances which will arise and will likely test the aforementioned legal principles. Until more cases are brought to the courts which include arguments determining the characteristics of the given cryptoassets in consideration or property law; there is little certainty With that said, at the recent statement was issued by the UK Jurisdictional Taskforce which sets out the considerations of law and Cryptoassets generally. This statement concludes by suggesting that cryptoassets are capable of being property in law.

Legal certainty amongst business has risen as a result of regulatory clarification; however, new cryptoassets providing for new characteristics and utilities will likely challenge the existing legal framework and encourage new pieces of legislation and regulation to form to deal with these challenges. As cryptoassets are becoming increasingly adopted by business, purchased by consumers, those using them will want to know that they have a way of enforcing their rights over them as property, or to at least know if they have any rights over them at all. Further, consumer protection is required to protect those subject to unethical activities.

As for the ethical considerations, the implementations and widening of the MLR remit to include cryptoasset businesses is a positive step towards curbing any unethical activities, however, there is little that can be done to prevent scammers from approaching consumers and defrauding them. this is not so much as a legal consideration, however a challenge that will only be met with the mass adoption of cryptoassets, and with that, the knowledge and understanding that comes with it.

Bibliography

Blandin, Apolline, Ann Sofie Cloots, Hatim Hussain, Michel Rauchs, Rasheed Saleuddin, Jason Grant Allen, Bryan Zhang, and Katherine Clou (2019). *Global cryptoasset regulatory landscape study*, September 2019.

Dean Armstrong, Q. C., Dan Hyde, and Sam Thomas (2018). *Blockchain and cryptocurrency: International legal and regulatory challenges*, 06 September 2018.

Financial Conduct Authority (2019). *Guidance on cryptoassets*: https://www.fca.org.uk/publication/consultation/cp19-03.pdf.

Financial Services and Markets Act 2000.

Proceeds of Crime Act 2002.

Quoine Pte Ltd v B2C2 Ltd [2020] SGCA(I) 02.

Sagar, Leigh (2018). *The Digital Estate*.

UK Jurisdiction Taskforce (2019). *Legal Statement on cryptoassets and smart contracts*: https://35z8e83m1ih83drye280o9d1-wpengine.netdna-ssl.com/wp-content/uploads/2019/11/6.6056_JO_Cryptocurrencies_Statement_FINAL_WEB_111119-1.pdf, November 2019.

Vorotyntseva v Money-4 Ltd (T/A Nebus.com) and others.

Warbach, Kevin (2018). *Trust, but verify: Why the blockchain needs the law*, 33 Berkeley Tech. L. J. 487.

Shaen Corbet and Larisa Yarovaya

The environmental effects of cryptocurrencies

1 Introduction

This chapter discusses the environmental aspects of cryptocurrency markets and as to how their rapid growth can influence the environment and through which channels this process manifests. While it is not popular discussion among investors, we find that environmental issues can be of interest by wider society, students, policy makers and stakeholders of FinTech companies. Environmentalism has a long history, and controversy around this subject is remains quite substantial, thus to not make our discussion over-complicated, in this chapter we will focus on the area where to date, we possess the most thorough data and evidence through which we can build the case, namely electricity consumption associated with the mining of cryptocurrencies. The total carbon footprint of the industry is now estimated to have surpassed that of many large industrial nations. This chapter investigates the multiple knock-on effects and consequential behaviour of this rapid growth in energy usage, such as an increase in global temperature, the growth of mining companies who have targeted third world infrastructures, and the complete shutdown of the internet as we know it. Saying that, we encourage investors not to ignore these environmentalism matters, since we also show that electricity consumption is proven to be one of the commonly used variable in valuation of mineable cryptocurrencies and identification of their fair value, which affect investments returns and should be considered in their trading strategies.

As cryptocurrencies as a financial market product continue to evolve, it is becoming more certain that innovative solutions are going to be needed to solve some substantial forthcoming issues with regards to energy usage and technological capacity. The energy usage of Bitcoin mining has increased from 4.8 Twh to 73.12 Twh over the last two years, and the whole network now consumes more energy than Austria.[1] The estimated energy footprint per Bitcoin transaction is over 600 Kwt, which is estimated to be equivalent to over 300,000 contactless payment transactions, or to the power consumption of an average household for over 22 days. Bitcoin in its current form is a very expensive transmission mechanism. The major fuel used by these networks, due to its relatively majority-based Chinese point of origin, is coal-fired power plants, which has resulted in an extensive carbon footprint for each transaction. This raises questions about the environmental sustainability of cryptocurrencies. The participation in the validation and mining process of Bitcoin requires both special hardware and a substantial amount of energy, therefore, there is on-going carbon production. The computing power required to solve one Bitcoin has quadrupled throughout 2019,

1 BitcoinEnergyConsumption.com, October 2019.

https://doi.org/10.1515/9783110660807-009

compared to the same period twelve months previous. This has led to some concern within the sector of the imminent need for broad international regulation in a bid to stall such exponential growth in energy usage. However, there are difficulties in providing definitive estimates. Further, the argument has been even more substantially muddied, as cryptocurrency proponents have stated that the usage of renewable energy has not been appropriately accounted for.

Research by Li et al. (2019) presented evidence through data analysis and experiments, that the estimated electricity for Monero, could consume 645.62 GWh of electricity in the world in a single year after the hard fork. If there is 4.7% mining activity happening in China, the consumption is at least 30.34 GWh, contributing a carbon emission of between 19.12 and 19.42 thousand tons in a single year. Stoll et al. (2019) utilised a methodology for estimating the power consumption associated with Bitcoin mining based on IPO filings of major hardware manufacturers. The authors then translate the power consumption estimates into carbon emissions, using the localisation of IP-addresses. As of late 2018, the authors estimate the electricity consumption of Bitcoin to be 48.2 TWh, and estimate that annual carbon emissions range from 23.6 to 28.8MtCO_2, similar to that produced by the nations of Jordan and Mongolia, a result that the authors consider to be conservative. Should other cryptocurrency markets such as Ethereum, Monero and zCash among others be considered, this figure could well double, a sum equivalent to that of Portugal. Further, Krause and Tolaymat (2018) had previously identified that that mining Bitcoin, Ethereum, Litecoin and Monero consumed an average of 17, 7, 7 and 14 MJ of energy to generate one US$, respectively. While presenting results largely in line with Stoll et al. (2019), it was also estimated that it took four times more energy for mining 1 US$ of Bitcoin than it did to mine one US$ of copper and double that of either platinum or gold. Mora et al. (2018) showed that when basing their calculations on projected Bitcoin usage, under the assumption that it follows the rate of adoption of other broadly adopted technologies, this new cryptocurrency had the potential to create enough CO_2 emissions to push warming above 2 degrees Celsius within less than three decades.

While opponents of such estimates largely point towards the omission in such research of renewable energy usage, it is highly probable given the relatively small share of renewable in most countries with large mining pools that the net effects of the growth of cryptocurrency is carbon positive and detrimental to our environment at its current rate of growth. Recent research has focused on issues such as the sharp growth in cybercriminality (Corbet et al. (2019)), and the use of cryptocurrency for illicit purposes (Foley et al. (2019)), but little research to date has been done on the environmental impacts of cryptocurrencies (Truby (2018); Easley et al. (2019); Greenberg and Bugden (2019); Li et al. (2019)).

1.1 Why should we care about the environmental effects of cryptocurrencies?

It is not surprising that environmental aspects are often put aside in finance academic literature and financial industries. While there are many goals that enterprise may have, firms in the financial sector are less likely to directly aim at environmental actions without incentivisation, such as improving air and water quality, wildlife and habitats protection. Investment companies and funds are interested in maximising financial returns and decreasing the risks of investments, while incorporation of environmental goals and values into their strategy in majority of cases seems unnecessary, excessive, and most importantly, too expensive. This is also reflected in the finance research and papers published in reputable finance journals, where the majority of those analysing the risk-return characteristics of financial assets rather than the environmental implications of their growth. However, the situation is ever evolving. With elevated attention to the importance of the environment among society, and acknowledgement of the climate change issues facing society by the majority of governments and institutions worldwide, we observed emergence of environmental and climate finance field, as well as expansion of the research addressing urgent multidisciplinary research questions in finance and environmental science simultaneously. Corporate social responsibility matters shaped not only business and accounting processes, but further encouraged emergence of various ethically-cleansed financial assets and instruments, that are available for investors, which cause the changes in their investment objectives. The investors more often follow the ethical values and beliefs in making investment decisions, and environmental factors could be a strong influence.

As to whether cryptocurrency investors care about the carbon footprint of this industry and its environmental impacts is a significant question. We can only guess, but the easiest assumption to make here is that they do not care about it. If they do care about the increased mining difficulty and electricity consumption, then only in the context of the increased cost of mining and its impact on the prices and consequentially investment returns, while wider environmental impacts might be not considered. The majority of mining pools are situated in China and around 80% of Bitcoins minded there, followed by 10% in Czech Republic, and Iceland, Japan, Georgia and Russia account approximately 2% of network hashrate each. The location of mining pools matters due to the energy sources, environmental standards, and clean energy alternatives available in the countries. Not only the power consumption itself is important, but also energy sources which determine the carbon footprint of this industry.

According to Mora et al. (2018) cumulative Bitcoin mining emissions likely to warm the planet by 2 degrees Celsius within 22 years if the current rate is similar to some of the slowest broadly adopted technologies, or within 11 years if adopted at the fastest rate at which other technologies have been incorporated. However, this estimates are based on assumption that the sources of fuel will be fixed and remained unchanged over the target period of time.Thus, it is still possible to decrease the environmental impacts of Bitcoin mining and it is critical to explore the ways to decrease the carbon footprint of cryptocurrencies.

1.2 Technological vs ecological environmentalism

The nature of debates around any new technological development can be better understood if by referring to an early study by O'Riordan (1985) who discussed the differences between technological and ecological environmentalism, comparing technocentrists and ecocentrists viewpoints and beliefs. Technocentrism denotes that humans and technologies can impact environment, and by using adequate management we can minimise the negative impacts of economic growth on nature. This assumes that humans relationships with environment related to utility and usefulness of resources that are provided by nature. Thus, as individuals and as society we would care about negative impacts on environment only if we are directly benefiting from it and our negative impacts are subsequently reducing those benefits. In contrast, ecocentrism provides more romanticised interpretation of environmental protection suggesting that it's moral obligation of all human kinds to respect and protect the nature regardless of its use and its value referring to wild nature as to integral companion of man. Thus, people should try to avoid causing any harm to nature and environments since they are directly harming their own natural habitat.

1.3 Are all cryptocurrencies equally bad for the environment?

There are various digital currencies available and some of those are less energy consuming than others. A useful classification of the digital assets provided by Corbet et al. (2020a) who explained that financial cryptocurrencies that are intended solely for the transfer of wealth and to be used as payments systems, are just one of the possible applications on the top layer of the blockchain stack. Authors classify each digital asset in one of three categories:

1. *Currencies*: Digital assets whose primary (and in most cases, only) use is that of financial payment or monetary transfer.
2. *Blockchains/Protocols*: Digital assets whose primary usage is that of a blockchain platform, or protocol, on which other applications can be built.
3. *Decentralised Applications (dApps)*: Applications combining a user interface, and a decentralised back-end, built upon an already existing blockchain.

For the first category, digital currencies, to possess value, they must be scare, a shortcoming of all previous attempts at creating digital currencies. The mining process creates, and ensures scarcity. Miners allocate resources, in the form of computing power, to this pursuit, in the hope of receiving a block reward (a payment of Bitcoin to the first node to arrive at the correct solution to the mathematical problem). Digital assets derive their value, and the scarcity necessary for value, from this mining process. Digital assets can be stored using a variety of methods: online wallets, online exchanges, hardware wallets and paper wallets (cold storage) being just a selection of the possible storage methods.

Thus mining process is what mainly cause the environmental unsustainability of the digital currencies. Bitcoin is the most well-known, but not the only mineable cryptocurrency that is currently traded. Another popular mineable cryptocurrency is Ether which is built on Ethereum protocol. Ethereum use the same proof-of-work algorithm as Bitcoin, and even though the carbon footprint per transaction is lower, the entire Ethereum network also consumes the amount of electricity comparable with whole countries. Overall, all cryptocurrencies can be divided by mineable and non-mineable currencies.

2 Proof-of-work algorithm

2.1 Bitcoin mining

Bitcoin's trust-minimising consensus has been enabled by its proof-of-work algorithm. The machines completing the algorithms consume substantial amounts of energy while completing their tasks. New sets of blocks are added to Bitcoin's blockchain approximately every 10 minutes by miners. The code that supports Bitcoin includes several rules to validate new transactions. Every miner individually confirms whether transactions adhere to these rules, eliminating the need to trust other miners, instead trusting the process. Every miner in the network is constantly tasked with preparing the next batch of transactions for the blockchain. Only one of these blocks will be randomly selected to become the latest block on the chain.

In proof-of-work, the next block comes from the first miner that produces a valid one. The difficulty is regularly adjusted by the protocol to ensure that all miners in the network will only produce one valid block every 10 minutes on average. Once one of the miners finally manages to produce a valid block, it will inform the rest of the network and other miners will accept this block once they confirm it adheres to all rules, and then discard whatever block they had been working on themselves. The lucky miner gets rewarded with a fixed amount of coins, along with the transaction fees belonging to the processed transactions in the new block. Then the cycle begins once again.

The continuous block mining cycle incentivises miners to mine Bitcoin. As mining can provide a solid stream of revenue, these miners are very willing to run machines that consume substantial amounts of energy in an attempt to generate reward. Over the years this has caused the total energy consumption of the Bitcoin network to grow to unsustainable levels, as the price of the currency reached new highs. It is widely considered that Bitcoin alone uses more power when mining than that of countries such as the Philippines, Chile, Venezuela, the Czech Republic and Austria. Bitcoin's biggest problem is perhaps not even its massive energy consumption, but the fact most mining facilities in Bitcoin's network are located in regions that rely heavily on coal-based power. A Bitcoin ASIC miner will, once turned on, not be switched off until it either breaks down or becomes unable to mine Bitcoin at a profit. Because of this, Bitcoin miners increase both the baseload demand on a grid, as well as the need for alternative (fossil-fuel based) energy sources to meet this demand when renewable energy production is low. In the worst case scenario, the presence of Bitcoin miners may thus provide an incentive for the construction of new coal-based power plants, or reopening existing ones. This impact would be even harder to quantify.

In late 2017, Credit Suisse estimate that a bitcoin price of $50,000 would increase the electricity consumption tenfold. And at a bitcoin price of $1.1 m, it would be profitable to use almost all the electricity currently generated in the world for mining. The bank views the latter prospect as not worth worrying about, for two reasons: it doesn't think bitcoin will ever reach that value, since the competition from other cryptocurrencies is too strong; and it thinks that power consumption of mining will fall over time as better technologies are used for miners. Credit Suisse explicitly compares bitcoin to marijuana cultivation and data centres, two other industries that once sparked fears they would have huge power draws.

2.2 Ethereum

The power usage of Bitcoin is somewhat in contrast to that of other large cryptocurrencies such as Ethereum. Ethereum has plans to change its proof-of-work algorithm to an energy efficient proof-of-stake algorithm called Casper. This change would minimise energy consumption and will be implemented gradually. For now, Ethereum is still running on proof-of-work completely. In its current state the entire Ethereum network consumes more electricity than a number of countries, based on a report published by the International Energy Agency while Bitcoin had been estimated to use 73 TWh per year, Ethereum's power usage was substantially lower at 7.65 TWh per year. Proof-of-work was the first consensus algorithm that managed to prove itself, but it is not the only consensus algorithm. More energy efficient algorithms, like proof-of-stake, have been in development over recent years. In proof-of-stake coin owners create blocks rather than miners, thus not requiring power hungry machines that produce as many hashes per second as possible. Because of this, the energy consumption of proof-of-stake is negligible compared to proof-of-work. Bitcoin could potentially switch to such an consensus algorithm, which would significantly improve sustainability. The only downside is that there are many different versions of proof-of-stake, and none of these have fully proven themselves yet. Nevertheless the work on these algorithms offers good hope for the future.

As cryptocurrency markets continue to develop, it is to be expected that solutions are imminently necessary to solve some substantial forthcoming issues. The energy use of Bitcoin mining has increased from 4.8 Twh to 68.9 Twh over the last two years and the whole network now consumes more energy than Czech Republic. The energy footprint per Bitcoin transaction is now in excess of 500 Kwt, which is equivalent to 350,000 visa transactions. Energy wise, Bitcoin in an expensive transmission mechanism. Nowadays, most mining pools, i. e. groups of miners working in specialised warehouses with extensive amounts of mining hardware, are situated in China. The major fuel used by these networks is thus from coal-fired power plants, which results in an extensive carbon footprint for each transaction. Some estimates say more than 60 percent of the processing power used to mine bitcoin is in China, where it relies heavily on the burning of coal. An estimated 85% of cryptocurrency mining occurs in China, where electricity is cheap and largely sourced from environmentally unsustainable sources like coal-powered plants. As the cryptocurrency industry grows, and the adoption of blockchain technology increases, it is increasingly important for cryptocurrencies' blockchain technology to be more environmentally conscious. By prioritising efficiency, these new cryptocurrencies also reduce their environmental impact. In doing so, the industry neatly exemplifies how improving the environmental output of an industry can be linked to enhanced productivity and effectiveness. Coal and other fossil fuels are also the largest generator of electricity for the rest of the world, and coal is a significant contributor to man-made climate change. Burning it produces carbon dioxide, a gas that is a primary contributor to global warming. This reliance on fossil fuels has given rise to speculation that bitcoin's energy consumption will continue to rise as it grows in popularity. This raises questions about the environmental sustainability of cryptocurrencies.

Participation in the validation and mining process of Bitcoin requires both special hardware and a substantial amount of energy. Thus there is embedded carbon and ongoing carbon production. The computing power required to solve one Bitcoin as of 2019 has quadrupled compared to twelve months previous. Evidence of this substantial growth in difficulty is presented in Figure 1. This has led to some concern within the sector of the imminent need for broad international regulation in a bid to stall such exponential growth in energy usage. However, there are difficulties in providing definitive estimates and the argument has been even further muddied as cryptocurrency proponents have stated that the usage of renewable energy has not been appropriately accounted for.

The rest of this chapter is as follows. Section 3 presents a thorough review of the literature relating to the growth of energy usage within the cryptocurrency sector along with the main identified issues that exist today. Section 4 presents an overview released data to date, with associated commentary as to what the trends have being presenting and as to whether multiple sources are generating the same conclusions.

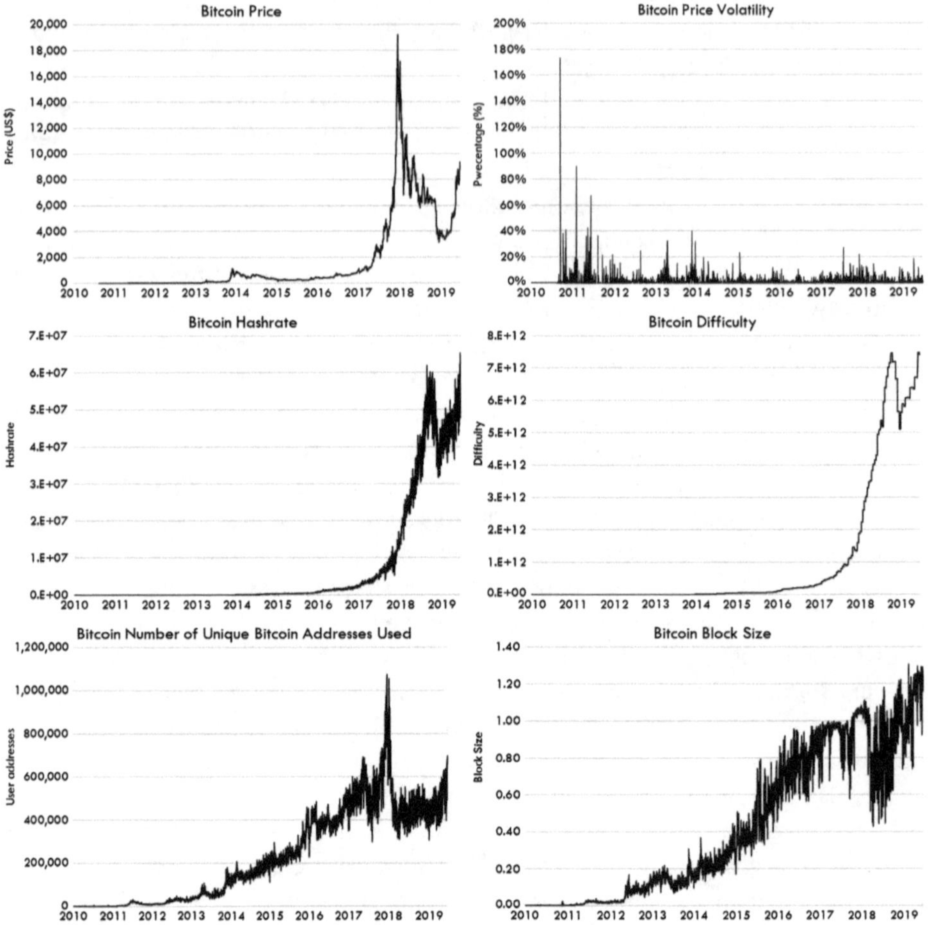

Figure 1: The Changing Characteristics of Bitcoin, 2010–2019.

Note: The top two figures represent the price and volatility of Bitcoin between 2010 and 2019. The middle pair of figures presents the hashrate and mining difficulty respectively. The bottom figures represents the number of unique addresses used to mine Bitcoin and the block size respectively.

Section 5 outlines and explains the multiple issues that have been identified to date. Section 6 presents a concise overview of the proposed solutions to the analysed issues, while Section 7 concludes.

3 Previous literature

Research by Stoll et al. (2019) utilised a methodology for estimating the power consumption associated with Bitcoin mining based on IPO filings of major hardware manufacturers, insights on mining operations, and mining pool compositions. The authors then translate the power consumption estimates into carbon emissions, using the localisation of IP-addresses. As of late 2018, the authors estimate the electricity consumption of Bitcoin to be 48.2 TWh, and estimate that annual carbon emissions range from 23.6 to 28.8MtCO_2, similar to that produced by the nations of Jordan and Mongolia, a result that the authors consider to be conservative. Should other cryptocurrency markets such as Ethereum, Monero and zCash among others be considered, this figure could well double, a sum equivalent to that of Portugal. Krause and Tolaymat (2018) had previously identified that that mining Bitcoin, Ethereum, Litecoin and Monero consumed an average of 17, 7, 7 and 14 MJ of energy to generate one US$, respectively. While presenting results largely in line with Stoll et al. (2019), it was also estimated that it took four times more energy for mining 1 US$ of Bitcoin than it did to mine one US$ of copper and double that of either platinum or gold. Mora et al. (2018) showed that when basing their calculations on projected Bitcoin usage, under the assumption that it follows the rate of adoption of other broadly adopted technologies, this new cryptocurrency had the potential to create enough CO_2 emissions to push warming above 2 degrees Celsius within less than three decades.

While opponents of such estimates largely point towards the omission in such research of renewable energy usage, it is highly probable given the relatively small share of renewable in most countries with large mining pools that the net effects of the growth of cryptocurrency is carbon positive and detrimental to our environment at its current rate of growth. This research sets out to specifically investigate as to whether the price volatility effects of such cryptocurrencies, proxied by Bitcoin, has generated dynamic correlations with electricity and utilities providers in countries that contain the largest international mining pools. Such increased demand through the cryptocurrency mining process should theoretically manifest in changing financial dynamics for these identified companies. We have also selected to investigate as to whether any dynamic relationship exists between Bitcoin and the markets for green energy ETFs and the market for ICE EUX Carbon Credits, where one lot of 1,000 CO_2 EU Allowances provides an entitlement to emit one tonne of carbon dioxide equivalent.

Recent research has focused on issues such as the sharp growth in cybercriminality (Corbet et al. (2019)), and the use of cryptocurrency for illicit purposes (Foley et al. (2019)), but little research to date has been done on the environmental impacts of cryptocurrencies (Truby (2018); Easley et al. (2019); Greenberg and Bugden (2019); Li et al. (2019)). Further, there is much evidence to suggest that this new financial product has continued to progress with evidence provided of growing efficiency (Bariviera (2017)) and product and pricing enhancement through the use of related derivatives products (Corbet et al. (2018); Akyildirim et al. (2019)). While the main stream of cryptocurrency research is currently focused on the dilemma as to whether this is a currency or speculative asset (Baur et al. (2018)); and conducting analysis of the multiple forms of pricing inefficiencies (Urquhart (2017); Sensoy (2019); Mensi et al. (2019); Katsiampa et al.

(2019)), Corbet et al. (2019) have provided a concise systematic review of the literature associated with cryptocurrency markets at large, and note that more research is needed to assess environmental and energy use issues. As this new financial product continues to develop through improved market efficiency (Ekinci et al. (2019); Corbet et al. (2020b)) and portfolio design (Akhtaruzzaman et al. (2019); Corbet et al. (2018)), it is imperative that we continue to understand the true risks associated. While considering the broad improvement in pricing efficiency and market efficiency, indicative of a rapidly developing financial market product, our paper assesses the financial long terms impacts of Bitcoin energy usage.

In Figure 1, we present the 1) mining difficulty; 2) hashrate; 3) the number of daily transactions; 4) the number of unique Bitcoin mining addresses and 5) block size of Bitcoin. Through each particular variable, we observe the growing maturity of this new financial product over time. Mining difficulty reflects how difficult it is to find a new block compared to the easiest that it could be, recalculated every 2016 blocks to a value such that the previous 2016 blocks would have been generated in exactly two weeks had everyone been mining at the same difficulty. As more miners join, the rate of block creation will increase, which causes the difficulty to increase in compensation to push the rate of block creation back down. A hash is the output of a hash function, and the hashrate is the speed at which a compute is completing an operation in the Bitcoin code. A higher hashrate when mining increases your opportunity of finding the next block and receiving the reward. The increased difficulty in mining has led to a need for more powerful technology and increased energy usage to mine cryptocurrency. Of course, the source of this additional required energy is central to the issues that Bitcoin, among other cryptocurrencies, faces.

Due to the growing number of mining pools across the world, we focus specifically on the six largest. China accounts for 81% of mining pool concentration, the Czech Republic 10%, while Iceland, Japan, Georgia and Russia account for 2% respectively. After a thorough analysis, only China, Japan and Russia possess publicly traded electricity companies or core utility companies that trade primarily in energy. Further, there have been issues identified with the very nature of such concentration. Stoll et al. (2019) found that the four largest Chinese pools now provide almost 50% of the total hashrate, with Bitcoin operating three of such pools.

4 What does the data tell us?

As of December 2019, it has been estimated that annualised global revenue available through the mining of Bitcoin alone was estimated to be $5.4 billion. The global estimated cost to generate this revenue is approximately $3.9 billion. Consider this, with one cryptocurrency, the potential rewards for mining is a spoil of a pool of $1.5 billion. Considering the incredibly rapid growth in the number of cryptocurrencies that exist today, it is easy to comprehend as to how large this market, and the profits that exist for the most efficient miners in the market. It is this market efficiency that has come into sharp focus with costs accounting for approximately 70% of revenues. Much of the cost surrounds the technological challenges that miners face. In terms of mining cryptocurrency, substantial energy is allocated towards heat reduction. Countries with warmer climates have been broadly linked with substantial technological issues and machine malfunctions. While considering that a basic miner can use approximately 1,500 watts per hour, much of this energy is converted directly to heat output, which can be in excess of 5,000 BTU per hour. When considering the fact that some mines possess up to 5,000 of these miners in close proximity, it is very easy to quickly identify the scale of the temperature issues that are faced. The task is not aimed at cooling the air, but rather to evacuate it from the areas surrounding the miners using industrial fans. Evaporative coolers are then used to cool the physical infrastructure surrounding the miners, controlling for moisture and evaporation from the heat exchange which can create disastrous consequences for the electrical infrastructure. If for example, a mine consumes 40 MW of electricity per hour, and given an energy consumption of about 1,500 watts per hour per Bitcoin mining machine, these miners can consume over 75% of the electricity consumption with regards to the cryptocurrency mining process. Therefore, the cooling process of the miners can account for up to 25% of the total energy usage costs of a mine. We must further consider as to how hard these miners are working. In some cases, to reduce machine wear-and-tear, some miners are set to run below their maximum operating capacity. This would cause such cooling estimates to vary quite considerably. For example, some mining machines have controllers that gauges the ambient temperature and sets the fan speed and the voltage and clock speed of the machine accordingly. During periods of warm weather, this process will result in mining machines running at slower speeds (as measured in terahashes per second) to keep the chips cooler and reduce the risk of significant damage.

Stoll et al. (2019) found directly estimated the significant carbon footprint. The authors demonstrated a methodology for estimating the power consumption associated with Bitcoin's blockchain based on IPO filings of major hardware manufacturers, insights on mining facility operations, and mining pool compositions. We then translate our power consumption estimate into carbon emissions, using the localisation of IP addresses. We determine the annual electricity consumption of Bitcoin, as of November 2018, to be 45.8 TWh and estimate that annual carbon emissions range from 22.0 to 22.9 Mt CO^2. However, this validation process uses this 'vast amounts of electricity', to earn cryptocurrency without spending any money. To estimate the electricity consumption, the authors used IP addresses and hardware data from recent IPO filings. The authors wrote that their study points to potential drawbacks of blockchain technology that should be considered by policymakers. As of late 2019, the total network hashrate (1,000,000 GH/s) was estimated to be 121,669 PH/s with an estimated energy footprint per transaction of 640 KW/h. This is found to represent almost 7.2 million households that could be powered by the equivalent energy that Bitcoin is accounting

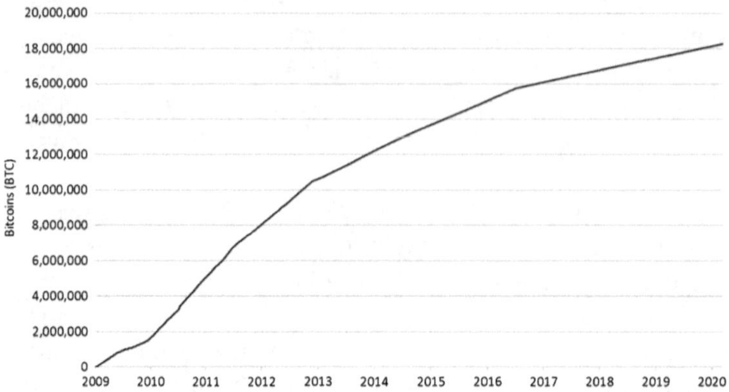

Figure 2: Bitcoins in circulation.

Note: The above figure presents the total number of bitcoins that have already been mined; in other words, the current supply of bitcoins on the network. The data is correct as of January 2020.

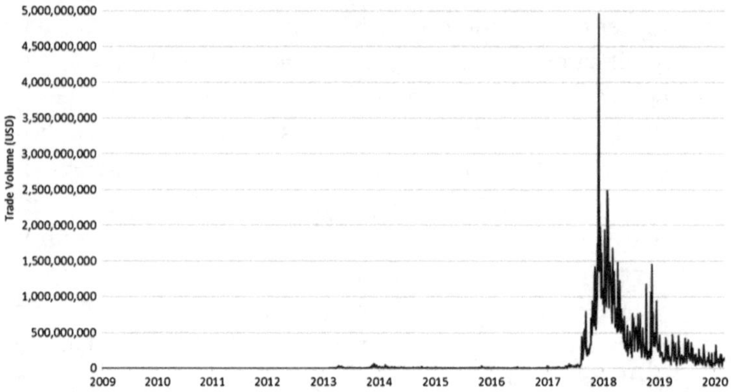

Figure 3: USD ($) Exchange Trade Volume.

Note: The above figure presents the total USD ($) value of trading volume on major bitcoin exchanges. The data is correct as of January 2020.

for, or otherwise 22 households could be powered for one day by the electricity consumed for a single transaction. This indicates that Bitcoin's electricity consumption[2] as a percentage of the world's electricity consumption was estimated to be 0.35%, with an annual carbon footprint 36,947 kt of CO_2, with a carbon footprint per transaction 303 kg of CO_2.

To analyse the sectoral growth of Bitcoin since 2009, we present a number of characteristics surrounding this new product in Figures 2 through 5. As Bitcoin obtained

2 Data obtained from https://digiconomist.net/bitcoin-energy-consumption

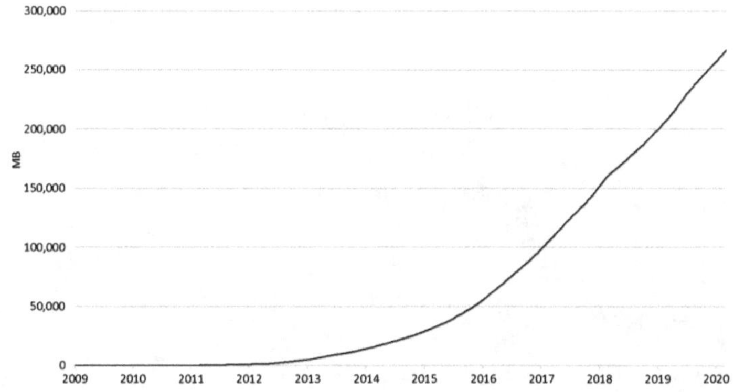

(a) Blockchain size

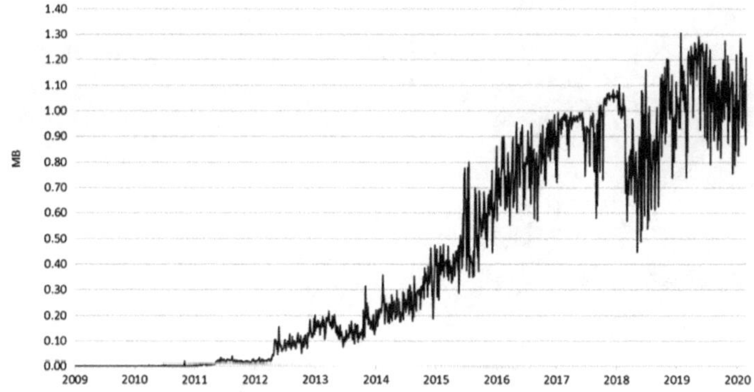

(b) Average block size

Figure 4: Blockchain size and the average block size.

Note: The above figures represent the total size of all block headers and transactions and the average block size in MB respectively. The data is correct as of January 2020.

more attention as a new financial product, its internal structure changed quite substantially. With this added attention developed a sharp increase in the number of transactions, trading volume and mining processes associated. In Figure 2 we identify the number of Bitcoins in circulation, with evidence of sharply elevated growth rates in the period between 2010 and 2013. However, in the period since 2017, this growth rate has somewhat plateaued. In Figure 3, we observe the USD ($) exchange traded value of Bitcoin. As expected, during the sharp price appreciation of late-2017, the value of the market grew from approximately $1 billion to almost $5 billion. In Figure 4, we observe some of the key statistics with regards to blockchain size. As of late-2019, the blockchain size of Bitcoin grew above 250 GB, while the average block size exceeded 1.20 MB per transaction. In Figure 5, we observe the average number of transactions per block which has consistently exceeded 1,000 transactions since late 2015, and has been above 2,000 transactions since mid-2018. Throughout 2019,

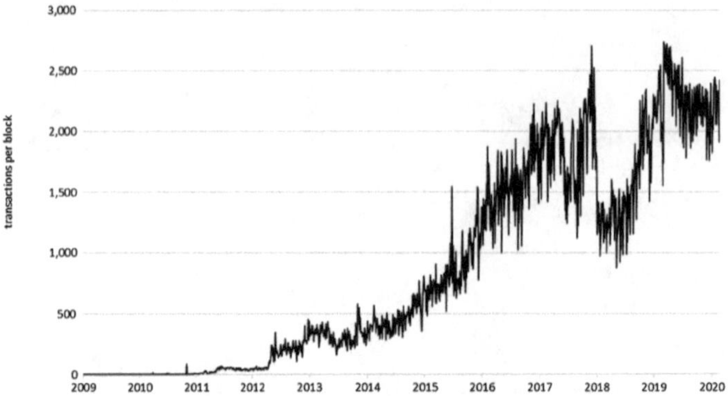

(a) Average Number Of Transactions Per Block

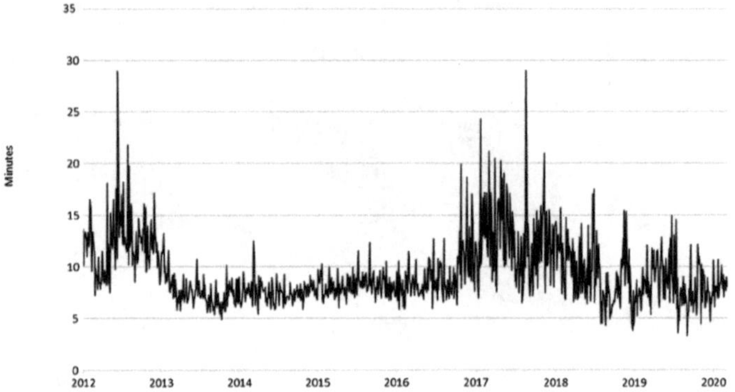

(b) Median Confirmation Time

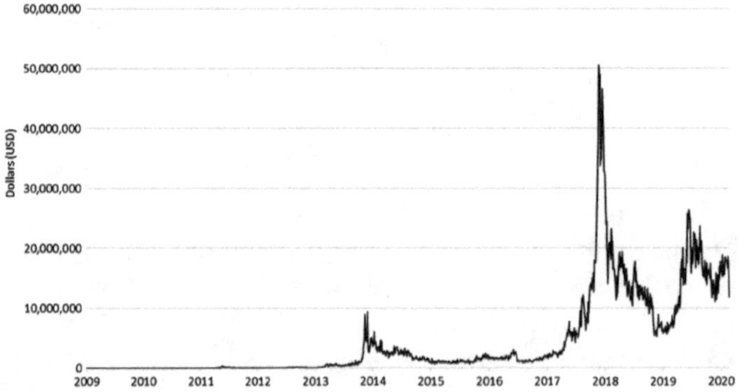

(c) Miners Revenue

Figure 5: Average Number Of Transactions Per Block, Median Confirmation Time and Miners Revenue.

Note: The above figure presents the average number of transactions per block, the median time for a transaction to be accepted into a mined block and added to the public ledger (note: only includes transactions with miner fees) and finally, the total value of Coinbase block rewards and transaction fees paid to miners. The data is correct as of January 2020.

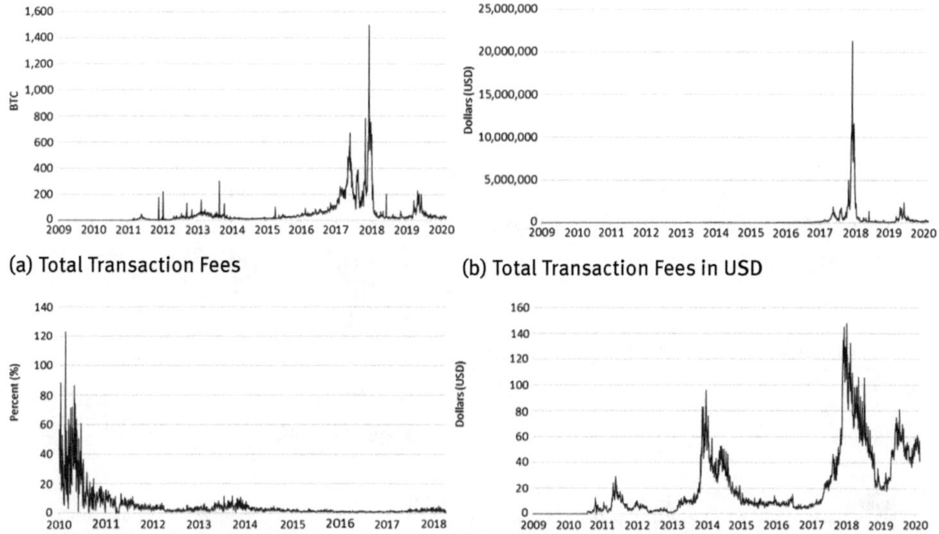

(a) Total Transaction Fees

(b) Total Transaction Fees in USD

(c) Cost as a % of Transaction Volume

(d) Cost per Transaction

Figure 6: Total Transaction Fees, Total Transaction Fees in USD, Cost as a % of Transaction Volume and cost per Transaction.

Note: The above figure presents the total value of all transaction fees paid to miners (not including the Coinbase value of block rewards), the total value of all transaction fees paid to miners (not including the Coinbase value of block rewards), miners revenue as percentage of the transaction volume and miners revenue divided by the number of transactions. The data is correct as of January 2020.

the median confirmation time has averaged approximately seven minutes, which was the consistently average range experienced between 2013 and late-2017. Miner's rev enue has also be consistently above $5,000 since Q2 2017, peaking during the period in which Bitcoin prices almost reached $20,000.

In Figure 6, we observe the key statistics with regards to transaction fees in the market for Bitcoin. We observe that the total transaction fees grew quite substantially during periods of sharp price appreciation, reaching over $20 million in late-2017. However, we also observe that cost as a proportion of the transaction volume has sharply declined over time while the cost per transaction has increased to a sustained high level since early-2017. In Figure 7, we can clearly identify the sharp growth in interest in the mining of Bitcoin as a product. There has been a consistent level of growth in the number of unique addresses mining the product, peaking during the largest price appreciations in Bitcoin. The has been echoed by the confirmed transactions per day in Bitcoin and the total number of transactions. In Figure 8, we see the behaviour of the number of unspent transaction output (UTXO) which is an abstraction of Electronic Money. Each UTXO represents a chain of ownership implemented as a chain of Digital Signatures where the owner signs a message (transaction) transfer-

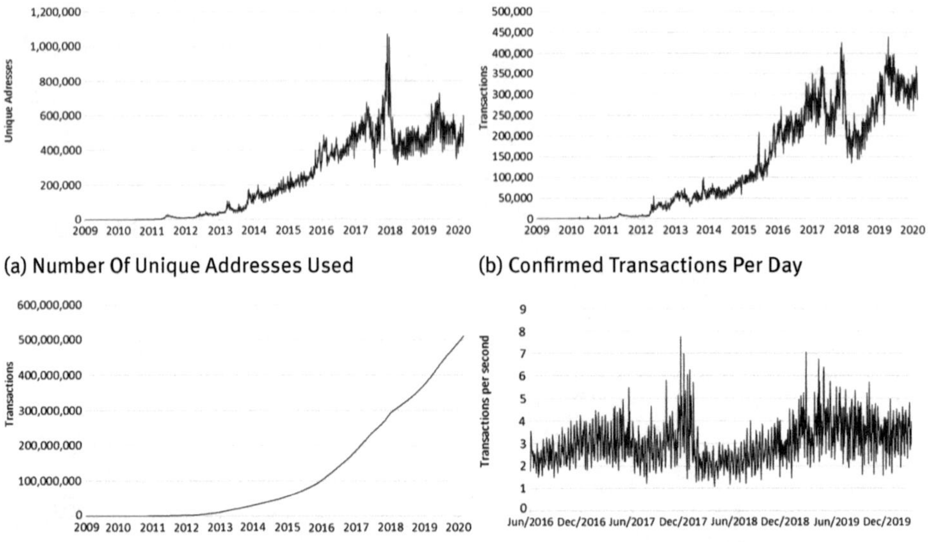

(a) Number Of Unique Addresses Used
(b) Confirmed Transactions Per Day
(c) Transaction Rate
(d) Total Number of Transactions

Figure 7: Number Of Unique Addresses Used, Confirmed Transactions Per Day, Total Number of Transactions and the Transaction Rate.

Note: The above figure presents the total number of unique addresses used on the Bitcoin blockchain, the number of daily confirmed Bitcoin transactions, the total number of transactions and the number of Bitcoin transactions added to the mempool per second. The data is correct as of January 2020.

ring ownership of their UTXO to the receiver's Public Key. The total UTXOs present in a blockchain represent a set, every transaction thus consumes elements from this set and creates new ones that are added to the set. The set thus represents all the coins in the system. In early-2018, while Bitcoin prices starts to decline from lifetime highs, the UTXO declined in a similar fashion, remaining elevated during some periods of short-term panic in mid-2019, but being quite low otherwise. Further, the mempool size, representing the aggregate size of transactions waiting to be confirmed has had a number of short-term spikes value over the past three years as measured in bytes per second. These large spikes can indicate that a number of miners have left the process. Further, the spike could also mean that the Bitcoin protocol is under threat, simply because transactions are not processing at their usual pace. It is also possible that the spike is because someone is spamming the network on purpose, to either raise fees or prevent certain transactions from processing.

We observe the number of unspent transaction outputs in Figure 9, which has been at a lifetime high of almost 70 million outputs in late-2019. Further, we observe the output value, which contains instructions for sending bitcoins. The value is the number of Satoshi (1 BTC = 100,000,000 Satoshi) that this output will be worth when claimed. ScriptPubKey is the second half of a script and there can be more than one

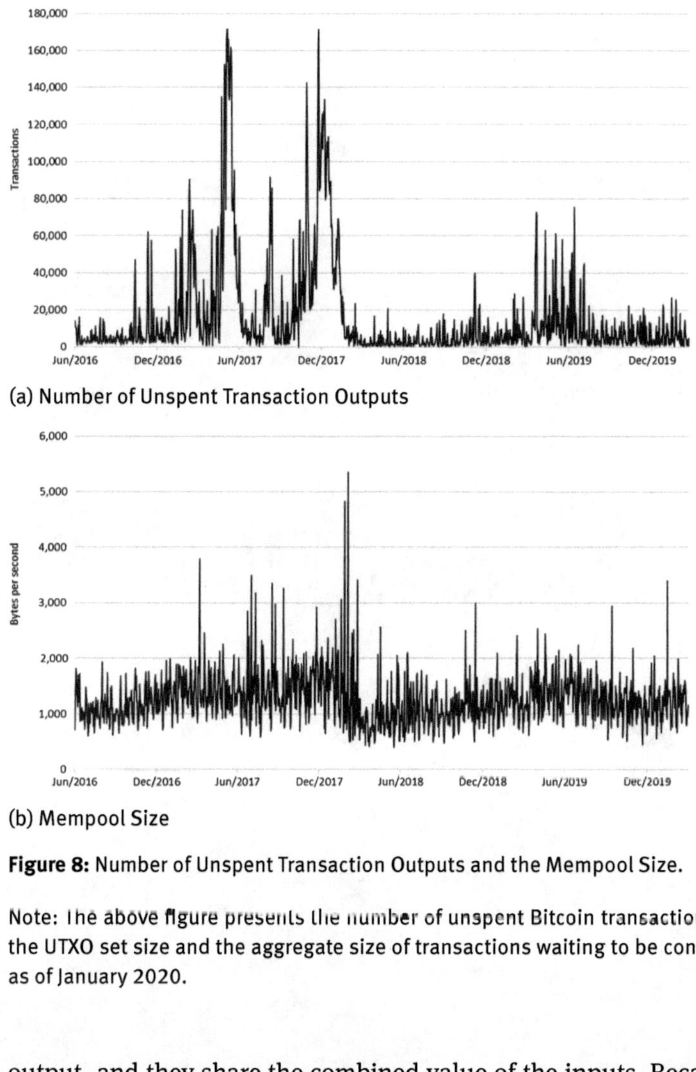

Figure 8: Number of Unspent Transaction Outputs and the Mempool Size.

Note: The above figure presents the number of unspent Bitcoin transactions outputs, also known as the UTXO set size and the aggregate size of transactions waiting to be confirmed. The data is correct as of January 2020.

output, and they share the combined value of the inputs. Because each output from one transaction can only ever be referenced once by an input of a subsequent transaction, the entire combined input value needs to be sent in an output if you don't want to lose it. There have been a number of distinct, sharp increases in this value, most notably in early-2016 and mid-2019. In Figure 10, we observe that the estimated transaction value has reduced consistently over time, however, as the price of Bitcoin increased, so did the estimated USD($) transaction value. Finally, Figure 11 presents the user count of blockchain wallet users over time. We can clearly see a sharp growth of user numbers in the period since 2014, peaking in excess of 45 million in the period since early-2019.

In Table 1 we observe the international estimates of international electricity consumption (as of the most recent estimates in 2017). We observe that China is the largest

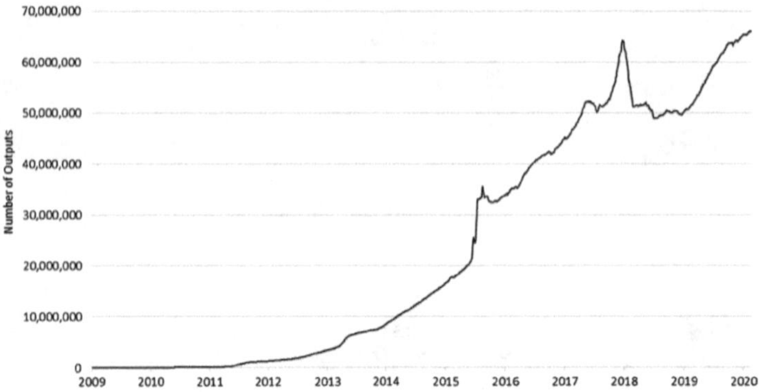

(a) Number of Unspent Transaction Outputs

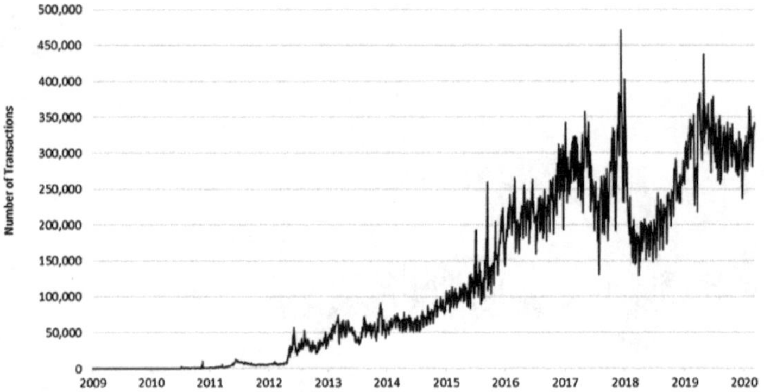

(b) Number of Unspent Transaction Outputs

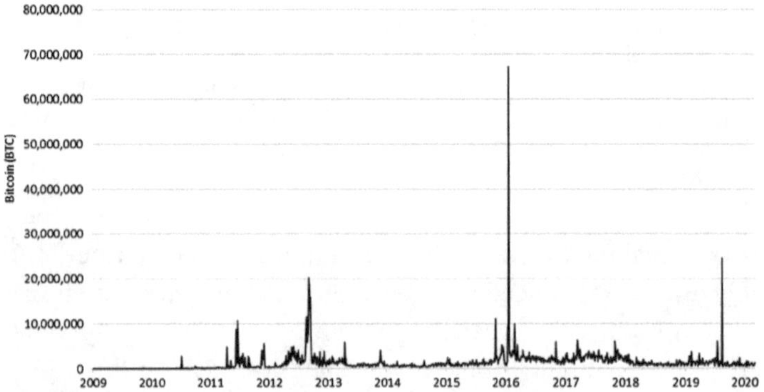

(c) Output Value

Figure 9: Number of Unspent Transaction Outputs, Number of Transactions Excluding Popular Addresses and the Output Value.

Note: The above figure presents the number of unspent Bitcoin transactions outputs, also known as the UTXO set size, the total number of Bitcoin transactions, excluding those involving any of the network's 100 most popular addresses and the total value of all transaction outputs per day (includes coins returned to the sender as change). The data is correct as of January 2020.

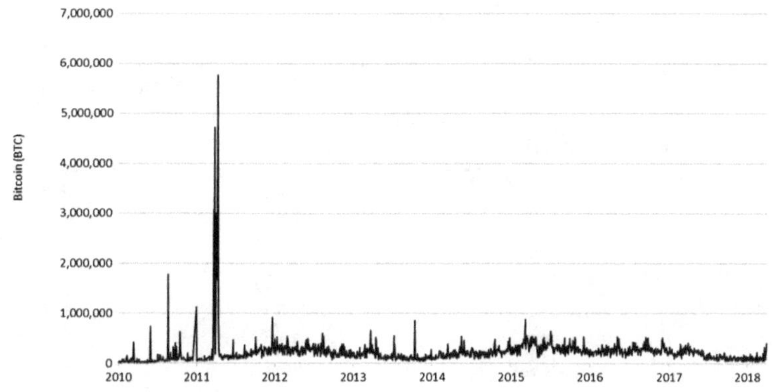

(a) Estimated Transaction Value

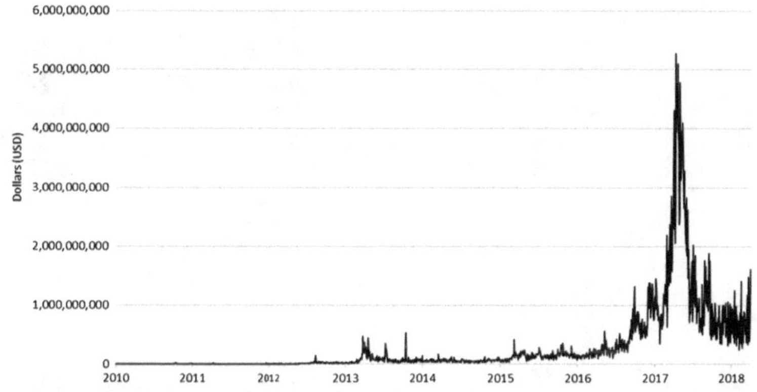

(b) Estimated USD Transaction Value

Figure 10: Estimated Transaction Value and the Estimated USD Transaction Value.

Note: The above figure presents the total estimated value of transactions on the Bitcoin blockchain (does not include coins returned to sender as change), and the Estimated Transaction Value in USD value. The data is correct as of January 2020.

consumer of electricity in the work, estimated to be in excess of 6.3 trillion kW hours per year. This is followed by the United States, then India, Russia and Japan. It is important to note that Japanese power consumption is almost twice that of the next group of countries that includes Germany, Canada, Brazil and South Korea. When considering the average electrical energy usage per capital, we observe a considerable change in the above rankings. Norway is the most significant user as measured per person, estimated to be in excess of 24,000 kWh per person per year. The UAE, Canada, Finland, Sweden and the United States follow, with emphasis on the need for heating consumption of electricity in Scandinavia, and cooling in the UAE. When considering China's usage per capital, it does not feature in the least efficient countries on this list. This is also the case with regards to the average power per capital.

Table 1: International estimates of electricity consumption, as of 2017.

Rank	Country	Electricity consumption (per million kW h/yr)	Average electrical energy per capita (kWh per person per year)	Average power per capita (watts per person)
1	China	6,310,000	4,475	510
2	United States	3,911,000	12,071	1,377
3	India	1,547,000	1,181	260
4	Russia	1,065,000	7,481	854
5	Japan	934,000	7,371	841
6	Germany	533,000	6,602	753
7	Canada	528,000	14,930	1,704
8	Brazil	518,000	2,516	287
9	South Korea	495,000	9,720	1,109
10	France	431,000	6,448	736
11	UK	309,000	4,795	547
12	Italy	291,000	4,692	535
13	Saudi Arabia	272,000	9,658	1,102
14	Taiwan	249,500	10,632	1,213
15	Mexico	238,000	1,932	220
16	Spain	234,000	4,818	550
17	Australia	224,000	9,742	1,112
18	Indonesia	221,070	1,058	117
19	Iran	218,000	2,632	300
20	South Africa	112,000	3,904	445
21	Turkey	347,400	2,578	294
22	Thailand	264,000	2,404	274
23	Egypt	143,000	1,510	172
24	Ukraine	143,000	3,234	369
25	Poland	142,000	3,686	420
26	Malaysia	131,000	4,232	483
27	Sweden	127,000	12,853	1,467
28	Norway	126,400	24,006	2,740
29	Vietnam	125,000	1,312	149
30	Argentina	116,000	2,643	301
31	Netherlands	108,000	6,346	724
32	UAE	96,000	16,195	1,848
33	Philippines	94,370	885	101
34	Kazakhstan	91,000	4,956	565
35	Pakistan	82,000	471	50
36	Finland	81,000	14,732	1,681
37	Belgium	81,000	7,099	810
38	Venezuela	78,000	2,523	288
39	Austria	69,750	8,006	913
40	Chile	66,000	3,739	426

Note: Data obtained from https://www.cia.gov/index.html.

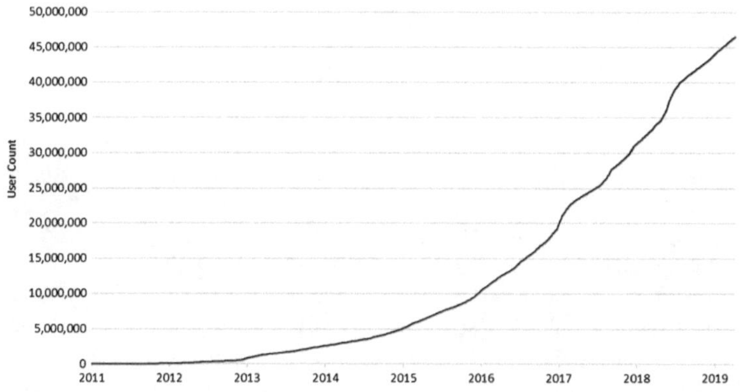

Figure 11: Blockchain Wallet Users.

Note: The above figure presents the total number of blockchain wallet users. The data is correct as of January 2020.

In Tables 2 and 3, we observe estimates of the electricity prices facing both households and businesses as of 2019. Within this list, we observe that countries such as Iran, Iraq and other middle eastern nations such as Qatar present evidence of substantially reduced household charges for electricity. Germany represents the most expensive country to buy domestic electricity per kW, closely followed by Denmark, Belgium, Portugal, Jamaica and Japan. In terms of the business charges in Table 3, although rates are broadly reduced in comparison to household estimates, Denmark is the most expensive at US$0.28 per kW. This is closely followed by Jamaica and Costa Rica. In terms of the cheapest countries in which to buy electricity, Venezuela, Libya and Ethiopia represent the cheapest countries in which to run potential cryptocurrency mining operations.

In each country, a substantial number of mining companies have harnessed a large amount of network hash power in their mining efforts, creating a more centralised structure of the mining process. The three countries with the largest production of Bitcoin include:

1. China: which mines the most bitcoins of any nation and has been driven, in part, by cheaper electricity in comparison to international counterparts. Chinese Bitcoin miners have gained an advantage by capturing a large percentage of Bitcoin's hash power. China is home to many of the top Bitcoin mining companies such as F2Pool, AntPool, BTCC, and BW. It's estimated that these mining pools own somewhere around 60% of Bitcoins hash power, meaning they mine about 60% of all new Bitcoins.
2. Czech Republic: accounts for approximately 10% of all mining and is home to Slush Pool, which was the first mining pool and currently mines about 11% of all blocks. Slush is probably one of the best and most popular mining pools despite not being one of the largest.

Table 2: Electricity prices for households as of 2019 (per kW).

Iran	$0.01	India	$0.08	Namibia	$0.13	Uganda	$0.20
Burma	$0.03	UAE	$0.08	Colombia	$0.14	Finland	$0.20
Iraq	$0.03	Sri Lanka	$0.08	Hong Kong	$0.15	France	$0.20
Zambia	$0.03	Vietnam	$0.08	USA	$0.15	Philippines	$0.20
Egypt	$0.03	Lebanon	$0.08	Cambodia	$0.15	Peru	$0.20
Qatar	$0.03	Taiwan	$0.09	Macao	$0.15	Greece	$0.20
Algeria	$0.04	Turkey	$0.09	Lithuania	$0.15	New Zealand	$0.21
Kazakhstan	$0.04	Argentina	$0.09	Iceland	$0.15	Kenya	$0.22
Azerbaijan	$0.04	Botswana	$0.09	Malta	$0.15	Switzerland	$0.22
Afghanistan	$0.05	Serbia	$0.09	Honduras	$0.16	Luxembourg	$0.22
Saudi Arabia	$0.05	Cameroon	$0.09	Brazil	$0.16	Austria	$0.23
Bahrain	$0.05	Indonesia	$0.10	Croatia	$0.16	Czech Republic	$0.23
Ukraine	$0.05	Ecuador	$0.10	Costa Rica	$0.16	Australia	$0.24
Malaysia	$0.06	Canada	$0.10	Chile	$0.16	Spain	$0.25
Ghana	$0.06	Tanzania	$0.10	Estonia	$0.17	Netherlands	$0.25
Pakistan	$0.06	Jordan	$0.11	Israel	$0.17	Liechtenstein	$0.26
Bangladesh	$0.06	Albania	$0.11	Senegal	$0.17	Italy	$0.27
Russia	$0.06	South Korea	$0.11	Romania	$0.17	United Kingdom	$0.27
Nepal	$0.07	Thailand	$0.12	Sweden	$0.18	Ireland	$0.28
Nigeria	$0.07	Morocco	$0.12	Poland	$0.18	Japan	$0.29
Tunisia	$0.07	Norway	$0.12	Singapore	$0.18	Jamaica	$0.30
Belarus	$0.07	Bulgaria	$0.13	Slovakia	$0.18	Portugal	$0.30
Georgia	$0.07	South Africa	$0.13	Latvia	$0.19	Belgium	$0.31
Mexico	$0.08	Hungary	$0.13	Uruguay	$0.19	Denmark	$0.33
China	$0.08	Ivory Coast	$0.13	Slovenia	$0.19	Germany	$0.35

Note: Data obtained from https://www.globalpetrolprices.com/electricity_{p}rices/ in US$ terms as of November 2019.

3. Iceland: accounts for 2% of cryptocurrency mining. The new industry's relatively sudden growth has been raising concerns for its environmental impact. Iceland's energy comes from hydroelectric dams and geothermal power plants, creating electricity without carbon emissions. It has been the relatively cheap, and abundant amounts of energy that have attracted multiple companies to Iceland.
4. Japan: accounts for approximately 2% of mining, driven by cheap electricity and low setup fees, both of which are a substantial advantage for venture businesses. There has been a large drive for Japanese companies setting up cryptocurrency mining processes both at home and abroad. Japanese companies moving into the business in anticipation of future growth. For example, DMM.com, has set up Japan's largest cryptocurrency mining operation in the central city of Kanazawa, while GMO Internet has one in Scandinavia.
5. Russia: accounts for 10% of international mining. Russia as a whole currently mines one-tenth of the world's bitcoin production. RMC previously raised $43 mil-

Table 3: Electricity prices for businesses as of 2019 (per kW).

Venezuela	$0.01	Russia	$0.08	Bulgaria	$0.12	Singapore	$0.15
Libya	$0.02	South Korea	$0.08	Burma	$0.12	Cameroon	$0.15
Ethiopia	$0.02	Czech Republic	$0.09	Thailand	$0.12	Poland	$0.15
Uzbekistan	$0.03	Canada	$0.09	Philippines	$0.12	Macao	$0.16
Zambia	$0.03	Ecuador	$0.09	Romania	$0.12	Switzerland	$0.16
Algeria	$0.04	Uruguay	$0.09	Taiwan	$0.13	Guatemala	$0.16
Qatar	$0.04	UAE	$0.10	Hungary	$0.13	Mexico	$0.16
Kazakhstan	$0.05	Turkey	$0.10	Chile	$0.13	Uganda	$0.16
Iraq	$0.05	Malaysia	$0.10	Bolivia	$0.13	Slovakia	$0.17
Paraguay	$0.05	Ukraine	$0.10	Peru	$0.13	Austria	$0.17
Azerbaijan	$0.05	Estonia	$0.10	Greece	$0.13	Malta	$0.17
Kuwait	$0.05	Tanzania	$0.10	Brazil	$0.13	Australia	$0.17
South Africa	$0.06	Serbia	$0.10	Croatia	$0.13	Liechtenstein	$0.17
Argentina	$0.06	China	$0.10	France	$0.13	Mali	$0.17
Georgia	$0.06	Lebanon	$0.10	Belgium	$0.13	Belize	$0.18
Iceland	$0.07	Bangladesh	$0.10	Slovenia	$0.13	Kenya	$0.19
Saudi Arabia	$0.07	Belarus	$0.11	Pakistan	$0.14	Ivory Coast	$0.21
Armenia	$0.07	DR Congo	$0.11	Finland	$0.14	United Kingdom	$0.21
Mozambique	$0.07	Nigeria	$0.11	Luxembourg	$0.14	Honduras	$0.22
Sri Lanka	$0.07	Israel	$0.11	Netherlands	$0.14	Italy	$0.22
Indonesia	$0.07	Botswana	$0.11	Colombia	$0.14	Germany	$0.22
Egypt	$0.07	Tunisia	$0.11	Ghana	$0.14	Japan	$0.22
Nepal	$0.08	Morocco	$0.11	Hong Kong	$0.14	Costa Rica	$0.24
Bahrain	$0.08	USA	$0.11	Latvia	$0.15	Jamaica	$0.24
Vietnam	$0.08	Bosnia & Herz.	$0.12	Spain	$0.15	Denmark	$0.28

Note: Data obtained from https://www.globalpetrolprices.com/electricity_{p}rices/ in US$ terms as of November 2019.

lion in an initial coin offering (ICO) in 2017, which was identified as the largest Russian ICO at the time.

6. Georgia: accounts for approximately 2% of Bitcoin mining and is home to a company known as BitFury who acts as one of the largest players in the Bitcoin mining business segment, known particularly for their role in the development and sales of efficiency streaming hardware to Bitcoin users and businesses. Bitfury is one of leading full service Blockchain technology companies and one of the largest private infrastructure providers in the Blockchain ecosystem. In late 2016, the company became famous as they were estimated to be mining approximately 15% of all Bitcoins in the world.

Within these companies, there are a number of substantial mining pools. A mining pool is a joint group of cryptocurrency miners who combine their computational resources over a network. Individually, participants in a mining pool contribute their processing power toward the effort of finding a block. If the pool is successful in these efforts and is rewarded with cryptocurrency tokens as a result, the mining pool divides up these rewards to individuals who contributed according to the proportion of each individual's processing power or work relative to the whole group. In some cases, individual miners must show proof of work in order to receive their rewards. There are broadly three types of mining pools: 1) Proportional mining pools are among the most common. In this type of pool, miners contributing to the pool's processing power receive shares up until the point at which the pool succeeds in finding a block. After that, miners receive rewards proportional to the number of shares they hold; 2) Pay-per-share pools operate somewhat similarly in that each miner receives shares for his or her contribution. However, these pools provide instant payouts regardless of when the block is found. A miner contributing to this type of pool can exchange shares for proportional payout at any time; and 3) Peer-to-peer mining pools aim to prevent the pool structure from becoming centralised. As such, they integrate a separate blockchain related to the pool itself and designed to prevent the operators of the pool from cheating as well as the pool itself from failing due to a single central issue.

1. Poolin: is a public pool which mines about 18% of all blocks. They are based in China, but have a website fully available in English.
2. F2Pool: is based in China. It mines about 17% of all blocks.
3. BTC.com: is a public mining pool that can be joined and mines 15% of all block.
4. AntPool: is a mining pool based in China and owned by BitMain. AntPool mines about 11% of all blocks.
5. ViaBTC: is a relatively new mining pool. It is targeted towards Chinese miners and mines about 9% of all blocks.
6. 1 Hash & 58 coin: This is a Chinese pool made from two pools: 1 THash and 58 coin.
7. Slush Pool: was the first mining pool and currently mines about 11% of all blocks. Slush is probably one of the best and most popular mining pools despite not being one of the largest.
8. BTC.top: is a private pool and cannot be joined. It mines about 7% of all blocks.
9. Bitfury: is a private pool that cannot be joined. Bitfury currently mines about 3.5% of all blocks.

While success in individual mining grants lead to complete ownership of the reward, the probability of achieving success is very low because of high power and resource requirements. Further, due to the increasing difficulty of mining in recent years as popularity of these digital currencies has grown, mining is often not a profitable venture for individuals. The costs associated with expensive hardware necessary to be a competitive miner as well as electricity oftentimes outweigh the potential rewards. The benefits of mining pools are found within a number of key characteristics. First, they require less of each individual participant in terms of hardware and electricity costs, thereby increasing the chances of profitability. Whereas an individual miner might stand little chance of successfully finding a block and receiving a mining reward, a mining pool dramatically improves the success rate as the cumulative effort leads to better chances of finding a block, though the joint effort comes at the cost of shared reward. However, by taking part in a mining pool, individuals give up some of their autonomy in the mining process. They are typically bound by rules established within the pool while they are further required to share any potential rewards, which reduces profits in comparison to working alone.

5 What are the main identified issues to date?

5.1 Do cryptocurrency miners take advantage of developing regions?

As we have been developing, cryptocurrency miners seek low cost electricity and permissive policy environments, which can also unfortunately create environmental hazards and substantial impacts upon local consumers without producing any benefit for communities. The energy needs of these miners means that mining is in fact quite mobile. China has been a dominant force in the cryptocurrency industry, acting as a home to the world's largest Bitcoin mining companies. Regions such as the Xinjiang or Sichuan possess substantial surplus energy which can be made available to these mobile mining operations. Since 2018, China has however begun to exert regulatory pressure on provincial governments to encourage the closure of crypto mining operations and has withdrawn incentivised taxation offers. Further, China has consistently attempted to enact financial regulations on cryptocurrencies. Notably, The People's Bank of China, China's central bank, implemented measures prohibiting domestic Bitcoin exchanges and banning the practice of raising public funds for the development new cryptocurrencies, while China's financial regulatory measures have been found to correlate with depreciation in Bitcoin's value. Due to these issues and similar problems in North America and Western Europe, these operators have been continuing to explicitly seek out countries with looser regulatory environments and physical environments that favour the cost of crypto-mining production.

Crypto-mining facilities potentially subsidise the development of renewable energy resources by seeking the cheapest resource, optimising consumption value. In 2017, 80% of China's Bitcoin mining operations were based in Sichuan, a province that generates approximately 90% of its energy production from renewable resources, thereby accounting for 43% of global Bitcoin mining operations. The profitability of cryptocurrency mining is dependent on the currency's market value in concurrence with the price of electricity. The most efficient mining operations are those that can operate at the lowest cost by obtaining the cheapest electricity capable of supporting extreme consumption. As a result, miners seek cheap electricity markets while benefiting from policy environments that do not regulate the ways in which electricity can be consumed. This can manifest in a number of quite unusual outcomes. With regards to countries without substantial asset resorts, the Democratic Republic of Congo for example, has been linked with a number of substantial projects that could help to protect children there from forced labour.

One particular project has the ambition to provide global manufacturers of high-tech devices like smartphones with a guarantee that cobalt used in lithium-ion batteries was not mined by children which has been an incredibly broad issues associated with cobalt development in the country. The Democratic Republic of Congo is reported to possess in excess of half of the world's cobalt resources, which will become ever more valuable as companies attempt to develop electric cars. Other substantial issues have been identified in Venezuela, where hyperinflation has prompted dramatic shortages of basic necessities and food, bitcoin and other cryptocurrencies could help ease the strain. Given its global usage and the relative ease of cross-border payments and transfers, cryptocurrency has been a viable alternative to an increasingly problematic local fiat money for many Venezuelan citizens. The Petro (PTR) has its origin in the idea of president Hugo Chavez of a strong currency backed by raw materials. The blockchain allows the transfer of value and information, without third parties, they provide the tools to successfully face the challenge of creating platforms and financial instruments that are transparent, efficient and inclusive. Petro was aimed to be a sovereign crypto asset backed by oil assets and issued by the Venezuelan State as a spearhead for the development of an independent, transparent and open digital economy open to the direct participation of citizens. It is also aimed to serve as a platform for the growth of a fairer financial system that contributes to development, autonomy and trade between emerging economies. Venezuelan oil assets will be used to promote the adoption of crypto assets and technologies based on the country's blockchain. The ambition of the State is to promote and encourage the use of Petro with a view to consolidating it as an investment option, savings mechanism and means of exchange with State services, industry, commerce, and citizens in general. Petro aspired to be an instrument for to develop Venezuela's economic stability and financial independence, while also providing an opportunity to create a freer, more balanced and fairer international financial system.

Further, Haiti, a country that has been still reeling from natural disaster, and possessing a gross national Income per capita of approximately $900, have also attempted to benefit from blockchain. The Haitian government has suggested that blockchain technology could be used to record and register property transactions, voting, intellectual property and other aspects of the national bureaucracy. Proponents of blockchain believe that its further development in such regions could enhance the distribution of government services, therefore helping to provide identity services and even help to enhance freedom of speech while counteracting corruption which has been prevalent in these jurisdictions.

5.2 Global warming effects?

A key element of many cryptocurrencies, including bitcoin, is that so-called miners compete to complete complex mathematical calculations to get the right to add a 'block' to the blockchain. The addition of the block stores information about a transaction, and the winning miner is rewarded for its work. The rise in cryptocurrency mining can therefore be seen as environmentally damaging in two ways. Firstly, the mining of cryptocurrency requires substantial volumes of electricity. Secondly, cryptocurrency mines are distributed in a way that enables them to take advantage of cheap electricity in countries that utilise power generation from non-renewable resources such as coal, effectively giving the industry a commercial preference towards unsustainable energy. Additionally, bitcoin mining falls outside conventional environmental regulatory frameworks designed to address traditional mining. While the physical damage on-site remains minimal, the indirect environmental damage these mines produce as a result of their electricity consumption remains unchecked. Similarly, bitcoin miners are not required to offset or mitigate their electricity consumption as other forms of mining or even industrial operations may be required to do. Consequently, not only do bitcoin mines use vast amounts of electricity, they are not held to any form of environmental standard for either where they source their electricity, nor are they required to mitigate the environmental damage they cause.

In a 2018 study that examined the entire chain of events that leads to the creation of Bitcoin, researchers at University of Hawaii at Manoa[3] examined how the projected growth of this cryptocurrency would harm the climate. By way of comparison, the scientists compiled data on the uptake of forty different technologies ranging from dishwashers and e-books to electric power and the Internet. Compiling data on the electricity consumption of the various computing systems used for Bitcoin verification at present and the emissions from electricity production in the countries of the companies that performed such computing, the authors estimated that in 2017, Bitcoin usage emitted 69 MtCO2e. They used this information to estimate the rate of uptake this cryptocurrency will see in the coming years. Based on their most conservative appraisal, the team found that the cumulative emissions from bitcoin would be enough to push global warming beyond 2C in 22 years. If the average rate of technology uptake is used instead, this number is closer to 16 years. To work it out, the scientists analysed the power efficiency of computers used in bitcoin mining, the location of miners around the world and the CO2 emissions from electricity in those countries. The finding that emissions from an expanding bitcoin could push the Earth beyond 2C of warming above the pre-industrial level is particularly stark given the Intergovernmental Panel on Climate Change's recent report on the impacts of such a temperature rise. The report's authors warned that to avoid the worst impacts of

3 Available at: https://www.hawaii.edu/news/article.php?aId=9588

climate change, such as coral reef extinction and Arctic ice disappearance, warming must be limited to 1.5C. Though bitcoin has growing rapidly in the decade since it was introduced, this growth has somewhat stagnated over the past 10 months, suggesting fears about its climate impacts may be premature. However, this research was met with some opposition. Given the decentralised nature of Bitcoin and the need to maximise economic profits, its computing verification process is likely to migrate to places where electricity is cheaper, suggesting that electricity de-carbonisation could help to mitigate Bitcoin's carbon footprint – but only where the cost of electricity from renewable sources is cheaper than fossil fuels. One of the key arguments proposed by opponents surrounded the efficiency of the mining process. While the future growth of cryptocurrencies like bitcoin is highly unpredictable, we do know that the global electric power sector is de-carbonising and that information technologies, including cryptocurrency mining rigs, are becoming much more energy efficient.

5.3 Could Bitcoin stop hinder functionality of the Internet?

The continuing argument surrounding the benefits and complications that the development of Bitcoin and other cryptocurrencies provide has provided much substantial debate. However, at times, it has often teetered somewhat on brink of exceptionally alarmist and sensationalist accusations, such as that which accused Bitcoin of containing enough disruptive force to hinder and even stop the functionality of the Internet. This accusation obtained far more credibility when in June 2018, the Bank of International Settlements released a report[4] which stated that amongst a number of substantial concerns, the rapid growth of Bitcoin could generate substantial issues with regards to the functionality of the Internet. One of the key elements of the report read: "To process the number of digital retail transactions currently handled by selected national retail payment systems, even under optimistic assumptions, the size of the ledger would swell well beyond the storage capacity of a typical smartphone in a matter of days, beyond that of a typical personal computer in a matter of weeks and beyond that of servers in a matter of months. But the issue goes well beyond storage capacity, and extends to processing capacity: only supercomputers could keep up with verification of the incoming transactions. *The associated communication volumes could bring the Internet to a halt, as millions of users exchanged files on the order of magnitude of a terabyte.*" This would manifest through the need for an incredible amount of computer storage for major cryptocurrencies to keep up with the speed of transaction-processing systems that are currently in place. This finding presents a major issue for the process surround the scaling-up of cryptocurrencies. Each miner is required to download and verify the history of all transactions ever made, including

4 Available at: https://www.bis.org/publ/arpdf/ar2018e5.htm

amount paid, payer, payee and other details. The issues then surrounds the growth of this enormous history, with every transaction more information, the ledger continues to grow substantially as time passes. As of January 2020, the size of the Bitcoin blockchain alone was 240 GB. Figure 12 presents the estimated energy consumption that this represents between 2017 and 2019. Other cryptocurrencies, such as Ethereum, Litecoin and Bitcoin Cash, for example, were 181 GB, 22 GB, 158 GB respectively. To deal with this issue, cryptocurrencies have limits on the throughput of transactions in order to keep the size and of the ledger and the time needed to verify all transactions manageable.

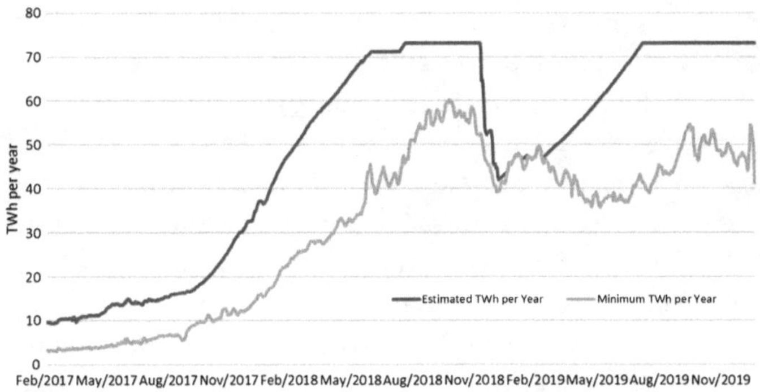

Figure 12: Bitcoin Energy Consumption.

Note: The above data was obtained from https://digiconomist.net/bitcoin-energy-consumption.

The disintegration of the actual processing power of cryptocurrency would manifest when considering the number of digital retail transactions currently handled by selected national retail payment systems. When considering the average computer used during the retail process, or indeed the mobile technology used for cost-efficiency throughout, one can easily understand how quickly that the size of the cryptocurrency ledger would overwhelm the storage capacity of such technology, it presents a clear example as to how the continued evolution of digital technology could actually lead to substantial issues without further technological evolution. Despite this extremely negative finding, the BIS did however add that blockchain and its associated distributed ledger technology could provide some benefits for the global financial system. It stated that the software have the potential to make the sending of cross-border payments more efficient, and with the regards to international flows could improve the exporting and importing industry.

6 Does there exist regulatory solutions?

There are a number of potential solutions to the problem as to how to reduce the environmental impacts sourced within the Bitcoin mining process. There are a number of schools of thought with regards to such a solution, but theory suggests that two prevail: first, policy-makers could stand aside and let the market attempt to solve the issue on its own, while secondly, the government could immediately stand in and regulate the entire market in a rigid manner should the stated issues continue to escalate.

When allowing that the market will solve these environmental issues on its own, it is assumed that the market participant will acquire information about the externalities on a voluntary basis, while then working to solve them without government involvement. Generally, such markets often become more efficient over time as they will theoretically correct government failures. The process of mining somewhat counteracts this theory. Bitcoin's blockchain system involves multiple miners competing to be first to successfully undertake verification work, where only the first successful miner will be rewarded, leading to significant delays in transaction processing times and costs. To counteract this, miners have become innovative and developed the technology that they use, but this advancement on its own is not enough. This approach remains problematic as it relies on the market naturally identifying cost driven solutions that are also environmentally beneficial. As outlined, this can work, but the most cost-effective solution will not always be an environmentally beneficial one, particularly as the cost-driven approach in the past has been for mining to occur in low cost jurisdictions like China, where the environmental costs of bitcoin mining are more pronounced. If markets identified more commercially effective means of improving efficiency this may see progress towards more environmentally efficient outcomes stall.

The alternative solution is to implement government regulation. Regulatory frameworks can help to internalise environmental costs, so that commercial-effective solutions directly take into account environmentally-effective ones. Such frameworks can introduce rules and requirements which have the effect of better controlling or mitigating the environmental impacts of cryptocurrency while they could also include conventional cap and trade schemes designed specifically for the cryptocurrency industry, to control the amount of electricity used by bitcoin mines. Alternatively (or additionally), incentivising the use of clean energy sources in bitcoin mining could be further encouraged as a more environmentally conscious developments in the industry. If one country introduces onerous regulations to improve the environmental impacts of cryptocurrencies, and this comes at a commercial cost, cryptocurrency miners may move offshore to a country that does not enforce or have such regulations in place (broadly like miners did to utilise low cost electricity in China). Regulations must therefore take into account the unconventional nature of bitcoin mines and their ability to easily relocate if regulations are unfavourable. Globally coordinated efforts to regulate cryptocurrency's environmental impacts may mitigate this outcome, though present regulatory agreement and diverse policy approaches make this unlikely in the short term. However, there are many other issues that must be addressed in a regulatory construct in advance of such deep-rooted industrial concerns. There have bee many issues with the generation of fake ICOs, where energy is wasted in a manner that eventually leads to those operating the ICO simply walking away with the funds of unsuspecting investors. Such types of fraud have been exceptionally damaging for the industry at large, creating a broad opinion that cryptocurrencies have been ripe with fraud. This image was not helped as substantial rumours began, later supported by evidence that the exchanges had been largely driven by fake volumes traded. There are now developing broad fears that such interactions might have been misstated due to the widespread allegations that now exist based on the presence of fake volumes. In a recent SEC report,[5] Bitwise Asset Management examined exchanges for fake volume, and found that roughly 95% of reported trading volume in Bitcoin is fake or non-economic in nature. Bitwise used screen scrapers to collect live trading data from over eighty exchanges for a period of several months. The only ten exchanges that passed Bitwise's tests were Binance, Bitfinex, Coinbase, Kraken, Bitstamp, bitFlyer, Gemini, itBit, Bittrex, and Poloniex. This research compared the number of website visits to trading volume across exchanges to identify suspects that participate in faking trading volume, as indicated by disproportionately high volume relative to website visits. In all, the report utilises forty-eight cryptocurrency exchanges, focusing on monthly traffic between November 2018 and April 2019. There were nearly 800 million cryptocurrency exchange website visits in that time period, while the total reported trading volume was $1.96 trillion, of which only $272.5 billion appears to be real trading volume on non-volume faking exchanges. About 86% of the trading volume looks to be fake with 65% of that total real volume originating on Binance and Bitfinex, both of which have virtually no regulatory oversight. Such fake volume is found to be either the fraudulent movement of cash or those generated from washing trades as per the definition in the Bitwise Report[6] who also argues that the prices on exchanges with fake volume do not influence the price of bitcoin in the real spot market.

To mitigate these continued developing issues, cryptocurrency market regulation would necessitate deep-rooted exchange regulation. Almost all foreign exchange flows through banks or currency houses where all transactions should run through an exchange that is regulated. In recent times, British banks are turning away cryptocurrency exchanges, and even closing customers' accounts for wiring to an exchange,

5 Available at: https://www.sec.gov/comments/sr-nysearca-2019-01/srnysearca201901-5574233-185408.pdf

6 "Fake volume refers to any reported trading volume that does not reflect legitimate price discovery in the market. This includes: 1. Fraudulent Prints: This is volume that is simply printed on the tape by an exchange, with no corresponding trading taking place, or 2. Wash Trading: Wash trading occurs when a single or affiliated trader executes trades with itself." from Bitwise Report.

so even if they'd prefer to be based in the UK, exchanges have to open accounts in mainland European countries such as Slovenia. Without tight regulation, they fear the funds could be used by criminals on the dark web or for money laundering. If they are part of that process, they could get fined or shut down. Exchanges should then be allowed to manage ICOs, to reduce the number of fake or fraudulent ICOs that exist. Investors would then follow Know-Your-Customer and Anti-Money Laundering processes. Many of the warnings issued by various countries also note the opportunities that cryptocurrencies create for illegal activities, such as money laundering and terrorism. Some of the countries surveyed go beyond simply warning the public and have expanded their laws on money laundering, counter-terrorism, and organized crimes to include cryptocurrency markets, and require banks and other financial institutions that facilitate such markets to conduct all the due diligence requirements imposed under such laws. For instance, Australia, Canada, and the Isle of Man recently enacted laws to bring cryptocurrency transactions and institutions that facilitate them under the ambit of money laundering and counter-terrorist financing laws. Some jurisdictions have gone even further and imposed restrictions on investments in cryptocurrencies, the extent of which varies from one jurisdiction to another. Some (Algeria, Bolivia, Morocco, Nepal, Pakistan, and Vietnam) ban any and all activities involving cryptocurrencies. Qatar and Bahrain have a slightly different approach in that they bar their citizens from engaging in any kind of activities involving cryptocurrencies locally, but allow citizens to do so outside their borders. There are also countries that, while not banning their citizens from investing in cryptocurrencies, impose indirect restrictions by barring financial institutions within their borders from facilitating transactions involving cryptocurrencies (Bangladesh, Iran, Thailand, Lithuania, Lesotho, China, and Colombia).

One of the final necessary changes would be to clean up the international tax ambiguity with regards to cryptocurrencies. Blockchains do not work without a token, and tokens need to be traded in and out of fiat (government backed currencies like the US dollar). This means there will always be a chance to profit (in fiat terms), so governments needs to clarify their stance. One of the many questions that arise from allowing investments in and the use of cryptocurrencies is the issue of taxation. In this regard the challenge appears to be how to categorise cryptocurrencies and the specific activities involving them for purposes of taxation. This matters primarily because whether gains made from mining or selling cryptocurrencies are categorised as income or capital gains invariably determines the applicable tax bracket. One, singular universal approach might warrant further investigation when analysing the variety of tax treatments for cryptocurrency. For example, in the UK, when using cryptocurrencies, corporations pay corporate tax, unincorporated businesses pay income tax, individuals pay capital gains tax. While in Argentina and Spain, the assets are subject to income tax, while in Denmark they are subject to income tax with the losses deducted. In Israel, they are taxed as an asset, in Bulgaria cryptocurrency is taxed as a financial asset, while in Switzerland they are taxed as foreign currency. It is very easy to see how the broad treatment of cryptocurrency can be deemed to be confusing, but also possessing many pathways through which illicit behaviour can occur once international tax treaty's and cross-border transfer legislation is also considered. Such international tax revenue could also be best served to be partially ring-fenced, acting as an insurance policy for any potential environmental damage that cryptocurrencies could generate. However, such legislative behaviour would necessitate a standardisation of the international approach.

7 Concluding comments

As cryptocurrencies as a financial market product continue to evolve, it is becoming more certain that innovative solutions are going to be needed to solve some substantial forthcoming issues with regards to energy usage and technological capacity. The major fuel used by these networks, due to its relatively majority-based Chinese point of origin, is coal-fired power plants, which has resulted in an extensive carbon footprint for each transaction. This raises questions about the environmental sustainability of cryptocurrencies. The participation in the validation and mining process of Bitcoin requires both special hardware and a substantial amount of energy, therefore, there is on-going carbon production. As the cryptocurrency industry grows, and the adoption of blockchain technology increases, it is increasingly important for cryptocurrencies' blockchain technology to be more environmentally conscious. By prioritising efficiency, these new cryptocurrencies also reduce their environmental impact. In doing so, the industry neatly exemplifies how improving the environmental output of an industry can be linked to enhanced productivity and effectiveness. Coal and other fossil fuels are also the largest generator of electricity for the rest of the world, and coal is a significant contributor to man-made climate change. This reliance on fossil fuels has given rise to speculation that bitcoin's energy consumption will continue to rise as it grows in popularity. This raises questions about the environmental sustainability of cryptocurrencies.

When observing estimates of the electricity prices facing both households and businesses, we observe that countries such as Iran, Iraq and other middle eastern nations such as Qatar present evidence of substantially reduced household charges for electricity. In terms of the cheapest countries in which to buy electricity, Venezuela, Libya and Ethiopia represent the cheapest countries in which to run potential cryptocurrency mining operations. This makes such countries attractive to cryptocurrency miners. However, the political stability of some might not be feasible. Further, cryptomining facilities potentially subsidise the development of renewable energy resources by seeking the cheapest resource, optimising consumption value. The profitability of cryptocurrency mining is dependent on the currency's market value in concurrence with the price of electricity. The most efficient mining operations are those that can operate at the lowest cost by obtaining the cheapest electricity capable of supporting extreme consumption. As a result, miners seek cheap electricity markets while benefiting from policy environments that do not regulate the ways in which electricity can be consumed. This can manifest in a number of quite unusual outcomes, such as those experienced in the Democratic Republic of Congo, Venezuela and Haiti. Proponents of blockchain believe that its further development in such regions could enhance the distribution of government services, therefore helping to provide identity services and even help to enhance freedom of speech while counteracting corruption which has been prevalent in these jurisdictions.

The rise in cryptocurrency mining can therefore be seen as environmentally damaging in two ways. Firstly, the mining of cryptocurrency requires substantial volumes of electricity. Secondly, cryptocurrency mines are distributed in a way that enables them to take advantage of cheap electricity in countries that utilise power generation from non-renewable resources such as coal, effectively giving the industry a commercial preference towards unsustainable energy. Additionally, bitcoin mining falls outside conventional environmental regulatory frameworks designed to address traditional mining. While the physical damage on-site remains minimal, the indirect environmental damage these mines produce as a result of their electricity consumption remains unchecked. Similarly, bitcoin miners are not required to offset or mitigate their electricity consumption as other forms of mining or even industrial operations may be required to do. Consequently, not only do bitcoin mines use vast amounts of electricity, they are not held to any form of environmental standard for either where they source their electricity, nor are they required to mitigate the environmental damage they cause. The disintegration of the actual processing power of cryptocurrency would manifest when considering the number of digital retail transactions currently handled by selected national retail payment systems. When considering the average computer used during the retail process, or indeed the mobile technology used for cost-efficiency throughout, one can easily understand how quickly that the size of the cryptocurrency ledger would overwhelm the storage capacity of such technology, it presents a clear example as to how the continued evolution of digital technology could actually lead to substantial issues without further technological evolution.

Overall, the total carbon footprint of the industry is now estimated to have surpassed that of many large industrial nations. This chapter has investigated the multiple knock-on effects and consequential behaviour of this rapid growth in energy usage, such as an increase in global temperature, the growth of mining companies who have targeted third world infrastructures, and the complete shutdown of the Internet as we know it. Considering the evidence provided, we encourage investors not to ignore these environmentalism matters, particularly due to the substantial electricity consumption from coal in countries such as China. Further investigation of these issues are exceptionally important, as should they continue to be made without fair supporting analysis, it could be considered to be an unfair attack on this developing industry. However, should such problems continue to transpire with evidence provided, it is of the utmost importance that regulators, policy-makers and governments alike take appropriate action.

Bibliography

Akhtaruzzaman, M., A. Sensoy, and S. Corbet (2019). The influence of bitcoin on portfolio diversification and design. *Finance Research Letters*, 101344.

Akyildirim, E., S. Corbet, P. Katsiampa, N. Kellard, and A. Sensoy (2019). The development of bitcoin futures: Exploring the interactions between cryptocurrency derivatives. *Finance Research Letters*, Available at: https://doi.org/10.1016/j.frl.2019.07.007.

Bariviera, A. F. (2017). The inefficiency of bitcoin revisited: A dynamic approach. *Economics Letters 161*, 1–4.

Baur, D. G., T. Dimpfl, and K. Kuck (2018). Bitcoin, gold and the us dollar – a replication and extension. *Finance Research Letters 25*, 103–110.

Corbet, S., D. J. Cumming, B. M. Lucey, M. Peat, and S. A. Vigne (2019). The destabilising effects of cryptocurrency cybercriminality. *Economics Letters*, 108741.

Corbet, S., C. Larkin, B. Lucey, A. Meegan, and L. Yarovaya (2020a). Cryptocurrency reaction to FOMC announcements: Evidence of heterogeneity based on blockchain stack position. *Journal of Financial Stability 46*, 100706.

Corbet, S., C. Larkin, B. M. Lucey, A. Meegan, and L. Yarovaya (2020b). The impact of macroeconomic news on bitcoin returns. *The European Journal of Finance*, 1–21.

Corbet, S., B. Lucey, M. Peat, and S. Vigne (2018). Bitcoin futures: What use are they? *Economics Letters 172*, 23–27.

Corbet, S., B. M. Lucey, A. Urquhart, and L. Yarovaya (2019). Cryptocurrencies as a financial asset: A systematic analysis. *International Review of Financial Analysis 62*, 182–199.

Corbet, S., A. Meegan, C. Larkin, B. Lucey, and L. Yarovaya (2018). Exploring the dynamic relationships between cryptocurrencies and other financial assets. *Economics Letters 165*, 28–34.

Easley, D., M. O'Hara, and S. Basu (2019). From mining to markets: The evolution of bitcoin transaction fees. *Journal of Financial Economics*, *134*(1), 91–109.

Ekinci, C., E. Akyildirim, and S. Corbet (2019). Analysing the dynamic influence of us macroeconomic news releases on Turkish stock markets. *Finance Research Letters 31*, 155–164.

Foley, S., J. R. Karlsen, and T. J. Putnins (2019). Sex, drugs, and bitcoin: How much illegal activity is financed through cryptocurrencies? *The Review of Financial Studies 32*(5), 1789–1853.

Greenberg, P. and D. Bugden (2019). Energy consumption boomtowns in the united states: Community responses to a cryptocurrency boom. *Energy research & Social Science 50*, 162–167.

Katsiampa, P., S. Corbet, and B. Lucey (2019). Volatility spillover effects in leading cryptocurrencies: A BEKK-MGARCH analysis. *Finance Research Letters 29*, 68–74.

Krause, M. J. and T. Tolaymat (2018). Quantification of energy and carbon costs for mining cryptocurrencies. *Nature Sustainability 1*(11), 711.

Li, J., N. Li, H. Cui, and Z. Wu (2019a). Energy consumption of cryptocurrency mining: A study of electricity consumption in mining cryptocurrencies. *Energy 168*, 160–168.

Mensi, W., Y.-J. Lee, K. H. Al-Yahyaee, A. Sensoy, and S.-M. Yoon (2019). Intraday downward/upward multifractality and long memory in Bitcoin and Ethereum markets: An asymmetric multifractal detrended fluctuation analysis. *Finance Research Letters 31*, 19–25.

Mora, C., R. L. Rollins, K. Taladay, M. B. Kantar, M. K. Chock, M. Shimada, and E. C. Franklin (2018). Bitcoin emissions alone could push global warming above 2c. *Nature Climate Change 8*(11), 931.

O'Riordan, T. (1985). Research policy and review 6. future directions for environmental policy. *Environment and Planning A 17*(11), 1431–1446.

Sensoy, A. (2019). The inefficiency of Bitcoin revisited: A high-frequency analysis with alternative currencies. *Finance Research Letters 28*, 68–73.

Stoll, C., L. KlaaBen, and U. Gallersdörfer (2019). The carbon footprint of bitcoin. Available at SSRN 3335781.

Truby, J. (2018). Decarbonizing bitcoin: Law and policy choices for reducing the energy consumption of blockchain technologies and digital currencies. *Energy Research & Social Science 44*, 399–410.

Urquhart, A. (2017). Price clustering in Bitcoin. *Economics Letters 159*, 145–148.

Shaen Corbet

Evaluating a decade of cryptocurrency development: Navigating financial progress through technological and regulatory ambiguity

In this final chapter, we present an overview of the key lessons that have been provided throughout this collection. The substantial surge in interest and continued media coverage surrounding cryptocurrencies, and in particular, Bitcoin, has generated an environment through which pricing bubbles, market manipulation and illicit usage could thrive. There have been many accusations of substantial inherent issues such as the generation of significant environmental effects and the potential shutdown of the internet and broad technology as we know it due to the sheer size of cryptocurrency ledgers. Further, legal and regulatory issues, including the lack of international consistency as to what exactly cryptocurrency represents as a financial product continue to obstruct the trust of many investors. The many cases of market manipulation and illegality that exist have also substantially diminished trust. However, after a decade in existence, the price of Bitcoin remains consistently elevated, acts as quite a useful diversification tool, and does present uses as a tool to covert international value, even if it is one of the most volatile alternative investments in existence.

While cryptocurrency as a product continues to expand at pace, it is of the upmost importance that we continue to expand our understanding of this youthful financial product, with particular emphasis on the contagion effects that can be sourced therein. The regulatory issues surrounding the growth and usage of cryptocurrencies has also been the focus of substantial attention in recent time. These chapters provided a broad cross-discipline perspective. We first analysed a range of questions such as what exactly is blockchain, or what best describes the Bitcoin mining process? We focused specifically on the provision of explanation outlining the role of cryptocurrencies and blockchains on real economic transactions, investigating as to how blockchain affects information friction and asymmetry in economic and financial transactions and further, as to how it changes the landscape of markets while considering spillover effects upon all market participants.

Further, we investigated the literature on both broad- and narrow-based cryptocurrency research from a bibliometric and scientometric perspective. Such analysis is used to establish the development of a visual representation and explanation of the flow of research direction during the past decade based on blockchain and cryptocurrency across all disciplines. We provide clear evidence of a growing but fragmented research area, while concluding that there is a significant difference in how researchers treat broad conceptual topics versus individual products. We finally provided a concise overview of the current topics that have been central to recent research efforts,

https://doi.org/10.1515/9783110660807-010

while attempting to provide oversight key areas that have presented evidence of particular deficiency. Regardless as to whether one believes that cryptocurrencies to be a passing fad, the future of money or somewhere in between, they have emerged as one of the most interesting and discussed financial assets of the last decade, with particular evidence that these assets have had greatly increased research activity focused on them over the last two years. This research however is characterised by being rather fragmented. It is fragmented in a significant sense across products and broad areas. The authors state that "while islands of research do connect they do so in very limited ways". This research is found to be parallel, mostly non-overlapping research initiatives drawing inspiration form the technical and the economic literature but limited "interdisciplinary" research. It is within this section of the research that this handbook goes some way to providing an overview of the areas of research and will spark greater cooperation to develop broad alignment. Such recommendations will hopefully provide direction for future research synergy.

Next, we investigated the financial characteristics of cryptocurrencies, identifying that they are best characterised by heavy tail behaviour, very high volatility, persistence, large and abrupt price swings, and vulnerability to speculative bubbles, among other properties, all of which lead cryptocurrencies to resemble more financial assets rather than fiat currencies. Moreover, cryptocurrency markets exhibit some informational inefficiencies, which, however, depend on several factors. Finally, cryptocurrencies are highly connected to each other but isolated from mainstream assets, with their hedging and safe haven properties varying over time. This research is further supported through two further piece of works, the first providing a test of the interactions between cryptocurrency and various US stock indices using Granger causality analysis; and the second specifically analysing the market microstructure of cryptocurrencies. Unsurprisingly, there is evidence of a relationship between Bitcoin and US tech stock indices. Specifically, there is clear evidence of predictability between Bitcoin and US tech stocks, which seems to vary across quantiles. US stocks Granger cause Bitcoin return, but this is not the case for other stock indices. Generally, Granger causality from one market to another is insignificant in both mean and variance. However, when one market is in its bear state, the other become more volatile. Furthermore, there is evidence of casualties when one market is in its bear market state, while the other is in its bear or bull market state. With regards to market microstructure, while analysing a broad range of specific questions, one of the key takeaways is based on the fact that there continues to be no central authority to register cryptocurrency exchanges, it is estimated that there are currently up to five hundred exchanges in circulation, characterised by varying platforms, geographical reach, and compliance with regulatory frameworks. Cryptocurrency markets share many similar characteristics with both foreign exchange and equity markets such as limit order books and matching algorithms, and exchanges that can be both centralised or decentralised. As these markets are still in their infancy, what shape or form they will take in future will depend on a combination of acceptance from consumers, the investment community, as well as worldwide regulators.

The next chapter sets out to establish the key issues that have become central within the market for Initial Coin Offerings (ICOs). Within this context, we provide a brief overview of the existing literature based on ICOs around the world, while explaining the motivations and styles of criminality that have occurred, the methods that have been widely used by cryptocurrency thieves, the potential for the innovation of theft within the sector and the related problems that such technological progress can potentially generate, and the types of market agents that have set out to potentially misuse ICOs for a variety of reasons at both the sovereign and corporate level. As cryptocurrency markets continue to evolve, it is imperative that policy-makers and regulators continue to monitor the potential development of sophisticated manipulation and cybercriminality techniques that have developed throughout the market for cryptocurrencies. A central theme throughout these listed issues and examples surrounds substantial damage to credibility within the market. We have observed cases of theft at the level of the exchange, within the whitepapers that have been provided, through the usage of celebrities to support marketing tactics, through the illegal cross-jurisdictional transfer of funds and indeed, the most simplest form of theft, where the ICO counter-party quite simply disappears with the accumulated assets of investors. While cryptocurrency-enthusiasts continue to promote the positive attributes that support the potential growth of this new investment asset, the same proponents cannot ignore that this entire sector has been rampant with levels and styles of fraudulent behaviour that is quite difficult to find in other international markets of similar scale and scope. But there have been significant positive developments in terms of the future scope of international regulation and the potential to eliminate fraudulent behaviour. It is essential that during the continued growth of the sector for cryptocurrencies that regulation, including a broad international set of standards, be developed and maintained to grow at pace with the market for cryptocurrencies. It is essential that regulations must compare effectively with the sophistication of the market that they attempt to monitor. Until the broad gap between regulation and the capacity for cryptocurrency market misuse is diminished, there will continue to be substantial and frequent loss of investor assets through mechanisms that represent those usually observed in an exceptionally juvenile market.

Finally, this book concluded with an investigation of the environmental aspects of cryptocurrency markets and as to how their rapid growth can influence the environment and through which channels this process manifests. The authors find focus on the area where to date, we possess the most thorough data and evidence through which we can build the case, namely electricity consumption associated with the mining of cryptocurrencies. The total carbon footprint of the industry is now estimated to have surpassed that of many large industrial nations. This chapter investigates the multiple knock-on effects and consequential behaviour of this rapid growth in energy usage, such as an increase in global temperature, the growth of mining companies who have targeted third world infrastructures, and the complete shutdown of the Internet as we know it. Saying that, we encourage investors not to ignore these environmentalism matters, since we also show that electricity consumption is proven to be one of the commonly used variable in valuation of mineable cryptocurrencies and identification of their fair value, which affect investments returns and should be considered in their trading strategies. Overall, the authors concluded The rise in cryptocurrency mining can therefore be seen as environmentally damaging in two ways. Firstly, the mining of cryptocurrency requires substantial volumes of electricity. Secondly, cryptocurrency mines are distributed in a way that enables them to take advantage of cheap electricity in countries that utilise power generation from non-renewable resources such as coal, effectively giving the industry a commercial preference towards unsustainable energy. Additionally, bitcoin mining falls outside conventional environmental regulatory frameworks designed to address traditional mining. The total carbon footprint of the industry is now estimated to have surpassed that of many large industrial nations. This chapter has investigated the multiple knock-on effects and consequential behaviour of this rapid growth in energy usage, such as an increase in global temperature, the growth of mining companies who have targeted third world infrastructures, and the complete shutdown of the Internet as we know it.

1 Concluding thoughts on the benefits associated with cryptocurrencies

It is very important that we present a balanced argument within the scope of such research on cryptocurrencies. While much research to date has focused on the pitfalls and specific issues that cryptocurrencies have produced, there have also been a substantial number of benefits provided. Some of the main benefits that have been observed to date include:

1. **Credibility:** One of the most substantial issues with the establishment of a new product is developing trust and recognition with a customer base. International traders and those who conduct cross-border trade are generally exposed to exchange rate risk while being subject to fees associated with exchanging one currency for another. Further, there may be challenges in exchanging currency dependent on availability in certain jurisdiction. Fortunately, for some large cryptocurrencies, this is not a particularly significant issues as the digital currency is universally recognised at an exchange-driven value. This minimises valuation risk and somewhat saves time in determining a price for a transaction, as well as any fees associated with exchanging money from one form to another. As cryptocurrency continues to expand and is increasingly adopted around the world, it has the potential to make financial transactions faster and simpler.

2. **Improved Security:** Unlike traditional payments, cryptocurrencies are digital and encrypted; meaning that you have a substantially reduced risk of having assets exposed to theft as would be possible in other transactions with other legacy payment systems. It is far more difficult to steal cryptocurrency compared to a physical wallet. However, there are issues with specific types of criminality that must be addressed before to ensure that credibility is maintained. However, identity theft and hacking are two specific issues that cryptocurrency users are constantly exposed. Credit cards operate on a 'pull' basis, where the store initiates the payment and pulls the designated amount from your account, necessitating credentials at the point of purchase. Cryptocurrency uses a separate 'push' mechanism that allows the cryptocurrency holder to send exactly what he or she wants to the merchant or recipient with no further information. However, there is no scope for error as misplaced trades cannot be retrieved without a resolution provided from a party that might not be able to be identified in a timely manner.
3. **Elimination of Transaction Fees:** While it is considered standard among cryptocurrency exchanges to charge so-called 'maker' and 'taker' fees, and other fees such as deposit and withdrawal fees, cryptocurrency users are generally not subjected to the traditional banking fees associated with fiat currencies, therefore, no account maintenance or minimum balance fees, no overdraft charges and no returned deposit fees, among many others. While standard wire transfers and foreign purchases typically involve fees and exchange costs, since cryptocurrency transactions have no intermediary institutions or government involvement, the costs of transacting are kept very low. This can be a major advantage for travellers. Additionally, any transfer generally occurs rapidly, therefore, eliminating the inconvenience of typical authorisation requirements and waiting periods usually experienced in the banking system. These services act like PayPal (who does not accept cryptocurrency) does when considering cash or credit card users, thereby providing the online exchange system. Cryptocurrency act as a direct threat to similar payment mechanisms.
4. **Improved accessibility:** As the international usage of technology continues to expand, many more populations are not only able to access cryptocurrency, but with the increased speed of such technological development, these same populations can use this new payment mechanism in a meaningful way. It is very possible that such product development mirrors the expansion of mobile phone technology in the latter period of the 1990s, where the new product spread rapidly through the developing world, and saturated markets where standard landline telephones had never been established. It is not unrealistic to assume that cryptocurrency can do similar. Because users are able to send and receive cryptocurrency with only a smartphone or computer, cryptocurrency is theoretically available to populations of users without access to traditional banking systems, credit cards and other methods of payment.

5. **Corporate advancement:** By being an early adopter of cryptocurrency, it is entirely possible that you can gain a competitive advantage over your competition. This also includes being able to access finance and data transfer, and other corporate elements of the Internet including marketing and advertisement which can be used to target anybody who has a viable data connection and ready access to their relevant websites and portals. It is very important to recall that there are an estimated 2.2 billion individuals across the world who have access to the Internet or mobile phones, while also not possessing access to traditional systems of banking or exchange. The cryptocurrency ecosystem holds the potential to make asset transfer and transaction processing available to this vast market of willing consumers, once the required infrastructure (digital and regulatory) is put in place.
6. **Improved User Autonomy:** which is one of the benefits of digital currencies as users possess more autonomy over their own money than fiat currencies do. Users are able to control how they spend their money without dealing with any form of regulatory intermediary authority such as government.
7. **Discretion:** Cryptocurrency purchases are discrete unless a user voluntarily publishes records of their transactions, while these purchases are never associated with one's personal identity, similar to purchases with cash, while and cannot easily be traced back to the point of origin. While is must be stated that cryptocurrency transactions are not completely anonymous or entirely untraceable, they are less readily linked to personal identity than other forms of payment.
8. **Adaptability:** Due to the exceptionally large range of cryptocurrency now available, there exists a range designed for specific usage, providing evidence of the wide-ranging flexibility of these new digital products. Some cryptocurrencies are specifically designed to mask the buyer and seller's identities, while others are specifically designated for specific purpose, such as charitable donation or a mechanism through which market participants can gamble for example.
9. **Broad decentralisation:** Blockchain technology incorporates a substantial technological network to manage the recording and collection of Bitcoin transactions. The technological system is managed by the network and not any one central authority, therefore operating on a peer-to-peer basis, similar to a ledger or a database that records property rights. The forms of mass collaboration this makes possible are just beginning to be investigated. The use of such a system eliminates brokers, the usage of solicitors and other parties who would normally increase the cost of transaction. There various advantages to decentralisation, where this system can ensures the those without access to fair banking systems can participate in the global economy: anyone can store and transfer wealth to anyone anywhere in the world. Another benefit of decentralised exchanges is that users are fully in control of their data as there is no central authority storing or managing it.
10. **Tailor-made asset transfers:** The blockchain cryptocurrency ecosystem may also be used to facilitate specialist modes of transfer. Cryptocurrency contracts can be designed to add conditions that include third-party approvals or can be

specified to pay at on exact date or time in the future. Though largely unrecognised as legal tender on national levels at present, cryptocurrencies by their very nature are not subject to the exchange rates, interest rates, transactions charges, or other levies imposed by a specific country. And using the peer-to-peer mechanism of the blockchain technology, cross-border transfers and transactions may be conducted without complications over currency exchange fluctuations, and the like.

11. **Increased Speed of Transactions:** The usage of broad decentralisation means that cryptocurrency transactions are one-to-one affairs, leading to greater clarity in establishing audit trails, greater accountability, and less confusion as to who owes who. Cryptocurrency users can pay for their coins anywhere that they have Internet access, however, personal information is not necessary to complete any transaction. Further, such transactions have the added benefit that they are immediately settled, which is in contrast to a number of other mechanisms where third parties or legislative delays are imposed.

2 Concluding thoughts on the issues associated with cryptocurrencies

Considering the listed benefits and many facts provided throughout the chapters provided in this book, there remains a substantial number of significant issues that must be rectified before cryptocurrencies can truly be represented in the same manner as traditional financial assets. Although the first decade of existence has contained many incredibly unique events attributed to the development of cryptocurrencies, there remain a number of substantial issues that continue to require resolution such as:

1. **Scalability:** One of the largest problems facing the cryptocurrency space today is the issue of scalability. The main concern within this regards is trust of the blockchain, that is, if there are only a few entities capable of running full nodes, then those entities could potentially collude to present themselves with a large number of additional cryptocurrency, and there would be no way for other users to audit such behaviour, namely, that a block is invalid without processing an entire block themselves. Currently, most of the cryptocurrencies can handle 10–100 transactions per second. This limitation stops blockchain networks from being used by solid companies and real-world business use cases. Obviously, that's a temporary thing that is close to being solved by various solutions, like Lightning network, Waves-NG, Graphene, etc. While the number of cryptocurrencies continues to increase at pace, the speed of a transaction is another important metric that cryptocurrencies cannot compete with on the same level until the infrastructure delivering these technologies is massively scaled. Such an evolution is complex

and difficult to do seamlessly. However, some have already proposed several solutions, including lightning networks, sharding, and staking as options to overcome the scalability issue. To resolve this issue, it is necessary to create a blockchain design that maintains Bitcoin-like security guarantees, but where the maximum size of the most powerful node that needs to exist for the network to keep functioning is substantially sub-linear in the number of transactions.

2. **Time-stamping:** It is of the utmost importance that the system maintains the current time to high accuracy. All cryptocurrency users have clocks in a normal distribution around some 'real' time with standard deviation of twenty seconds, that is, there are no more than twenty seconds between two nodes on the blockchain. The system should continuously provide a time which is within the designated standard deviation (or less if possible) of the internal clock of >99% of honestly participating nodes. External systems may end up relying on this system; hence, it should remain secure against attackers regardless of incentives. For example, Ethereum possesses a thirteen second block of time and with no particularly advanced time-stamping technology implemented. It uses a simple technique where a client does not accept a block whose stated timestamp is earlier than the client's local time. However, to date, this has not been tested under serious attacks. The recent network-adjusted timestamps proposal tries to improve on the status quo by allowing the client to determine the consensus on the time in the case where the client does not locally know the current time to high accuracy; this has not yet been tested. But at this point in time, issues surrounding time-stamping are not currently at the foreground of the key challenges to cryptocurrencies, however, they do open an avenue through which cybercriminality can prevail.
3. **Transparency:** It has been well-established in the preceding literature that the majority of ICOs end up unsuccessful and some of them even fraudulent. Many cryptocurrencies often state that they are decentralised, however, it is estimated that 80% of the top fifty coins are held by the top twenty wallets. It is further estimated that the twenty biggest wallets held more than 90% of total token supply. The lack of transparency, accountability and professionalism from renowned institutions can deeply influence perceptions of the industry, which in turn greatly reduces the benefit of digital currencies. The undermines blockchain adoption in different industries. One current situation that is being broadly monitored is that of the issue of fake volumes traded being identified across many exchanges.
4. **Credibility:** The continuous manner in which cybercriminality and even basic levels of theft across the industry continue to deeply diminish trust within the cryptocurrency industry at large. There have been widespread issues with regards to trading fees and the costs of transactions. While some exchanges charge a single flat fee, on average, of 0.25% of the transaction value, on all trades, but there has been a breach of trust and loss of credibility when some exchanges split their trading fees into two separate fees (the maker fee and the taker fee), where maker fees can be higher than the taker because the maker adds liquidity to the market.

As we begin to understand these processes, the credibility of those who provided incorrect information in the past is duly diminished.

5. **Liquidity:** A lack of liquidity can generate an imbalanced environment, where orders are not placed/executed on time, and there is an increased possibility where large cryptocurrency owners can manipulate prices. Further, such reduced levels of liquidity can create a scenario where markets become more volatile and see more price slippages. A secondary issue is that power within the cryptocurrency sector falls into the hands of exchanges with large liquidity, generating substantially escalated fees for the listing of cryptocurrencies on such exchanges.
6. **Price volatility:** Price volatility, and subsequently, a lack of an inherent value, is an important issue, but one which can be overcome by linking the cryptocurrency value directly to tangible and intangible assets. Increased adoption should also increase consumer confidence and decrease this volatility. The market continues to be quite small in comparison to other more developed financial markets, even considering that it has grown exponentially. The construction of a cryptographic asset with a stable price might go some of the way to eliminating such exceptional short-term volatility, however, such a response must be wary of the generation of implicit contagion effects.
7. **Regulations:** In the continuing cases of hacks and breaches of exchanges, there continues to be quite a stark absence of regulation. In 2019, both the European Banking Authority (EBA) and the European Securities and Markets Authority (ESMA) have publicly called for better assessments of cryptocurrency technology and its impacts to develop appropriate regulations. The Securities and Exchange Commission (SEC) in the US is applying their regulatory guidance to cryptocurrency projects as it considers another form of securities. It is this broad absence of regulation is the most important aspect that prevents merchants from accepting digital currencies.
8. **Transaction Delays:** The cryptocurrency market is plagued with a litany of delays across almost every type of transaction. From opening a trading account to verifying your identity and being able to make deposits and withdrawals, the system seems to be quite slow. While cryptocurrency transactions are known for being fast, delays can happen and can be a way to protect users from hacking or fraudulent transactions. Exchanges sometimes delay transactions if they suspect the user did not authorise the transactions. Some issues with regards to scalability have been identified by experts as being the cause of transaction delays. As the blockchains become longer, more transactions are being held up in the queue awaiting approval. It is vital that key stakeholders in the market continue to work on efforts to combat these issues.
9. **Physical usage of cryptocurrency:** It has become a very obvious trend in recent times, but there has been a substantial decline in the growth of cryptocurrency acceptance. This has been attributed to excessive fees and high volatility. Cryptocurrencies through their very design, are supposed to simplify the transaction

process significantly by reducing fees to a mere 1% and eliminating the need for extra hardware. However, due to the novelty of blockchain technology, substantial issues were passed towards customers. Depending on the blockchain, you can end up paying from $0.01 (Dash) to up to $30 (Bitcoin) in commission, which would indicate that those cryptocurrencies denoted to be cheapest or those who provide free transactions will be eventually used by the masses. However, the credibility of some less well-known cryptocurrencies has created an issue with regards to adoption and some companies and countries appear fearful to be a first-mover.

10. **Cybercriminality issues:** Arguably, the most substantial issue to date, as continued criminality in this sphere has greatly reduced confidence across all agents. There have been multiple ICOs breached and have cost investors hundreds of millions of dollars in losses. Mitigating this will require continuous upkeep of security infrastructure and the development of enhanced security measures that go beyond those used in the traditional banking industries. There have been a number of high-profile cryptocurrency hacks and heists that have resulted in millions of dollars being stolen. Traders and investors have lost funds and some platforms have ceased to operate. In a bid to counter the activities of these criminals, traders and platform operators have to take a number of precautionary measures. However, there are side effects to these policy changes as they have created a number of bottlenecks that hamper the cryptocurrency trading process. This then creates a trade-off between security and efficiency. Due to the activities of hackers, some traders prefer to store the bulk of their cryptocurrency holdings in offline wallets. This means that when trading they have to move from offline storage to online storage before participating in the trade, increasing the risk and cost of efforts. It must be considered that transactions on a blockchain are immutable and as such if funds get stolen, there is little chance of ever recovering such funds. This not only applies to cryptocurrency traders. Cryptocurrency trading platforms constantly have to improve their security framework in order to stay ahead of the hackers and thieves. It is important to remember that as technology becomes more sophisticated, so do hackers. Exchanges are essentially so vulnerable to hacks because they centralise the risk, so further decentralisation can be an option in the pursuit for maximum security. Some of the key cybercriminality risks have been identified as:

    I *Price manipulation:* The light regulation of exchanges has created an environment where abusive and illicit manoeuvres can manifest. It is reported that crypto exchanges use algorithms to manipulate the prices of coins. In a number of situations, cryptocurrency traders exposed a promotion on some exchanges which inflated the trading volume on the exchange, where there was a connection between fake trading volumes and paybacks as trading fees as an airdrop. Further, when a tradeable asset can drop by as much as fifty percent in less than 24 hours, we must ask significant questions. There are a number of reasons that contribute to the excessive volatility in the market but perhaps the biggest contributor is the activities of 'whales', who are individuals that have large cryptocurrency holdings. They are able to swing the market by manipulating the price of a cryptocurrency. They do this by means of buying and selling walls. The problem with this regularly occurring scenario is that the whales can drive up the price without actually investing in the market. The actual trades that have boosted the price of the cryptocurrency has come from the smaller traders. Further, one of biggest reasons why this sort of asset price manipulation is possible is due to the lack of position price limits/fees on many cryptocurrency trading platforms. If adequate limits or fees are put in place, it would discourage the movement of large buy and sell market positions.

II *Pump and Dump ICO Schemes:* ICOs have emerged to become an integral part of the cryptocurrency market. Many tokens are introduced to the market via ICOs with investors buying these tokens in exchange for fiat money. Pump and dump ICO schemes continue to be a problem for the market due to the lack of regulation. During the ICO, the entrepreneurs behind the token speculate massively on the coin, driving the prices up and getting investors attracted. Once this is done, the same investors cash out, therefore leaving the investors with worthless coins that have little or no value. There has also been a substantial increase in the level of spoofing payment information and phishing.

III *Loss/corruption of a wallet file:* Most users store their cryptocurrency wallet files on their computers. Therefore, they can be stolen using malware or lost if the hard disk crashes. So most advanced users make hard copies of their secret key and purchase USB hardware wallets.

IV *Spoofing/manipulating a user address:* Collection of funds in an ICO usually opens at a specified time and closes when the required amount has been collected. The collection address is posted on the project website when it opens. There have been a number of situations where such user addresses have been intercepted and the precedes stolen. This has also manifested in the hacking of payment gateways.

3 In conclusion

Overall, cryptocurrencies have a long way to go before they can replace the traditional mechanisms through which global finance flows. However, as outlined throughout this book, even considering the many, substantial issues that exist within this developing sector, there have also been a number of benefits and unexpected side-effects generated. To briefly conclude, the regulation of the product and the subsequent reduction of cybercriminality appear to immediately necessitate action, even before the need for technical improvement. It would appear that the reduced usage of cryptocurrency has manifested directly from the substantial theft and illicit usage that is central to the product's usage. Media coverage has been based largely on such issues, not necessarily on the implicit benefits contained therein. Most individuals, without deep financial knowledge base their views of such products on such basic news coverage, which has mainly surrounded the volatility of these products and the cybercriminality contained within. Should confidence be restored, this could lead to increase usage, allowing cryptocurrencies to potentially grow in a more organic manner. It must be noted that the use of such technology presents benefits to countries with a lack of basic infrastructure, such as easy access to banking networks. However, the very nature of the technology also makes it a very useful tool for many forms of illicit behaviour. Governments and regulatory bodies in the medium-term will most likely reach a crossroads as to how to balance these positive and negative outcomes. While some investors in 2009 did not foresee the longevity of digital currencies as a viable financial product, many most certainly did not envisage their survival for a decade. Cryptocurrencies have presented much resilience, continuing to thrive even considering the many issues that they have faced. It is within the forthcoming decade that we will understand as to whether cryptocurrencies can grow to be the ground-breaking future of finance that proponents claim the product can become.